D0791102

DESIGN AND
FIGURE CARVING

Art when really understood is the province of every human being. It is simply a question of doing things, anything well. It is not an outside extra thing. . . . He does not have to be a painter or sculptor to be an artist. He can work in any medium. He simply has to find the gain in the work itself, not outside it.

—ROBERT HENRI

Fig. 1 · The "Tree of Life" one of the largest wooden statues in the world, in process of carving for the New York World's Fair 1939 by Lawrence Tenney Stevens from an elm planted by Hessian prisoners in South Windsor, Conn., in 1781. It is 60 ft. high and represents a great ethereal spirit.

DESIGN

AND FIGURE

CARVING

BY

E. J. TANGERMAN

Author of *Whittling and Woodcarving*

NEW YORK

DOVER PUBLICATIONS, INC.

Standard Book Number: 486-21209-2
Library of Congress Catalog Card Number: 64-18869

Manufactured in the United States of America
Dover Publications, Inc.
180 Varick Street
New York, N.Y. 10014

PREFACE

"WILL you please send me, or refer me to, designs suited to this particular piece? I can't originate, but I can copy anything." So runs a letter typical of many I've received since publication of *Whittling and Woodcarving* three years ago.

These letters, the steady increase in the acceptance of whittling and woodcarving as hobbies and leisure-time pursuits, and my firm belief that, with a little practice, any amateur can learn to carve a wide variety of patterns and figures have led me to write this second, and more specific, volume. Though complete in itself, it is intended to supplement and amplify the earlier book, particularly Chaps. XIII and XIV, dealing with caricatures, and Chaps. XVIII to XXI, progressing from surface decoration to in-the-round carving of figures. It is also graded in content from very simple exercises through typical classical and modern designs to museum pieces. Designs are classified *by tool*, to assist in training, tool by tool.

Three years' use and acceptance of *Whittling and Woodcarving* have been convincing evidence that the ancient Confucian precept, "One picture is worth ten thousand words," applies in full measure to carving. Thus, this volume again incorporates dozens of new sketches and hundreds of new photographs of carved objects from all over the world, supplemented by a minimum of explanatory text. They provide literally thousands of readily usable ideas.

Here let me reiterate that anyone who can sharpen a pencil or peel a potato can learn to carve. Only a little practice will show you that you have plenty of skill. Don't worry about your inability to draw. Drawing is admitted by artists to be harder than carving—my own sketches prove that beyond question.

I repeat, carving is easy. A year or two ago, I spent an evening talking to a group of Girl Scouts, none of whom had ever whittled before. They were anxious to try, so I passed out little Scottie-dog blanks. Though their knives were so dull that it was hard work, fourteen of the eighteen girls whittled Scotties that were readily recognizable, complete with the proper number of feet and ears. I have had the same experience in other cases and have been told of scores more.

Why not try it? All you need is a bit of wood, a knife or chisel, and an idea. The last-mentioned you can get right here, and for them thank the dozens of companies and individuals who have made this book possible. I am particularly indebted to The Metropolitan Museum of Art, The American Museum of Natural History, Harmon Foundation, German Railroads Information Office, State Woodcarving School at Brienz, Switzerland, Albert Wood & Five Sons, Cunard White Star Line, Ford Motor Company, National Soap Sculpture Committee, *Popular Mechanics*, *Compressed Air Magazine*, Adam Dabrowski Studios, Jacqueline Overton of the Children's Library (Westbury, N.Y.), Major Henry A. Barber, U.S.A., Allen H. Eaton of the Russell Sage Foundation, Professor Glenn L. Jepson of Princeton University, Rev. E. J. Flanagan of Boys' Town, *The Saturday Evening Post*, *The New Yorker*, Béla Z. Reiter, Walter F. Koch, Faith Bisson, John L. Knight, Mary Quist, J. A. Lucas, Fred Colvin, B. C. Brosheer, M. K. Cumming, W. Parker Lyon, and many others. Their cooperation has permitted the inclusion of many fine pictures. I am also indebted to my wife for tracing most of my sketches, as well as developing many basic designs.

E. J. TANGERMAN.

PORT WASHINGTON, NEW YORK,
February, 1940,

CONTENTS

CONTENTS

〖 x 〗

DESIGN AND
FIGURE CARVING

F_IG_. 2 · *Interior of Vama Temple of Vadi Parsvanatha at Patan, India* (1594–1596), *an amazing example of woodcarving design. Courtesy Metropolitan Museum of Art.*

CARVING TODAY · *Trends*

INEVITABLY, mass production has brought "style" with it—a periodic change of appearance or motif having more to do with merchandising than with permanent beauty. It is change to excite cupidity rather than respect. Often, too, style sacrifices structural excellence in its passion for change. Thus advertising may be all testimonials one year, cartoons the next, beautiful women a third. Similarly, the radiator lines of most automobiles change constantly in comparison with the traditionally square, peaked Packard front.

As Albert Wood, well-known craftsman, says, "Styling is a merchandising trick. Once upon a time we had craftsmen; now we have draftsmen. There is no "style" in craftsmanship; it is permanently good, useful and beautiful."

Look, for example, at the Vama Temple of Vadi Parsvanatha (Fig. 2), 350 years old, still an outstanding example of fine design in wood. Or at the English Coronation Chair[1] (Fig. 3), on which

[1] Perhaps we may digress a moment to tell the legend of Lia-Fàil, the little chunk of gray-brown, mica-flecked syenite that is in the Coronation Chair and is now called the Stone of Scone, symbolizing rulership of Scotland. Legend has it that this is the stone on which Jacob rested his head the night between Beersheba and Haran when he had his dream of the ladder reaching from earth to Heaven. He set it up as a pillar, where it stood until the Children of Israel took it with them into exile in Egypt.

There its power held good, for Moses became captain-general of the armies of Pharaoh Orus and defeated the invading Ethiopians. After Moses was banished, his young aide, Gathelus, exiled son of King Cecrops of Athens, came into favor and won Pharaoh's daughter Scota. Eventually, Orus was succeeded by his grandson Chencres, a lavish man who brought on his countrymen the ten plagues of the Bible. Soon, Chencres' army was swallowed up in the Red Sea, and Gathelus decided it would be healthful to leave at once. He took only his family—and the Stone of Jacob, about whose virtues Moses had told him.

Gathelus first landed in Lusitania, now Portugal. His descendants moved onward to Brigantia, then to Tara Hill, always taking along the stone, the last mover being Simon Brecht, son of Milo the Scot. In the fifth century, the Stone, now called Lia-Fàil, was taken to Dunstaffnage in Scotland, to lend éclat to the coronation of Fergus McErc. In 840, it was carried to the Abbey of Scone by Kenneth II. In the reign of Edward I, it was moved to Westminster, where it has since remained to grace the coronation of the kings of England. The arguments of skeptics are still triumphantly refuted with the fact that syenite is found in the mountains northwest of the Dead Sea in Palestine.

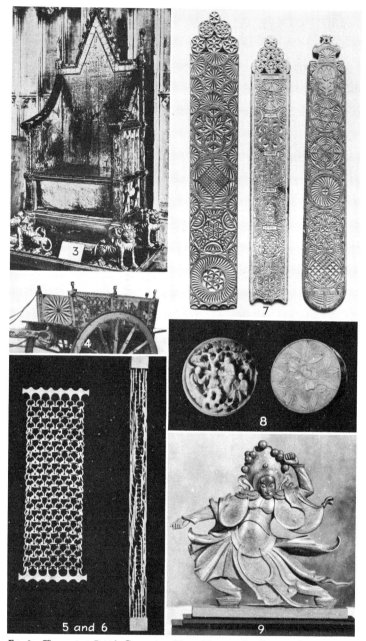

FIG. 3 · The ancient British Coronation Chair. Note initials. Courtesy Acme. FIG. 4 ·
Sicilian painted bridal cart, with carved heads on side stakes, carved edgings, borders, etc.
Courtesy Edison Museum. FIG. 5 · 279-link chain. FIG. 6 · David Strausset of Shoemakers-
ville, Pa., made this intricate specimen, with 44 main links, each composed of 8 interlocking
rings. Both courtesy Delta Manufacturing Company. FIG. 7 · Chip-carved, eighteenth-
century, Dutch mangle boards. Courtesy Metropolitan Museum of Art. FIG. 8 · Simple
scratch-carved bottom and intricate relief-carved top of Chinese ivory box. Courtesy Mary
Quist. See also Fig. 300. FIG. 9 · Teak copy by Walter Koch of low-relief carving of a Chinese
dancing girl, by Allan Clark.

George VI was crowned in 1937, as were many of his ancestors. Its basic design contrasts sharply with the whittled initials on its back, some famous, but lacking in design nevertheless!

No one people can claim exclusive knowledge of design. Our caveman ancestors began to acquire it in making tools, many essentially unchanged in design through succeeding ages. Says Hendrik Willem van Loon,[1] "Unless you have seen some of this prehistoric work with your own eyes, you will hardly believe how far these cave dwellers had advanced as draftsmen, as sculptors and as plain, ordinary whittlers. For they were still in the whittling stage of development, not yet full-fledged sculptors."

Man, ever since he developed edged tools, has carved everything around him, though wood and soft stone have been his favorite materials. He is still at it, though progress has brought machines and much more leisure time. And it has not all been the carving of essentials (see Fig. 6). Carved ivory pieces have often, throughout the ages, been purely, or almost purely, decorative. From Travancore, India, source of the world's smallest coin, came also the seed called Adenanthera Pavonina, hardly $\frac{1}{4}$ in. in diameter, which contains 90 tiny ivory elephants, each perfect in detail under a glass. According to Sirdar Kumar Jag-Jit Singh, only one man still living in India can produce this fine and ancient art.

Much ivory carving is so delicate that it is reminiscent of the carving of Grinling Gibbons, which trembled when anyone slammed a door (Fig. 8). In larger European cities, ivory carvers now often restrict their labors to the hours between midnight and dawn, when traffic vibration is at a minimum.

Modern developments have added new materials to those available for carving—the plastics, celluloid, fiber, even soap—as well as having broadened the availability of the older materials. No longer is a carver's work necessarily produced in materials available locally. And some of the materials, as well as the results, surpass all imagining, for example, an 8-ft. statue carved from cheese, mannequins carved of bread, and a carved soap pistol that helped Dillinger escape from a county jail.

[1] *The Arts*, p. 23.

Many carved works are quite original in design. Lithuania, for example, has long been celebrated for the variety of its carved wooden votive crosses, some 20 ft. high. In a recent study, 3,000 were photographed without showing any duplicates. This like-wise holds true for the carved totem poles and war clubs of the American Indian, for the canoe paddles and images of the Poly-nesian, and for the mangle boards of the Netherlands (Fig. 7).

Mention of totem poles brings up the news report from Illinois of their modern contemporaries. Park officials there have at last ended the sentimental carving of initials on trees and sign-boards by providing whittling posts of cedar, 7 in. in diameter and 4 ft. high. So enthusiastic have the whittlers been that some posts set in May had to be replaced before Labor Day.

A white man's totem pole on a grand scale is the man-god carved of a giant elm by Lawrence Tenney Stevens for the New York World's Fair (Fig. 1). One of three figures, it rises 60 ft. above the ground, and is probably the largest wooden statue ever made. The tools were a bit unconventional, starting with a crosscut saw and ax and progressing through hatchets and gouges to carving chisels and a 3-lb. hammer. Weighing 25 tons, it is flanked by two 10-ft. figures, male and female, in eucalyptus.

New York also claims the world's largest pocketknife. Parker & Battersby, at Radio City, have it. Weighing 6 lb., it is $7\frac{1}{4}$ by $3\frac{1}{4}$ by $1\frac{1}{2}$ in., with 110 blades. There are nine regular knife blades, hunting knife, jeweler's hammer, buttonhook for shoes, another for spats, four dissecting blades, a dozen screw drivers, nut turner, speemer, corkscrew, bottle opener, sail needle, scraper for clarinet reeds, dog's currycomb, fork, steak knife, leather reamer, spatula, calipers, castrating knife, file, and a surgeon's tonsil-removing blade. Each has its own spring, and the knife a special brass case. Cost is $350!

There are several close rivals for the title of the world's largest pocketknife. A knife in Sheffield, England, has 1,937 blades (one for each year A.D.), but stands 6 ft. tall, hence is no pocketknife. Bing Crosby, quite a knife fancier, has a Henckels knife which has four blades not included in the one detailed above—namely, three sizes of toothpick and an eyebrow tweezer—in all, a total of 114 blades.

These are typical of many newspaper items which have appeared during the last several years, indicating the revival of interest in whittling and woodcarving. Other evidences are the increasing frequency of cartoons such as Figs. 31, 32, 1105, and 1107. Here are other news items: John L. Baldwin, celebrated around New York as one of three or four foremost practitioners of the vanishing art of "primitive" water-fowl carving, sold (only to customers whom he liked) excellently made wooden decoys, miniatures, and birds on the wing. Harris V. Johnson of Duluth began to carve fishermen, miniatures, and plaques. Now he is carving figures, and making it a lifework! Eight prominent men in Houston have formed a Whittler's Club, its only rule being that a member caught without his whittlin' knife buys a round of drinks for the others present.

Leslie Garland Bolling, negro shipping clerk of Richmond, has had several exhibitions of whittled figures (see Figs. 1108, 1119–1127). William Steig, well-known cartoonist, has just had his first (Figs. 1068–1075). Anna Larkins of McPherson, Kans., earns her living carving wooden animals. A recent one is a wooden cow, with a man on a stool milking her and a cat sitting near by waiting for the froth. At 83, Miss Larkins is still using a saw she brought from Sweden 73 years ago.

At least two former carpenters have turned woodcarvers and sculptors, who make miniature busts of famous personages for sale. One uses only burin-size tools made from an old telephone guy cable; the other uses ultrasharp wood chisels, gripped like pen-holders. Another whittler of miniatures is McDonald Taylor of Des Moines, Ia., who carves furniture from matchsticks under the microscope—and mounts a whole dining-room suite on a pinhead!

Behind all these news reports runs the increasing desire of the amateur for fundamentals—enough design, enough patterns, and enough ideas to maintain his interest. It is this need the subsequent chapters attempt to fill.

FIG. 10 · *The dwarfs carve a bed for Snow White. Courtesy Walt Disney Productions.*

CHAPTER I

DESIGN · *Principles*

WHEN a friend asked John Opie, the painter, what he mixed his colors with, the painter replied, "With brains!" The same formula works well in design for woodcarving.

What is design? It is the working out, from basic natural or artificial forms, a new form expressing the imagination of the designer—good or bad, depending upon his skill and imagination. If, working according to the laws of design, the designer produces a fine thing, the product of his labor is a work of art.

Since an object is designed, first of all, to serve some useful purpose, this practical cause of its existence must be the main consideration in determining its character. This cause may be either utilitarian or purely decorative, depending upon the nature of the project.[1] If a chair is being designed, it should certainly be, first of all, a comfortable chair in which to sit (Fig. 14). There should be no carving on the seat (Fig. 12), no deep carving on the back (Fig. 13; see also *Whittling and Woodcarving*, page 180). If a panel is being designed, its purpose should be to announce something in no uncertain terms. Everything in the way of arrange-ment and light and shadow which will help to make it more easily seen and understood should be used; any decorative elements that add confusing detail should be eliminated (see Fig. 11). Think first: Does it fulfill to best advantage the purpose for which it was intended? Figure 15 does that without question.

We demand, besides mere utility, another quality in things designed—*beauty*. The human mind craves it, and indeed, most things around us, at least in nature, abound with it. The graceful lines of plant growth, the geometric perfection of snowflake crystals, the expanding spirals of shells, the intricate pattern of light and shadow on an outcropping of rock, all are examples. To repeat them, it is the purpose of design to create things that are both *useful* and *beautiful*.

To make any design most effective, there should be a real idea behind it. For example, in Fig. 14, the motifs on the chair back are based on the Vermont ancestry of the men for whom the set was made. Likewise, the flying-bird motif of Fig. 15 was developed to symbolize the freedom of spirit of the lady who ordered the slipper cabinet. In each case, some dominant fact in the purchaser's background suggested a basic idea for the motif.

In your own decorative carving, seek for some theme or idea, and that will often suggest a motif. Consideration of that and the surface to be decorated will soon provide an answer to your question of what to carve. Of course, there is one further con-sideration if you are planning to make a carving harmonize with

[1] Design data based largely on Chap. I, *Commercial Art*, by C. E. Wallace.

FIG. 11 · *Carved Italian Renaissance cassone, from Venice (sixteenth century), showing simplified scrolls, bosses, masks, shell and Flemish S motifs.* FIG, 12 · *Chip-carved seventeenth-century chair, Swiss or Italian.* FIG. 13 · *An English walnut chair of the William and Mary style (1689–1702). All courtesy Metropolitan Museum of Art.* FIG. 14 · *Dining-room chair. Motifs symbolize Vermont origin of family.* FIG. 15 · *Slipper cabinet; bird motif symbolizes a soul not earthbound. Both in teak, by Albert Wood & Five Sons.*

other articles of furniture. Then it must be in proper "period" or style, and your motif must be subordinated to the characteristics that denote that particular style. It is still possible, however, to produce a design that suggests the style and, yet is distinctive— or better still, an original design which harmonizes with the style and yet sets a style all its own, or all *your* own.

The woodcarver makes use of lines, areas, and depth as elements from which to build designs. It is essential to study these elements to determine the means of securing beauty of design through them.

Lines may be classified as straight, crooked, or curved. A straight line, though essential to the structure and utility of many forms, certainly cannot be considered beautiful in itself. Its uniformity makes it monotonous (Fig. 16). On the other hand, a crooked line usually isn't beautiful because it keeps changing in a disorganized way. It has no unity (Fig. 17).

A curved line, however, possesses a degree of beauty, depending upon rhythm, variety, subtlety, and harmony of the parts (Fig. 18). Of curved lines, the arc of a circle is least beautiful because it lacks variety and subtlety. Ellipses, parabolas, hyperbolas, and compound curves attain a high degree of beauty because of their subtle rhythm.

Beautiful curved lines occur everywhere—in well designed vases, in a skyrocket's flight and burst, in a flower stem, in the female silhouette.

While carved lines are important in edgings, bands, borders, and in simple surface design, more important are carved *areas*. Areas in design depend for their interest and beauty upon good proportion of masses and harmony of shapes. Good proportion simply means an interesting variety of related shapes. There must be dominant and subordinate elements, major and minor parts; even in an allover pattern such as a diaper design (see *Whittling and Woodcarving*, Fig. 263) the little patterns dominate the subordinated interlaced network. Equal sizes are monotonous, but the difference in size must not be so great as to make the parts unrelated (Fig. 20).

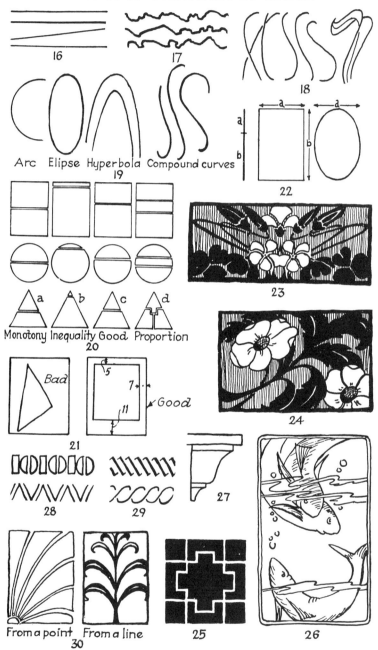

FIG. 16 *shows monotony,* FIG. 17 *inharmony,* FIG. 18 *interest.* FIG. 22 *gives proportions of the* Golden Section

Several rules have been developed to aid in the interesting division of space. All are based on the same principle, that, to be well divided, space must be broken to have variety, subtlety, and harmony of parts. Of course, in the last analysis, no rule can cover all cases. For example, the rule that only a third of the area should be carved is successfully violated by allover chip-carving designs (Figs. 7, 12, 334, and 335) and by most Chinese and Indian patterns (Figs. 2, 8 and 9). The designer must rely upon his judgment and good taste in sizing and placing his carving properly. In fact, in some cases, carving may do more harm than good, for, unless on a purely decorative panel or figure, it should accentuate the piece, not stand out of itself.

An old architectural rule of thumb, the "Golden Section," keeps turning up wherever form and proportion are discussed. Fundamentally, the Golden Section is nothing more than a ratio (Fig. 22) between the width and the height of a rectangle or between the minor and major axes of the ellipse of 0.618 to 1. In other words, for every inch of height of the rectangle or length of the major axis of an ellipse, the width of the rectangle or minor axis of the ellipse is about $\frac{5}{8}$ in. long. The same principle can be applied to the subdivision of a line and to other geometric shapes.

No matter how applied, this ratio, in days gone by when the significance of numbers was regarded with awe and superstition, was believed by many to possess attributes of the divine and to be the fundamental basis of natural beauty. Actually, it is the proportion preferred by most observers. It was preferred by Leonardo da Vinci and most other artists and scholars of the Renaissance.

Whether use of the Golden Section by many generations of distinguished artists has been intuitive or reasoned, their success recommends it as a practical aid to less-inspired craftsmen, a rule not to be followed slavishly, but used wherever it is consistent with the functional and dynamic elements of the design.

The Golden Section is helpful in a surprising number of problems. It may be applied to the spacing of lines and to subdivision of lines and areas, as well as to the proportions of ovals, rectangles,

FIG. 31 · RABBIT MOTIF IN VARIOUS AREAS

and ellipses. It provides an interesting variety in dimensions to-gether with an effect of unity and balance.[1]

[1] The Golden Section has a long and curious history. It has been construed to be identical with the Sacred Quotient, Seqt., which a papyrus in the British Museum records was used in building the earliest pyramid in 4750 B.C. Contemporary artists have found it oft repeated in their measurements of the Parthenon and classical Greek sculpture.

As a mathematical concept, it appeared in Euclid's elements. It is a proportion in which the smaller part is to the greater as the greater is to the whole, or a : b :: b : a + b. Fra Luca Paccioli, in the first noteworthy mathematical treatise after Euclid's, named this the "Divine Proportion." "Like God," he says, "it has a peculiar and unique unity; its com-ponent parts ally with the Holy Trinity; as God cannot be defined by words neither can this proportion by numbers, for it is an irrational; like God it is all in all, and all in every part." (The proportion is actually 0.618 +.)

It was not, however, until about 1850, when Zeising became acquainted with Paccioli's book, that the empirical rule for achieving beautiful proportions and the mathematical formula were correlated. Measurements seemed to point to the Golden Section as a prin-ciple underlying all creations of beauty. The London Royal Botanical Society found the Golden Section expressed in the arrangement of seeds, buds, and leaves of many plants, and critics found it "in every intersection of Titian's 'Assumption'," in Raphael's "Madonna of the Cradle," and in works by Hals, Botticelli, and Turner.

Fechner, the German physicist, made some of the earliest attempts to discover aesthetic principles by scientifically controlled experiments in the latter part of the nineteenth century. One experiment involved the selection of the most pleasing of twelve white rectangles of varying proportions on a black background. The Golden Section was chosen in 35 per cent of 350 cases. Allowing for the two distinct subgroups of individuals, those preferring asymmetry (average 0.621) and those preferring the symmetry of the square (average for both groups 0.632), modern analysis, as reported in the *Bell Laboratories Record*, would indicate that the best proportion lies somewhere between 0.610 and 0.632.

All sorts of psychological experiments have been made and reasons advanced. Suffice it to say, that the Golden Section is often used—for example, the telephone handset is based on a Golden Section ellipse. If a square is taken from a Golden Section rectangle, the remaining rectangle will be the same shape as the original. This process may be repeated infinitely, and a curved line joining the centers of the subtracted squares is a spiral coming to a focus at what we commonly call the "optical center" of the original rectangle.

In the framing of a decorative panel, for example, the so-called "Greek" proportion of 5 to 7 to 11 is one of the rules (Fig. 21). While there is, without doubt, a certain subtlety and interest in such a proportion of areas, it is too limited in its conception. This rule, often applied to marginal spaces, obviously doesn't apply in such a case as Fig. 15, in which the panel is a part of a larger piece.

Another rule states that when space is divided so that one part is more than half and less than two-thirds of the whole, the resultant division will be interesting (Fig. 20, c and d). Other rules stress the importance of having prominent corner-to-corner diagonals or a triangular- or diamond-shaped principal element even in a panel involving human figures, with the center of interest—in most cases the head of the dominant figure—at the apex of the triangle or at the optical center (slightly above the true center).

Nature is filled with beautiful proportions of areas and interesting space division—flowers, plants, leaves, fish, birds, animals, and landscapes all yield rich motifs for design. I have shown in Figs. 31 and 32 several motifs taken from nature and inspired by Walt Disney's "Snow White and the Seven Dwarfs." This motion picture was particularly rich in carving motifs—even though the sequence of Fig. 10 ended up on the cutting-room floor. In Figs. 31 and 32, I have attempted to show how a single motif may be varied to suit a space of any given shape.

In area design, *harmony* of shapes is as essential as good proportion. It is attained by placing together only forms that are consistent in character and style, or that have elements in common. If possible, designs should be kept structural; that is, the shape of one part should "fit" the shape of adjoining elements (Fig. 21).

Depth is the carver's equivalent of the painter's color or tone. Beauty in depth depends upon a proper proportion of light and shadow. Every good design will show a balanced distribution of attractions secured by carefully planned "value" relationships. Strong contrasts of light and shadow—obtained by deep carving or high relief—are appropriate in some instances (Fig. 13), while very close values—obtained by low relief or shallow carving with wide outlining—are better in others (Fig. 15).

Sometimes designs which look all right on paper, work out poorly when carved, owing to the change in effects of light and shadow. The carved design may require deepening or "shallow-ing" in spots—and may again have to be corrected when the carving is put in its final setting, owing to a change in lighting. Even Malvina Hoffman, famous sculptress, reports the necessity of climbing 80 ft. into the air over the entrance to Bush House, London, to deepen the shadows on draperies, shields, and inscriptions on two 15-ft. stone figures. The figures were made in her American studio in sunlight, but were placed facing north, where sunlight never struck, so that details had to be cut deeper and made more legible. Carving to be placed so far above the eye level tremendously complicates the problems of perspective also (see *Whittling and Woodcarving*, pages 200–202, and Fig. 264).

Many professional woodcarvers actually endeavor to duplicate in their studios the dominant lighting of the place of installation of a carving in order to avoid such difficulties. Further, they periodically place the carving at the same level above or below the eye as it will ultimately occupy, to correct carving depths accordingly.

While much of the foregoing might be classified under "principles of design," the following topics deserve special consideration, so are grouped here for convenience.

Balance in design means an equal arrangement of "attraction powers" on either side of a center or fulcrum. Any element has attraction power because of its contrast to other things about it. Large size does not necessarily imply power to attract—the midget in a circus receives more attention because he is *different*.

There are two forms of balance of attractions, *bisymmetric* and *occult*. In bisymmetric balance (Fig. 23) the attractions are arranged equally on either side of a vertical axis. Because of its quiet and dignified effect, this is often called "formal" balance. The human figure, a ship, a piece of pottery, are all examples. Sometimes, as in a tile pattern, the design is arranged equally on either side of two or more axes. It is then *symmetrical* (Fig. 25).

Occult balance is felt rather than measured. It expresses freedom and power and holds great possibilities for general design use.

There are unlimited arrangements, but in general it is the balancing, on either side of a fulcrum, of two unequal attractions by
varying the size, value, and distance from the center (Fig. 24).

In determining proper occult balance, size, color, value, shape,
and distance from the center must be considered. Just as a brilliant
color "weighs" more than a neutral color of the same area, so a
contrasting value, either decidedly lighter or darker (in light or
shadow) than the general tone of the design, has strong attraction
power. An odd shape attracts the attention more forcibly than a
regular form. Since all these factors are different, the attractions
resulting from each must be considered and adjustments made until
the final result seems satisfactory to the eye. This will generally
require that parts which have greatest attraction power be kept
nearest to the center, or balanced with an equally strong counter-
attraction on the opposite side of the center or fulcrum.

In any design there must be a single dominating part to which
the other elements are subordinated, just as the chorus in a revue
is subordinated to the star. The feature of the design must be
accented to serve as the center of interest or the dominating
theme—through size, color, contrast, or shape (Fig. 24).

Rhythm and *movement,* though harder to define, are as essential
in design as they are in music. Rhythm may be defined in carving
design as that quality of line and arrangement of a design which
causes the eye to move easily from one part to the next. Borders
and edgings are invariably rhythmic. Figure 26 shows the rhythm

Fig. 32 · *Further motifs suggested by "Snow White and the Seven Dwarfs."*

of swimming fish caught in a design. Figures 28 and 29 represent the measured beat or rhythm in border designs. Movement in carving may be obtained by means of dominant lines carrying the eye through the design, or by means of an obvious or repeated sequence of tones of light and shadow.

Transition is a principle closely associated with movement. When two main lines meet in a design, the union is likely to be too abrupt. The Greeks felt this and produced moldings and capitals to soften otherwise harsh angles caused by stone meeting stone. Figure 27 shows an example of transitional elements which lead the eye easily from one main element to another.

Just as do dominance and subordination, the principles of *repetition* and *variety* express opposing ideas. To be good, a design must repeat a motif or maintain the same spirit throughout, yet it must have a variety of form to keep it from becoming common-place and uninteresting. It is the designer's problem to secure a happy balance of these two factors. In music, the uninterrupted repetition of a single note or chord soon becomes unpleasant. Yet every composer makes use of repetition of chords and themes in order to hold his composition together. Figures 28 and 29 show a series of simple border effects to illustrate repetition with variety. In an area design, the repetition of the same

Fig. 33 · "*Little Lulu*," by Marge, and her first carving design. *Reproduced by special permission of "The Saturday Evening Post," copyright, 1937, by the Curtis Publishing Company.*

element, such as a similarly shaped area, or other like "eye appeal," aids the composition. Repetition tends to produce unity and harmony; variety adds interest and zest.

In allover patterns, there are several systems of repeats of units that may be employed, such as: placing units in vertical rows, in horizontal rows, in "drop" repeats in which each successive vertical or horizontal row is dropped a fraction of the height of the preceding row, and the familiar diaper arrangement, in which motifs are repeated continually or in series within a lattice.

When the elements of a design spring from a line or point, it is called a *radiating* design. Radiation tends to produce unity, because the parts of the design are tied in to a common center (Fig. 30). In nature, sea shells provide radiation examples.

The result of proper application of the foregoing principles of design is *unity*, or organization of lines, areas, and depths into a harmonious whole. You must learn to visualize, to make mental pictures strong enough for you to translate at least into basic drawings, because more work with the pencil means less with the tools. Until you attain the visualization strength of the sculptor who, without preliminary sketches, attacks a squared block of stone, good front and side sketches of the figure, and rough outline cutting will save endless, fruitless removal of small chips.

Fig. 34 · *"Boss! I've been wanting to get this off my chest for years." By Davis. Reproduced by special permission of "The Saturday Evening Post"; copyright, 1937, by the Curtis Publishing Company.*

FIG. 35 · *Sunflower design, and* FIG. 36 · *Tulip design, from a seventeenth-century American chest.*
FIG. 37 · *Gothic bands from a Swiss fifteenth-century piece.* FIG. 38 · *English horn cup with scratched*
design. FIG. 39 · *Seventeenth-century American desk box.* FIG. 40 · *Same as Fig. 37. All courtesy Metro-*
politan Museum of Art.

CHAPTER II

STAMP · *Punch and Tracer*

IT seems particularly inappropriate to begin a series of chapters on carved patterns and carving tools with a form of decoration which is not carving at all. But stamping is closely associated with carving, certainly belongs to the same family, and is occasionally very useful. Early American carvers, as well as the Chinese, East Indians, and aboriginal peoples, made common use of this method of surface decoration.

The American carvers learned it from their forebears in Europe, for it was common during the Middle Ages and later, for chest, box, and cabinet decoration. Punch designs were used—particularly where only a difference in *texture* was needed—to set off a design, to indicate a drapery, to delineate a shadow. They provide a difference in apparent color or tone due primarily to the variation in surface. They undoubtedly often replaced a carved or sunken background because of the simplicity and rapidity of their execution—anyone who can hit a nail with a hammer can do them, practically without instruction.

Another possible reason for the use of stamped designs, particularly in those cases where they were used to finish a background previously sunk with a gouge or firmer, is that they effectively hide a poorly or hurriedly leveled ground. Perhaps this latter reason may account for the present unpopularity of wood stamping among the more aesthetic carvers.

Though stamping is an unsponsored technique, it has its uses, for example, in decorating very thin wood, such as a book or album cover or other thin panel, where carving would appear to be too heavy or might even seriously weaken an already light section. It is also useful if you *must* decorate a stool top, chair seat, table top, or tray surface, for the marking is so shallow that it

FIGS. 41–45 and 52 are early American, FIGS. 46–49, 51, and 53 are old English. FIG. 50 is a typical lettered band. FIG. 54 is ancient Greek. FIGS. 55–65 are Jacobean style.

won't cause a glass to tip or the pattern to be impressed on a sitter—even in a bathing suit. Lastly, it is one method of delineating extremely complicated, small, or detailed designs.

Actual tools for stamping, also called *indenting*, have been described in *Whittling and Woodcarving*, page 165. Any plain pointed or pattern-ended stamp will do, even a nail, for the whole object is simply to roughen the surface of the background so that the smooth design stands out (or occasionally to roughen the *design* so that the smooth background stands out). The technique is exactly like that of stamping damp leather, or *repoussé*, or sheet-brass stamping.

The wood you indent should be fine-grained, such as elm, cedar, beech, birch, or hickory, and preferably light in color, such as holly. It should, of course, have no knots, flaws, or prominent "figure." All the diaper patterns (*Whittling and Woodcarving*, Fig. 264) are suitable motifs, as is any other recurring pattern, a strapwork or ribbon-work design, a border, edging or decorative band, or any other simple motif. Figures 41 to 65 detail 25 historical motifs, mostly early American and Jacobean. As another example of application, 27 poses of figures are shown in the panels of Figs. 66 to 74. The latter are taken from a sculptural frieze by Albert Stewart around the new Post Office, Court House, and Custom House building in Albany, N. Y.

Both series demonstrate the salient fact that any punch pattern can also be executed with the gouge or firmer as a typical surface carving, with the veiner or sharp vee chisel as a line or outline pattern, or often with the scroll saw as an openwork design for a grille or "squint." Likewise, almost all the patterns detailed in chapters devoted to these particular tools can likewise be done with the punch. Stool seats, for example, are shown in Chap. III, decorative bands of other styles in Chaps. III, VII, and IX. Further, an element of any of the designs shown here can be expanded to fit a desired shape, as was shown with the rabbit and owl patterns of Figs. 31 and 32.

Even when made with a small-pattern punch or a point, the edges of a stamped design are likely to look ragged and uneven

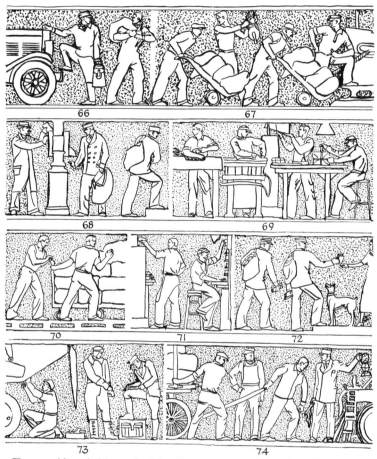

The original low-relief figures, by Albert Stewart, were 8½ ft. high in a 565-ft. frieze.

unless they are finished with a tracer or pattern wheel. Any dull-pointed or dull-edged tool can be used as a tracer—even a blunt-ended, round-corner screw driver. Just run it along the outline of the design to smooth rough edges. Professional carvers usually edge a punched design with a veiner, outlining the design first with the veiner, then stamping the ground.

Tight corners are likewise important, and hard to work. Regardless of the form of punch you use for the ground, you can stamp even the tightest corner with an ordinary small nail.

Medieval carvers often finished a stamped background, particularly on picture frames, with gold. The ground was first gilded, then raw sienna or burnt umber rubbed into the punch marks. The surface color was rubbed off, so that the ground became a dark-brown pattern and outline on a gold background.

An old ivory effect can be similarly obtained with a base coat of ivory paint, brown pigment mixed with drier being rubbed into the punch marks. Modern carvers may rub white lead into a stamped background on dark woods such as walnut, or brown paint into a pattern on light wood, for accent. In either case, the wood first receives a coat of linseed oil. Excess color is removed and the background polished with a stiff bristle brush.

Stamping, of course, has its equivalent in carving other materials. In ivory or bone, for example, backgrounds were often crisscrossed with a scratched pattern put on with a sharp-pointed or toothed tool, straight or hooked. Figures 8, 38, and 300 are examples. Modern plastics can be finished in the same way, the purpose being to produce a dull background texture to contrast with the surface shine or polish. Even soap lends itself to such treatment—though all you need for a tool in working with soap is a bit of old comb or a broken hack-saw or scroll-saw blade.

FIGS. 75–77 · *Large mural carvings in the starboard gallery, Promenade Deck, R.M.S. "Queen Mary."* All were designed and executed by John Skeaping. *Courtesy Cunard White Star Line.* FIG. 78 · *Welsh teak dresser, designed and built by Albert Wood & Five Sons, an example of ultrasimple modern design. Carving motifs are moldings, like Fig. 198, but square and done with the firmer, and a Greek scroll, done with the veiner.*

CHAPTER III

KNIFE AND FIRMER · *Chip Carving*

IN other centuries, woodcarvers customarily used intricate high-relief patterns. The unbelievably delicate and detailed work of Grinling Gibbons illustrates this type of carving (*Whittling and Woodcarving*, Figs. 2, 4, and 5). But tastes have changed—we have reacted from the ultraornate decoration particularly characteristic of the Victorian era. Today carvers prefer essentially simple designs—compare Figs. 75 to 78, for example, with the heavy, ornate, high-relief carving of yesteryear.

Tastes in carving follow a simple cycle. Primitive, savage decoration is simple, low relief—or even just surface scratching. Stamping and chip carving are examples. Most basic designs go back far beyond written record; the guilloche, or meander, as a case in point, is supposed to have come down to us from the Assyrians, with the Greeks supplying many variations, the Romans fewer, the Renaissance carvers still fewer. Geometric and strapwork patterns originated similarly, and variations have likewise been progressively fewer. The linen and parchment folds, Flemish Y and curve, and other common motifs were developed several centuries ago. Later carvers were able to do little but copy and elaborate these known designs. They increased the relief and added more and more confusing detail, until many Victorian examples were only grotesque and gimcracky, just as were Victorian houses. Some carving was good, but most carvers did not have Gibbons' ability to make involved details harmonious, nor the courage to strike out in a new direction.

To such ornate, dust-catching froth there must inevitably come a reaction. Ours began by elimination of the normally tightly closed "company parlor," with its stuffed peacocks and closed shutters. Greater understanding of the need for fresh air, sunlight, and dustless atmosphere doomed the whatnot and heavily carved dust-catching furniture. We entered a "streamlined" age, with far smaller houses or apartments, square-cornered, untempered "modern" furniture, and severe simplicity. Pieces were functional in the extreme, having little grace, less harmony, and minimum beauty. More recent pieces, however, show the trend back toward more graceful curves, with transition elements such as fillets and moldings, and monotony-relieving decoration.

This trend is exhibited in furniture just as strikingly as in buildings, where the blank-walled boxy structure is giving way to the pastel-toned, mural- or low-relief-decorated curved type. We are coming back from exact geometry to proportion, the same path that was followed by the ancient Greeks. Their early, geometric structures were later supplanted, in the Golden Age, by buildings with greater rhythm and balance. Façades and pillars were even designed with compensating curves to correct the optical illusion of concavity produced by a long straight line.

Almost certainly, we shall go too far in the opposite direction— again covering every visible portion of an object with decoration. Our only hope of avoiding such an overcompensating swing is to remember the old basic principle: Only a third of a large area should be decorated with carving; smaller objects may be covered with increasingly large proportions of carving. Thus, a snuff box (or its present-day equivalent, the compact) may well be carved all over, but a temple had best have some blank spaces to accentuate the beauty of the decoration.

There are many times and places where carving is not only unnecessary but definitely out of place. A beautifully figured or grained wood panel needs no carving, nor does an elaborately shaped or turned piece. The shape, figure, or color of the wood itself may be decoration enough.

Some time ago, we planned to refinish a four-poster bed that had been in the family for a hundred years or more. Many years ago, it had been carefully painted black with red markings to simulate mahogany. When this paint was scraped off, the bed was found to be maple, beautifully figured. We refinished it simply by oiling and waxing, because the turned corner posts, scroll-outline head and footboards, and the side rails with pins that once held the rope mattress are certainly decoration enough.

We planned a carved door, 3 ft. 6 in. by 6 ft. 6 in., to be solid teak and swung in a carved frame. The door incorporated three octagonal panels, one above the other, each set off with a heavy chamfered molding. All around the door frame is a 2-in. rope molding, made as shown in Fig. 224, and relieved at the corners with low-relief dogwood flower and leaf motifs (Figs. 491 and 495). When the molding was placed and the door brought up by oiling to its natural rich red-brown color, we found that any carving on it would be superfluous—its color, the three panels, and the framing molding were all that was needed. Any carving would tend to break up the planes and would detract from, rather than enhance, the beauty of the door.

Such examples could be multiplied endlessly. Look at the simple beauty of the pieces in Figs. 78, 233 to 235, and 248, designed and carved by Albert Wood & Five Sons. See how small a proportion is given over to carving, and how shallow that carving is? Or look at the panels of Figs. 75 to 77, from R.M.S. "Queen Mary," again essentially simple. Still other examples are the modern veneered pieces with simple veiner or vee-tool patterns outlined through the outer sheet of veneer (Chap. VII).

There is good precedent for this simplicity, as explained in preceding paragraphs. The trend toward simplicity explains, too, why much of the present-day carving can be done with the knife or firmer alone, or at most with only occasional assistance from the gouge and veiner. Even a pair of ordinary wood chisels will serve, if one of the chisels is ground with corners slightly rounded to permit its use for grounding out. So to patterns and techniques, which, as explained in the foreword, are taken up from the standpoint of the tools necessary to carve them.

Among the earliest of surface-decoration techniques is chip carving (see *Whittling and Woodcarving*, pages 166–168). Though apparently originated by natives of the South Sea Islands, chip carving has appeared in widely separated parts of the world, and

is probably best known to us as a Scandinavian, Frisian (the petaled-flower forms are still called Frisian carving, from the Netherlands state, Friesland, where they originated), or Pennsylvania Dutch technique. All designs are geometric (composed of circles and triangles), are incised, and cover a whole surface with reasonable uniformity. There are slight elaborations occasionally, rosettes, little geometric flowers, and monograms, but in general the outstanding characteristic, and primary claim to artistic worth, of this class of carving is the small scale of the elements (usually from $\frac{1}{16}$ to $\frac{1}{4}$ in.) and the obvious patience required to execute them.

It has been explained that the development of chip carving in England came about 1525, after Henry VIII began to suppress the monasteries, which had since the Middle Ages been the home of all English artistic crafts. Monks and lay brethren were driven forth as outlaws and outcasts. Gothic arts were destroyed. Cultured people of the next generation turned to the new manner, the Renaissance, while the untutored stayed faithful to the Gothic, which they remembered only dimly and whose principles were by now misunderstood. Chip carving, with designs patterned by divider and usually executed by knife, came in during this period, combining with the common motifs some crudely executed Gothic designs and even cruder Renaissance motifs such as heads enclosed in circular cartouches—nothing but the chip carving being executed successfully.

Possibly the fact that an untutored and relatively unskilled carver can produce acceptable chip-carved pieces is in itself a justification for chip carving in general. The obvious labor and patience that have gone into their execution may make up for their lack of originality. Chip-carved pieces have a quiet simplicity and beauty that are difficult to evaluate unless one remembers that the basic principle of all design is repetition. Always on small, serviceable objects such as paddles, mangle boards, or desk boxes, chip-carved patterns seem to be in harmony with the *purpose* of the utensil. The carving expresses man's respect for, and desire to beautify, the things with which he works each day. Even the savage has this feeling, and uses a repetitive motif subordinated to the object and varied only just enough to avoid monotony. He is trying to express his respect and win the admiration of others for the *utensil*, not for the decoration.

Be the reasons what they may, I feel that every carver should have some knowledge of chip carving. I have therefore included Figs. 79 to 128, which are 50 of the simpler motifs, as well as Figs. 7, 12, 334, and 335, showing their application to actual carved pieces (see also Figs. 223–226, *Whittling and Woodcarving*).

The basis of all chip-carved patterns is the incised triangle (Fig. 103). This has been modified by allowing a border between triangles (Fig. 104), by adding a side to make an incised square (Figs. 95 and 96), or by changing the shape of the triangle or its relationship to others. Thus a group of slender triangles radiating from a point produces the circular elements of Figs. 81, 84, 86, and 94, the six- and eight-pointed stars forming the centers of Figs. 101 and 116 to 118. Also, the sides may be curved, forming elements like the border in Fig. 86, the quadrants in Fig. 91, etc.

In contrast to the regular patterns for Figs. 95 and 103, rosette patterns of radiating types and odd shapes can be combined in an irregular, over-all pattern like that of Fig. 100. Judicious selection of patterns and interspersion of uncarved bands develops the involved patterns of Figs. 90, 91, 92, 93, 94, and 101. The addition of the chip-carved flower, which is really nothing but an uncarved square, diamond, or triangle with notches cut in each of its sides and a tiny incised triangle in its center, produces such designs as Figs. 80, 89, 117, while the same flower can be used to fit an otherwise round element into a square panel (Figs. 79 and 82). Use or dropping of a border between elements produces the variations shown in Figs. 105 to 110.

For chair or stool seats, the patterns of Figs. 90, 91, 94, and 101 are well fitted, each representing (except Fig. 101, which shows a bit over half) a quarter of the complete design element. Variation in length of triangles produces the cross element of Fig. 102, adaptable as part of an allover design, as a unit, or a border unit. Other typical borders are shown in Figs. 105 to 128, including

Fig. 125, which is really simply a triangular molding, notched with a series of triangles. It is included here because it can be used very well with chip-carved panels. The interesting fan border of Fig. 86 occurs again in curved form in Fig. 94.

The Frisian flower element shows up in Figs. 79 and 91. This use is typical of many, others showing up in the Dutch mangle boards of Figs. 8, 334, and 335 (as well as in the chip-carved pieces of Figs. 218, 222, and 223, *Whittling and Woodcarving*). The Gothic influence appears in the borders of Figs. 111 to 114, which show the Gothic arch produced by curving two sides of each incised triangle fanwise.

Not only may an individual triangle be varied in shape, but also an entire pattern. Notice the variation in Figs. 87 and 88, produced by varying proportions of the same unit. The border of Fig. 118 uses the same design in two widths alternately. An interesting variation of the radiating triangles is also produced by radiation from the outer corners instead of the center, as shown in Fig. 83, which is essentially half of a square panel, although it may make an oblong panel as drawn, or half of it may be used as a square flanking some other design.

Chip-carved patterns are very adaptable. Obviously the irregular pattern of Fig. 100 can be fitted into a space of any shape. Figure 85 demonstrates how a standard pattern can be elongated to fit a regular curve, and the corners outside the cross of Fig. 102 illustrate how it can be brought into a square or rectangle. Modern-furniture makers often use chip-carved motifs (see Figs. 903–908), Fred von Hoefer has even succeeded in making such designs as fighting cocks and a mandarin head, with chip carving as a basis (see *Whittling and Woodcarving*. Figs. 225 and 226).

In general, chip carving should fit freely into the space to be filled, and rough or irregular work—providing it is not just slipshod—will look about as well as many of the highly elaborate patterns. The main principle is precise, clean cutting, and individual units which are relatively small. An allover pattern of triangles an inch or so from point to point begins to look incongruous; the same pattern in $\frac{1}{4}$-in. triangles is very interesting.

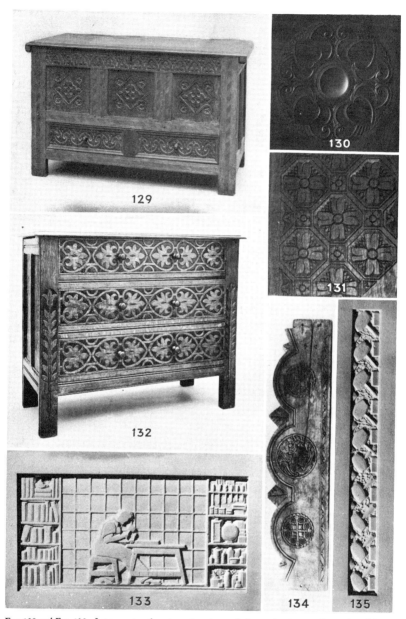

FIG. 129 and FIG. 132 · *Late seventeenth-century American oak chests, showing simple motifs with background grounded only about ⅛ in., then painted. Courtesy Metropolitan Museum of Art.* FIG. 130 and FIG. 131 · *Lovebird and tulip motifs by Albert Wood & Five Sons.* FIG. 133 · *A book headpiece in plaster, designed by Albert Wood.* FIG. 134 · *A seventh-century Egyptian (Coptic) panel. Courtesy Metropolitan Museum of Art.* FIG. 135 · *Footpiece for bookplate, designed by Albert Wood.*

One form of special finish for chip carving—beyond the usual oiling and waxing—may well be mentioned here. It is particularly useful for chip-carved chair seats or trays because it fills the chip-carved pattern to smooth the surface. Powdered rice, size, and lime, if mixed together with water and patted into the design, will dry to an ivory color. A putty and glue mixture gives a tan. Plaster of Paris, size, and paste mixed will give a dead-white surface. These are, of course, best in chip-carved designs in dark woods such as walnut or mahogany, particularly in those designs which incorporate uncarved bands or borders and strong, un-broken surface lines. After application of the filler, finish by sand-ing flat, then oiling and waxing. Any of these mixtures can be colored with oil pigments to produce a dark filler for light woods such as lime, holly, or apple.

One last caution may be in order before we leave chip carving. Chip-carved patterns look best in a close-grained, non-figured wood such as mahogany, holly, apple, or maple. Don't try them in such strongly grained woods as yellow pine, or in highly figured panels, such as quarter-sawed oak or burl walnut. They, or almost any other carving for that matter, will only interfere with the simple beauty of the wood itself.

Later peoples, among them the early settlers in America, used all sorts of simple patterns for design, such as the sunflower and tulip motifs of Figs. 35 and 36, and the modified tulip and acan-thus patterns of Figs. 129 and 132. In many cases, they sunk the ground slightly with a flat chisel, then stamped or painted it to make the design stand out boldly. Elaborate, high-relief patterns were relatively rare.

The reasons for the use of these simple designs by the American colonists go back to the reasons for the founding of America, to the desire for religious and political freedom, to the types of people who emigrated to the colonies, and to the inevitable mingling of races which followed. America needed carpenters and joiners in the early settlements, and these we got. There were practically no cabinetmakers, at least among the English colonists. In England, the cabinetmaker, the chair maker, and the woodcarver were all members of separate trades. None of the three was a "general utility" man. Unless he was escaping from something in England, he would not be among the immigrants. From other European countries came the craftsmen who taught us what little we knew about carving and cabinetmaking. Even when the wood-working trade began to segregate in Philadelphia in the latter half of the eighteenth century, the traditions which arose were not those of the English cabinetmaker, chair maker, or woodcarver. Our pieces were no less skillful or artistic, but were totally dis-tinct. Our woods reacted differently to the tools. Pennsylvania Chippendale is very different from any English work.

It was not until the middle of the eighteenth century that the exodus of craftsmen began to Pennsylvania and Massachusetts. The Revolutionary War and subsequent difficulties, coupled with the shortage of books or catalogues of standard English designs, resulted, however, in American designs distinctively different from the English. Our different woods were also factors.

Most woodcarving designs are not geometrically exact. Too much regularity makes a pattern uninteresting. This is one basic fault of the machine-produced carving of today. It is so precise and exact that there is never anything unexpected, hence interesting, about it. Note the obvious crudities and inexactness of the panel in Fig. 134; yet it is very interesting.

The ancient Greeks understood this principle, too. Their mean-der rarely continued uninterruptedly for an entire border (Fig. 147). They would carve a half dozen or so guilloches, then run the bands parallel or enclosing a long, flat boss, then repeat the guilloche. This also provided a simple way of turning the corner, always a problem in any evenly proportioned border design.

There is much more to the turning of a corner than most busi-nessmen realize. Many carvers, as well as designers in other materials, avoid corner problems in borders and bands by stopping the repetitive motif and inserting a special corner motif. The strapwork elements of Figs. 165 to 170, for example, have often been so used. But, with a little advance planning—done with the pencil, *not* the firmer—most patterns will readily go around the corner. Figures 173 and 174 show two typical methods, the upper simply dropping the ribbon downward instead of passing it back, while the lower utilizes extra-large loops of the ribbon.

Scandinavian, Swiss, and North-Italian carvers were the developers of ribbon carving or strapwork, which apparently originated in similar stone carving in Greece and Rome (see *Whittling and Woodcarving*, page 205). Undoubtedly, one factor in the development of ribbon carving was the endeavor to picture woven reeds as a surface pattern. The simplest weaving pattern is shown in Fig. 141, in which the woven appearance is obtained simply by shaving off the surface of the reed which would normally go under the adjacent one. Lines between reeds are made with the scratch with a pointed bit (see *Whittling and Woodcarving*, Fig. 231). This will be found somewhat easier to do if the pattern is made similar to open weaving (Fig. 143). In this case, the small squares shown between reeds are simply cut lower than the pattern with the tip of a knife blade or with a small vee tool or chisel.

Some of the commoner variations in weaving are shown in Figs. 136, 142, and 144, the latter two showing basket weaving. Figures 137 and 138 show the patterns of Figs. 141 and 136 turned 45 degrees and making a diagonal pattern. Any of these is highly satisfactory as an allover design; the narrow bands of Fig. 141, 142, and 144 make good borders.

The development of the guilloche or meander is shown in Figs. 147 to 150. More elaborate designs involve shaping of the ribbon by hollowing out the center of the band with a gouge, or lining just inside each edge of the strap with a veiner or vee tool. The plain modern design of Fig. 150 approximates the conventional rope molding of Fig. 151, except that the latter is more rounded and the carved lines are long S curves. Get the proper shape by copying an actual piece of rope. Such a pattern can also be applied to a half-round, quarter-round, or flat oval molding, with telling effect. Carving of the lines should be fairly rough to increase the resemblance to rope. The braided patterns of Figs. 152 and 153 are used similarly. Another whole group of patterns, particularly for borders, is developed from common

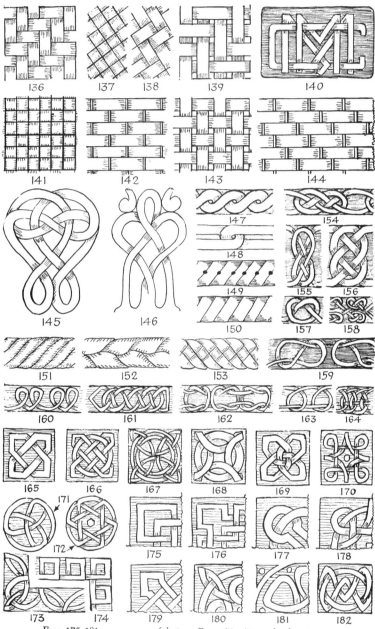

Figs. 175–181 are quarters of designs; Figs. 173–174 are border corners.

knots. Figures 154 and 163 show a few typical ones. Note from the three Carrick bends and the two simple knots (German—1600) how the same knot may be placed differently to make an entirely different pattern. Figures 160 and 161 deal with unknotted ropes, the first being simply loops, and the second two inter-woven slings. The latter is often modified by insertion of a bar through the center, the two ropes winding under and over it as well as under and over each other. Two end styles, one to fit a corner, the other against a straight border, are shown.

The remaining figures in this group deal with geometric strapwork patterns, commonly used in Switzerland and the Scandinavian countries. Figures 165 to 170 are square motifs, suitable as corner fillers or low-relief tray patterns, etc. As previously mentioned, they also provide good corner elements for a running strapwork pattern. Figures 171 and 172 are similar circular patterns. They can readily be redesigned to fit a square space, or corner fillers can be added. The designs of Figs. 165 to 170 can also be modified to go into circles.

Larger and more involved motifs are shown in Figs. 175 to 181. Each represents a quarter of a full design. The round motifs can readily be made square, and the square round. Further, a design incorporating circles can readily be changed to incorporate squares, and vice versa. Figure 177, for example, can also be modi-fied by leaving off the parallel ribbons which connect the small circle to the center. The panel motif of Fig. 182 (from Bologna) is a pattern to fill a rectangle or trapezoid; Figs. 173 and 174 in the opposite corner show two strapwork borders.

As examples of the application of strapwork in design, two chair backs are sketched. Figure 145 shows the entire back of a seventeenth-century Swiss chair; Fig. 146, the splat of a Chippen-dale chair. Both of these designs have the background removed completely by sawing out with a fret saw, a method which will be dealt with more in detail in the next chapter.

Strapwork has been extensively used for initials. Figures 140, 227, and 231 show monograms so made. Many old-time mottoes were carved in a continuous running band of old English

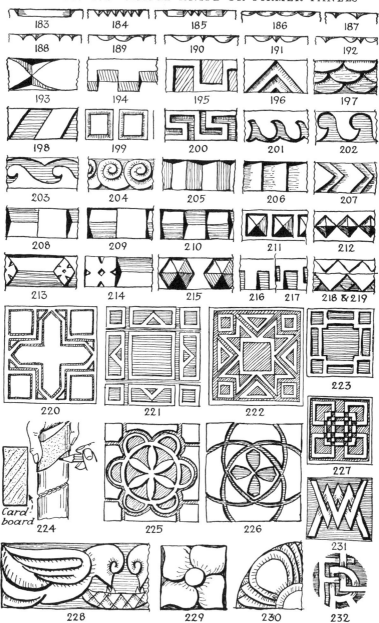

letters (see Fig. 392, *Whittling and Woodcarving*), the background being punched or otherwise dulled and the ribbon or strap being carved in relief.

With this prelude of the two great groups of classical designs, we can pass on to common firmer or knife patterns. First come edgings or chamfers, all variations of the common chamfered edge that anyone can do with a plane. But these are interrupted cham-fers, so must be done with the firmer. (All can also be done with the gouge, to create a hollow chamfer.) The first, in Fig. 183, shows one of the series of long bands. Figure 184 is a series of notches made with the knife or firmer. The series may be con-tinuous, or interrupted by unnotched edges. Combination of these two motifs gives Fig. 185.

Figure 186 is simply a series of concave chamfers, such as might be made with a wide gouge working from the side. Figure 187 is a convex chamfer, Fig. 188, a modification made by alternating long and short convex elements. Figures 189 to 192 combine concave and convex elements with the notch.

The next group, including Figs. 198 to 219, shows 27 borders or bands. Figure 193 is a modification of chip carving, in which the long ovals are formed by incising triangles with two curved sides. Figures 213 and 214 combine the chip-carved flower with a trough or long triangular incision, the first being hollowed at the center, the second rising to a peak in the center like a gable roof and being made by incising two parallel troughs with the outer sides of each perpendicular to the surface. Figures 208 and 209 are simpler modifications; Fig. 210 is a direct alternation of the two patterns; and Fig. 205 is like a series of miniature roofs set side by side. This latter pattern can be broadened out into a wide band, or with "roofs" of varying length makes an interesting decoration for a panel. Figure 206 is simply a shingled roof laid on its side. Figure 207 is the same pattern at staggered intervals, with each shingle pointed.

Figure 194 is quite similar to the battlements on an old castle, each element being chamfered to the surface of the wood. This design is most suitable as a molding.

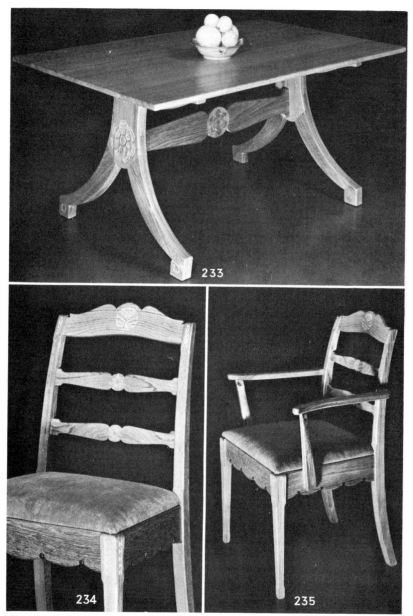

Fig. 233 · *Teak trestle table, and* Figs. 234 *and* 235 · *Teak chairs. All have conventionalized flower designs and were designed and built by Albert Wood & Five Sons. The Greek scroll appears on the table feet, and a plain chamfer and the Greek square of Fig. 199 on the chair legs.*

A series of common Greek designs is shown in Figs. 195 to 197, 199 to 204, 218, and 219. Figures 201 to 204 are variations of the wave motif, in which the shaded portion indicates where wood is removed. All can be grounded with the flat chisel or firmer with rounded corners.

Figures 211 and 212 are small four-sided pyramids, made by cutting away a groove on each side, the point of the pyramid being at the original surface of the wood. Figure 215 is an example of a similar hexagonal design. Figure 198 is simply a variation of a rope pattern. Figures 216 and 217 show two variations of a molding design which simply involves removal of a sloping chip at regular intervals.

The patterns of Figs. 220 to 223 and 225 to 227 are all geometric; in all of them the shaded areas are cut down slightly below the surface with a flat gouge or a firmer with rounded corners. The design itself is first outlined with the knife or the pointed firmer. These patterns may be used as table-top, stool-seat, or tray designs, and may be filled like chip carving (page 35) or inlaid (Chap. X).

Figure 224 illustrates the method of carving an "architectural rope." Note that the strands are about three times the width of the usual strand. Cut a rectangular piece of light cardboard as wide as the diameter of the bar and long enough to go around it. Put this at the angle of the usual rope spiral and draw a line along its edge. Then simply transfer the cardboard so that its top aligns with the pencil line, and draw the new line below. Cut out a deep, but rough, V groove along this line—and there you are. If used as a frame, the rope spiral should *rise* away from the door.

Many of the patterns of Albert Wood & Five Sons are based on a groove with one straight side, the other side being sloped up to the surface. Such grooves can readily be seen in Figs. 14, 15, 233 to 235, and 909 to 911. Three motifs from these pieces are shown in Figs. 228, 229, and 230. All are very simple. The shaded side of the line indicates the chamfered portion, the line itself a vertical cut about $\frac{1}{8}$ in. deep. These are applied in the sofa shown in Figs. 248; the details are shown in Fig. 249.

236

237

238

239

240

241

242

243

244

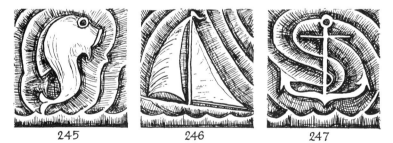

245

246

247

Figures 236 to 247 show another group of Wood motifs, these being designed by Gardner Wood to form a frieze around a mahogany desk handmade for me about two years ago. Each panel represents a hobby, and each was originally twice its present size, or $2\frac{1}{4}$ in. square. Figure 236 represents a crossed gouge and pocket-knife; Figure 238, a concertina; Fig. 239, a palette and brushes; Fig. 241, a Boy Scout First Class badge; Fig. 242, a quill pen, ink bottle, and book; Fig. 244, the crossed cannon of the Field Artillery; Fig. 245, trout fishing; and the next two sailing on small and large boats. The rose of Fig. 243 was used as a spacer between the other motifs, Fig. 240 as the monogram on the drawer front, and Fig. 237 for the monogram on the top rail of the matching desk chair. Figures 240 and 237 show how a motif can be modified to fit a differently shaped area.

All these motifs are produced by first outlining with knife or firmer, then cutting a wide, shallow, sloping plane in to the vertical line. The whole depth of the carving is not over $\frac{1}{16}$ in., the sloping planes creating shadows which define the design. These are in accord with the modern shallow-carving principle that the harder the wood the shallower should be the carving.

The designs of Figs. 133 and 135 would tend to bear out this principle, being relatively deep and in plaster. They are included here, however, not for this reason but to show how successfully a design may be worked out from commonplace things.

Figure 133 is a scene in the wood shop, conventionalized. Figure 135 is simply a mallet and block. Figures 133 and 135 suggest also another excellent plan—trying a complicated design in a soft, easily carved material *first*—to avoid later troubles with elevations and shadows on the carved hardwood piece.

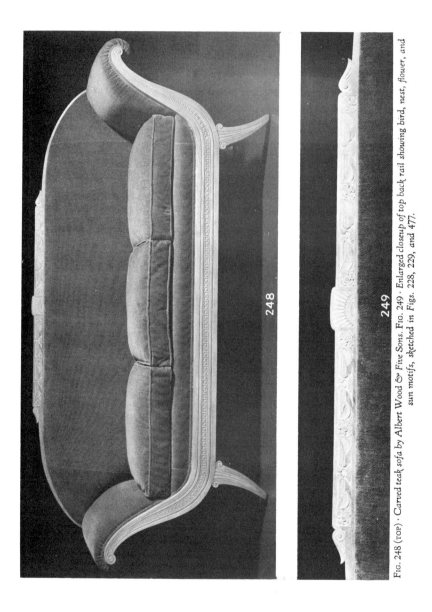

248

249

FIG. 248 (TOP) · Carved teak sofa by Albert Wood & Five Sons. FIG. 249 · Enlarged closeup of top back rail showing bird, nest, flower, and sun motifs, sketched in Figs. 228, 229, and 477.

CHAPTER IV

THE GOUGE · *Simple Designs*

FLUTER is the old English name for a half-round gouge—a gen-eral-utility tool that can do anything from grounding a deep-cut design or grooving a meander strap to rounding off a grape or berry. Usually, fluters in the diameters from $\frac{1}{4}$ to $\frac{1}{2}$ in. are ground with the corners rounded or with the center of the cutting edge projecting. This prevents dragging of the corners and permits the gouge to be used either right side up or upside down.

The urge of most amateur carvers to produce elaborate and showy designs has caused them to forget simple gouge decoration, just as they've forgotten punch work. Yet the gouge alone can produce hundreds of simple and useful designs, and in any ground-ing or modeling, the gouge is your most useful tool. For that reason, it behooves you to become as skilled with it as you are with a knife and fork.

Further, the gouge is the best tool to use with a carver's mallet, which is very useful whenever you're doing deep grounding or rough modeling. The mallet isn't very useful except where a lot of waste wood is to be removed or where very hard wood is being carved, but for those particular jobs it can save much valuable time. Professionals customarily use the mallet, but also usually do heavier carving and have had much more training in the control of blow strength. Until you've learned just how hard a blow to strike to accomplish a given result, you're likely either to split the piece, ruin a detail, or produce a jagged cut.

For most of the designs on the following page, a $\frac{1}{4}$-in. or $\frac{3}{8}$-in. half-round gouge with corners cut back is the best tool. Figures 252, 263, 277 to 279, 280 to 283, 288, 291, 293, 297, and 299 re-quire gouges of two sizes or more. Be sure the tool is very sharp

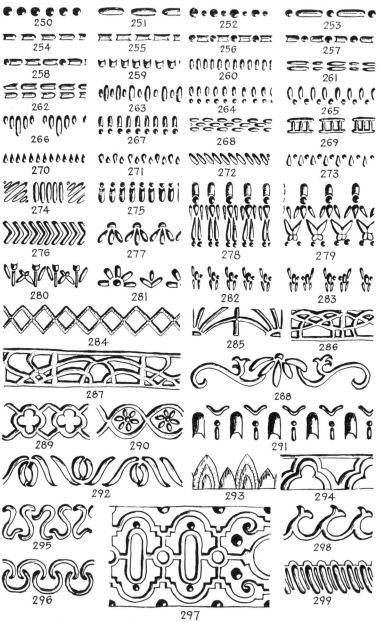

FIGS. 291, 297, and 298 are Jacobean; FIGS. 293–294 are Gothic.

and that the piece you are working is not heavily figured or full of knots. Mahogany, fine walnut, teak, pear, apple, holly, and straight-grained maple are suitable woods. And—don't stick the tool in deeply and then try to clear it by lifting on the handle! You're likely to snap the edge off.

These designs are carved with three basic cuts. The first is a dot, made by holding the gouge vertical over the piece, then pushing down and rotating simultaneously. This will cut out a little washer of wood the same diameter as the gouge (Fig. 250). By scooping a little, you can round up the bottom of the dot. The second cut is a groove, made simply by pushing the gouge along the wood, controlling depth of cut and direction with the left hand while you push with the right (Fig. 251). The third cut is a sloping one, in which the gouge starts at the surface and makes a sloping cut into the piece, or starts deep and "runs out." Figure 271 is a basic example of this design, which looks like nothing so much as the top of an exclamation mark.

One other caution—in gouge cutting, particularly with gouges of deep sweep, you'll find that one side of the gouge will probably tear the wood a little when you're cutting across grain. To smooth up that side of the cut, simply reverse the tool and cut along that side from the opposite direction.

Figures 250 to 253 are all variations of the basic cuts. Figure 254, a book-top-shaped border, has double points on its left end. These are made by pushing the gouge straight down into the wood at that place *first*, then cutting the long groove, and when the two cuts meet, swinging the gouge from side to side to clean out the little corners.

Figure 274 is a border, but the left-end element may also be used as a corner motif for patterns such as Figs. 260 to 269, 275 to 277, etc. The standing soldiers of Fig. 278 and the marching ones of Fig. 279 are examples of motifs designed from familiar things and created with simple gouge lines. These would be particularly suitable for a child's toy box or chest of drawers. Figures 277, 280, and 281 are simple flower motifs; Figs. 282 and 283 are the old Halloween cats, first in line, then inclined toward argument.

Radiation from points is the theory back of the border in Fig. 285. This may be expanded into a panel filler of any shape by adding more rays and lengthening those already shown. Figures 286 and 287 are just free gouge lines worked into a pattern. Though these happen to be geometric shapes, the same principle can be used in imitating the old-time runic carving, which was just a series of queerly angled and interlacing grooves all over a surface or enclosed within a geometric shape. Sometimes runic motifs may be repeated within the quarters of a square or the quadrants of a circle. Figure 245 *i*, in *Whittling and Woodcarving*, shows a simple runic border.

A motif like that of Fig. 288 is particularly suitable for the top of a panel or for a pediment. Figures 291, 297, and 299 are typical Jacobean motifs, the latter usually being made on a quarter-round molding. Figures 293 and 294 are Gothic, the former being made with gouges of three widths, each smaller one cutting within the larger, so that the smallest arch is deepest. An alternate design, with all three arches the same depth, can be made by using a gouge for the smallest arch, then forming the two others with a vee tool or veiner. The border of Fig. 294 is made simply with double gouge lines.

These borders may be carved around the edges of a panel, may border a chest or other article of furniture, may become all-over designs for a stool, tray, or other surface, or may be elongated to decorate the legs of any piece of furniture. In the latter case, the vertical motifs, such as Fig. 264 or Fig. 260, usually work out best. Sketch them in by drawing parallel lines and shading between with a pencil—that will give you a fairly accurate picture of what the results will be.

CHAPTER V

THE SAW · *Openwork*

MANY designs, particularly Gothic tracery, the chair stretchers, top rails, and grills of other styles, and modern screens, utilize the knife or firmer, with or without the gouge, and with the scroll or fret saw (or jig or band saw if you have them) to create openwork designs. This simply means that the background, instead of being set down below the surface of the piece, is cut away entirely. Of course the design must be such that it will permit such treatment, and it must be a suitable "light" motif or combination of motifs.

Eastern countries, particularly China and India, are famous for their openwork carving. Notice, for example, the elaborately carved openwork in even such a small object as the square puzzle of Fig. 300, or that incorporated in the brackets of Fig. 302. Even scenic carving is customarily in ultrahigh relief with backgrounds pierced.

Carvers of Western nations have also done much openwork at times. Heavy ornamentation, as in the Italian needle sheath of Fig. 305, makes this almost a necessity, if fully modeled elements are to stand out properly. The Gothic style, still almost exclusively used in religious edifices, incorporates much openwork and semi-openwork. Much Gothic tracery, as shown in Figs. 337 to 381, was made lighter and more "airy" by openwork backgrounds, or by setting the ground down so far that it looks as if the carving were appliquéd on the surface of a panel. In fact, much of the Gothic carving nowadays is so made.

Before attempting any of the designs shown here, go back to Chap. XX of *Whittling and Woodcarving* for basic instructions. Also see there Figs. 62, 209, 212, 274, 281, 285, 288, 295, 302, 314 to 320, and 322 to 324 as further examples. Openwork can be made

FIG. 300 · *Chinese ivory puzzle, a box with two layers of pierced inserts. The two large triangles form the first, the five small pieces the second, as shown in Fig. 324. Courtesy Mary Quist.* FIG. 301 · *Italian Gothic chest panel, fifteenth century.* FIG. 302 · *Indian brackets from Bombay; note the fernlike design and delicate veiner tracery.* FIG. 303 · *Three late-fifteenth-century French Gothic panels.* FIG. 304 · *Door of an English mid-sixteenth-century dole cupboard, built by an arkwright from "remembered Gothic" designs.* FIG. 305 · *Italian seventeenth-century needle sheath, about full size. All but Fig. 300, courtesy Metropolitan Museum of Art.*

into marquetry by inserting sections of wood, plastics, or ivory, etc., of contrasting color, and many strapwork patterns (see Figs. 139, 143, 147, and 154–182 of Chap. III) can be made open-work by cutting away the ground, as long as sections are left joined to the borders, with only veiner lines separating them.

Openwork carving gives bold relief—makes the elements of the design stand out sharply—by putting them in profile against light or darkness. This gives greater contrast than the usual background, hence shows up imperfections much more strongly. It is for this reason that outlines must be most carefully designed. Not more than half the wood should be removed in the usual design, and the parts removed should be uniformly distributed over the area. A large opening in one place must be balanced by another large one, or by several small ones, in another. The design should be so constituted that very light or very thin sections are supported by heavier ones or by frequent joining with other elements. Thus the border design of Fig. 319 is really very fragile, but frequent crossing with other elements and tying in with the sides give it support.

It is often advisable to balance some particularly light section of openwork with solid carving. Figure 313 is an example. Open-work and solid carving are frequently combined. Thus a border may be openwork, while the carving it frames is solid. The Chinese did this quite commonly (see Fig. 302, *Whittling and Woodcarving*). Chippendale, probably the greatest western user of openwork, also combined openwork with solid carving on occasion, as did Sheraton, Hepplewhite, and Duncan Phyfe (whose designs are largely based on Sheraton's).

Because of the exactness of openwork, woods used should be unfigured, free from knots, and straight-grained. Among the best are the "fruit" woods—apple, pear, and cherry. White oak, mahogany (fine-grained, *not* Philippine), and black walnut are suitable. Ivory of course works well, as do all the modern free-cutting plastics, fiber, hard rubber, and celluloid.

Openwork and pierced designs from various countries and various "periods" are pictured in Figs. 300 to 305. The intricate

306

307

308

309

310

311

312

313

314

315

316 317

318

319

320

321 *C1695*

322

323

324

325

326

327

328 *C1685*

329 *C1690*

330 *C1690*

331

332

333

double Chinese puzzle of Fig. 300, pictured only slightly smaller than the original, is indicative of the detail these carvers custom-arily produce. The box is made up of a scratch-carved lower panel held in four bamboo-pattern side pieces, into which the high-relief cover slides. The side pieces are joined with dovetail joints, no adhesive being used.

A crude Italian Gothic panel, shown in Fig. 301, combines the whirling-cross motif with a central shield and rope and gouge "petal" borders. Compare it with the delicate but precise French panels of Fig. 303 and the "remembered Gothic" arkwright designs in the dole cupboard of Fig. 304. As explained in Chap. III, Henry VIII's destruction of Gothic architecture in 1525 put the next generation of carvers at a loss for designs, except for what they could dimly remember.

To indicate the necessity of openwork in elaborate, high-relief carving, the Italian needle sheath of Fig. 305 is pictured almost full size so that its detail is readily visible.

The miscellaneous group of openwork designs shown in Figs. 306 to 333 is an attempt to indicate the scope and variety of this work. These designs include units from various styles through the last 300 years. Figures 306, 331, 332, and 333 are compara-tively modern and American, the latter three being executed in stone on the South Tower of the Palace of Mines, Metals, and Machinery at the Golden Gate International Exposition, San Francisco (1939). As is usual in picturing such designs, the blacked-out areas are to be removed, except of course when they are merely black lines, as between the circles and shield of Fig. 332. In that case they are deep veiner lines. Note that the arrows of Fig. 333 are not in one plane, but two—a cross section would be in the form of a W.

Figures 313 and 323 are contemporary American designs also, being adapted from pen-and-ink sketches in *Commercial Art*, by C. E. Wallace. In Fig. 313, lines of the iris must be put in with the veiner, and the pistils can be either drilled through or made as small gouge dots. Shading indicates slight sinking of the surface, as in strapwork. Note in this design that the flower forms the optical

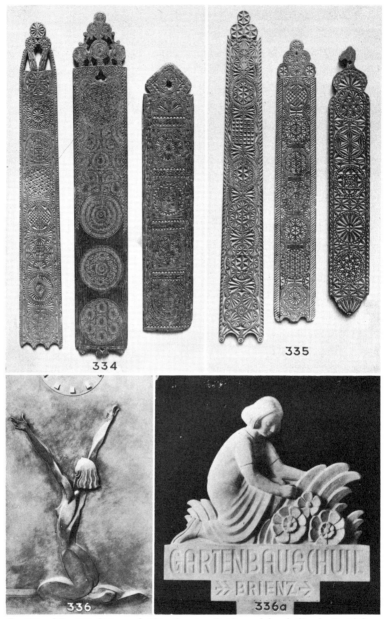

Fig. 334 and Fig. 335 · Chip-carved eighteenth-century Dutch mangle boards. (See also Fig. 7.) Courtesy Metropolitan Museum of Art. Fig. 336 · Hardwood figure affixed to nickel-surfaced plywood panel on tourist A Deck Lounge, R.M.S. "Queen Mary." By Rebel Stanton. Courtesy Cunard White Star Lines. Fig. 336a · A contrasting modern female figure topping a signpost leading to the Gardening School in Brienz, Switzerland.

center, with the large cutout area below balanced by a smaller one above and three much smaller ones at the right. In Fig. 323, the vein down the leaf is a plain saw cut and the flower center a drilled hole. No modeling of the surface is either indicated or required.

The Japanese motif of Fig. 308 is inserted here for contrast. It is a stylization of the Japanese word *Miyako*, meaning city, and gives an interesting motif. The two Chinese motifs of Figs. 309 and 310 are taken from the ivory frame and the support pedestal of an eighteenth-century screen by Chien Lung. Contrast their flowing simplicity with the "Chinese manner" Chippendale fret bracket of Fig. 317 or the Chippendale table leg of Fig. 322. The lamp base of Fig. 311 is contemporary Chinese, again showing the water-lily or poppy motif. Figure 312, showing the elaborately fretted back splat (center vertical element of one type of chair back) of a "Chinese manner" Chippendale settee, indicates the overdone fragility of some of this openwork. The same style also is responsible for the fretted bracket of Fig. 316, used on many "neo-Gothic" chairs, as was the pierced stretcher (crosspiece between chair legs) of Fig. 318. This shows the familiar four-petaled flower, which Chippendale himself usually alternated with an upright diamond.

The seventeenth century was particularly prolific in the development of elaborately fretted and carved stretchers. Figure 307 reproduces the stretcher of the late Jacobean chair sketched in Fig. 395. It shows Flemish and Dutch influences and probably dates from about 1650. Figures 321 and 328 to 330 show later stretchers, the approximate date of their design being indicated in each case. All incorporate the Flemish scroll and indicate unmistakable Dutch influence.

Hepplewhite (17?–1786), like Chippendale a master of the curved line, was also his equal in elaborate openwork. The two floral patterns from a Hepplewhite mahogany bedstead, Figs. 319 and 320, are examples. The first was used to decorate the upper portion of the head-end stretcher, the second as a running pattern around the tester from which the curtains hung.

Fretwork and strapwork have very much in common—as mentioned before, patterns designed for one can readily be executed in
the other. Figures 314, 315, and 325 to 327 provide good examples.
The first two are bandings on an early American highboy, the
others have appeared on various early American pieces. They are
of the exact, geometrical nature that characterizes the chip-
carving era (see Chap. III and also Figs. 334 and 335).

Mention of chip carving reminds one of the periodic use
of the saw in setting off chip-carving designs. Figures 7, 334, and
335 offer good examples of the ultimate development of the chip-
carving and saw-piercing combination, at least so far as the
Netherlands are concerned.

By way of contrast with the fretwork and pierced work discussed in preceding paragraphs, I have pictured two female figures,
both carefully executed with the carving tools, and both only
outlined with the saw. Figure 336, the modern pleading figure,
is of hardwood fixed to a nickel-surfaced plywood panel on
R.M.S. "Queen Mary" (Lounge, Tourist "A" deck). By Rebel
Stanton, it is part of a clock panel in which the girl is supplicating
beneath a clock, presumably begging for more time. Figure 336*a*,
while exhibiting the planes and flowing lines so typical of modern
carving, is much more conventional. Executed in the state woodcarving school at Brienz, Switzerland, it is one of the thousands
of hand-carved signs now in use throughout Switzerland and
Germany. This particular one directs the way to the gardening
school. In every case I have seen, these signposts are thus sil-
houetted, the sharply defined figure contrasting with the darkness
behind it. For other examples of such signboards, see Figs. 1109,
1165 to 1182, 1192, 1194, and 1200.

Perhaps it may not be amiss here to mention one important,
but often neglected, use of the saw in carving. Where heavy
carving is to be done, it is often preferable to saw away as much
of the waste wood as possible to avoid the risk of breaking the
piece with heavy mallet blows. When such carving incorporates
thin sections or extensive openwork in addition to the heavy
modeling, then use of the saw to remove "chunks" of waste wood

is almost imperative. Many other "hints" on the use of the saw are given in Chap. XX, *Whittling and Woodcarving*, so will not be repeated here.

Certainly the greatest period of openwork carving was that in which the famous English cathedrals were constructed. These Gothic traceries are almost unbelievably fine and detailed, yet when analyzed are relatively simple. All employ the characteristic Gothic arch, the drop-shaped or eye-shaped open section, with or without cusps, or some elaboration of these elements.

Peculiarly enough, the woodcarver was a humble craftsman indeed in the early days of Gothic art. He did his best to make his carving look like stone. The misericord of Fig. 379, from Hemingborough, Yorkshire, dates back to the thirteenth century, and clearly indicates the hand of the stonemason in its execution. Except for its deep undercutting, it could have been in stone; it certainly shows complete disregard for the fibrous structure of wood.

About the same time, the first good English woodwork was done in Winchester Cathedral. Again it shows the geometric exactness of stonework, with strong, bold outlines and almost perfect modeling of detail. This encouraged carvers to work in wood, for wood took detail much better than stone, was easier to work, and lastly, was found to be almost ideal for tracery, originally invented by the mason for stone. At first, this tracery was elaborately molded, as in Figs. 376 to 378, and was supported on turned posts. Figure 378 is an early fourteenth-century example from Kirk Ella, Yorkshire; Fig. 379 from Ashton, Devon; and Fig. 376 from Beverly St. Mary, dating from the mid-fourteenth century. Figure 380 is from a desk end in Manchester Cathedral.

Early traceries were cut from thick planks to permit the heavy moldings, but later ones were done in thin wood, the carver paying more attention to the design and less to its frame.

By the fifteenth century, the woodcarver had displaced the stonemason to such an extent that wood elements were framed up naturally, without any effort to simulate stone. Further, even the small churches and abbeys began to copy the work of

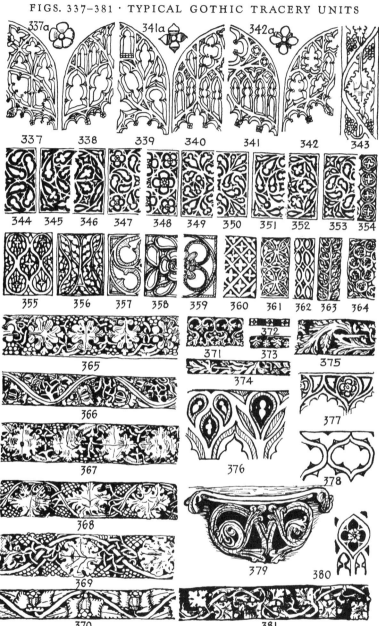

the great cathedrals, though concentrating the carving where it was most likely to show. There was much copying, engendered no doubt by local pride and the giving of commissions on the basis that a similar carved element at such-and-such a near-by church was to be excelled, but this copying led to ever-finer work. Throughout the fifteenth century designs steadily became more elaborate and delicate, traceries (whether pierced or solid) became more involved. All the older motifs, plus many new ones, were used, and a motif once developed was used over and over again. It was the peak of England's age of Gothic art, a peak that presaged its fall early in the sixteenth century.

With this little introduction, we can perhaps appreciate better the involved traceries of Figs. 337 to 381. Figures 337 to 342 are half sections of arched screens in Chester Cathedral, with details of the pendant flowers sketched above. This elaborate detail is typical of the finest of the late fifteenth-century work. Compare the grape border of Fig. 343, also at Chester, with the grape borders of Figs. 365 and 367 to 369, and note the continually increasing elaboration of detail. The latter borders are com-pletely modeled, and all, of course, are pierced through as indi-cated by the black shading, the completed border being carried in a double molding. Figures 365 to 367, and the detailed fringe tracery of Fig. 371, are all from Kentisbere, Devon; Figs. 368 and 372 to 375 are from High Ham, Somerset (all being bressummer [a beam supporting the rood loft] enrichments); Figs. 354, 360 to 364, 369, and 370 are from Llananno, Radnor (from the coving of the rood screen). The oak-leaf pattern of Fig. 381 is from the bressummer of Llanrwst, Denbigh. All this foliage was completely modeled down to its ultimate details, and required the complete kit of carver's tools for its execution. It contrasts sharply with the traceries of Figs. 337 to 342, which can be executed with the saw, firmer, and gouge, except for such details as the flowers. Other examples can be found in *English Church Woodwork*, by Howard and Crossley.

In all these traceries, the edges of pierced portions are chamfered, first by cutting away the margins with the firmer, then making

FIG. 382 · Egypto-Arabic eleventh-century panel of the Fatimid period. FIG. 383 · Mesopotamian early eighteenth-century teak panel. FIG. 384 · German twelfth-century horn or oliphant. FIG. 385 · Persian fifteenth-century doors made by Muhammed ibn Hussein. All courtesy Metropolitan Museum of Art. FIG. 386 · Mahogany low-relief plate and teak miniature head, both by Gardner Wood.

the chamfer faces slightly concave with a relatively flat spoon gouge. This adds to the thinness and lightness of effect of the tracery, while still permitting plenty of thickness and strength necessary for self-support.

Modern traceries of this style, used occasionally for grills and screens as well as for appliqué on paneling in ecclesiastical commissions, are usually made by boring out with an expansive bit and sawing across the cusps, then smoothing up the sawed surfaces and chamfering as described in the preceding paragraph.

One other point should be mentioned in connection with these screens—note that at every loop or joining of the eye motif there is a chip-carved triangle to remove the "kink" from the design. This is simply an incised pyramid of suitable shape, cut in with the firmer, or preferably, with the knife.

The tracery half motifs of Figs. 344 to 353 are from the coving of a rood screen formerly at Daresbury, Cheshire. They are typical of the light and airy screenwork eventually developed. Because of their smallness, the chamfer is indicated by the width of the outline, rather than by a second parallel line. Figures 354 and 360 to 364 are motifs suitable for continuous screens or bands to obscure an opening, to decorate a shaft outlet, or for some similar purpose.

Figures 355 and 356, from the parclose screen at Colebrooke, Devon, are suitable grills or squints. They include strong separat-ing elements of foreign detail (which dates them as sixteenth century) combined with the standard Gothic cusping.

Figures 357 to 359 are panels from a late fifteenth-century bench back at Fressingfield, Suffolk. Of a bolder, more open design, they contrast sharply with the very detailed traceries of Figs. 344 to 353. These traceries are mounted on panels, in contrast to most of the pierced-work ones preceding. Further Gothic designs are shown in Chap. VI.

For contrast with these Gothic motifs, I have chosen several pierced designs from other lands and other peoples. Figure 382 is an eleventh-century Egypto-Arabic panel of the Fatimid period; Fig. 383, a Mesopotamian teak panel from the first half of the eighteenth century. The German horn, or oliphant, of Fig. 384 dates from the twelfth century and incorporates several animal and bird motifs. A low-relief carving, its elements might just as readily be used in pierced carving, including the two borders at the bell of the horn.

Made by Muhammed ibn Hussein, the Persian fifteenth-century doors of Fig. 385 show exceedingly delicate openwork appliquéd on a supporting panel. Combining Arabic lettering with tracery forms, they offer an endless number of intriguing patterns.

Without the saw, woodcarving is rather largely limited to square panels. The round mahogany plate and miniature teak bust in Fig. 386, both by Gardner Wood, would be much harder forming jobs without a saw to assist in rough shaping. There are always those carvers who insist in carving a head like that of Fig. 386 from the square, persisting in the belief that cutting away waste wood (which has no function in the completed piece anyway) with a saw isn't playing fair. The only excuse that can be offered for this attitude is probably a heritage from whittling, where using any other tool than the knife is considered "cheating."

Perhaps the most graphic way to point out the development of openwork in furniture construction is to sketch a series of carved chair backs. I have done this in Figs. 387 to 428, which picture 42 half backs (having nothing to do with football) from the Italian *sgabelli* of A.D. 1450 to the typically rectilinear backs designed by Sheraton.

It is probably advisable to pause here and point out that the *Sgabelli* were really the first movable chairs—at least for several thousand years, because, as usual, the Egyptians once had chairs very similar to our own. In the British Museum is the chair frame of Queen Hatshepsu, who reigned jointly with her father in Egypt *sixteen centuries before Christ.* It had four legs as ours do, twin back supports, and apparently was elaborately carved and painted. Later civilizations likewise produced beautiful furniture— but only for kings. In ancient Babylon, for example, guests rested on huge golden couches while they ate. These couches, with carved lions' feet, were heavily inlaid and spread with rugs and draperies—or so the records say. The Greeks produced similar luxurious couches, as did the Romans. Their *triclinia* were high, four-legged, elaborately decorated small couches, usually placed around the table in a U shape (see Fig. 868, Chap. X). They also had an X-shaped seat called a *curule*, which is the real ancestor of the beach chair we know today.

Before A.D. 1450, most seats in Europe were huge, blocky affairs against walls, and there weren't many of those. The nobility sat on chests over which rugs or skins were thrown, the common people on logs, rude stools, or their haunches.

The first notable European chair was therefore the *sgabello*, really just a stool with a back added (Fig. 387). Several of these, with elaborately carved backs and panel supports (Fig. 711, Chap. VIII) were grouped around the table at the center of the great hall. They were very similar to the Swiss chair of 200 years later (Fig. 12)! (French *sgabelli* replaced the panel supports with three or four turned legs set at rakish angles, much like our present Windsor chairs.)

Other chairs were X-shaped, with beautifully inlaid pieces adapted from the Roman *curule* and designed in two forms, the Dantesca (Fig. 866, Chap. X) and the Savonarola (Fig. 867). Both carried surface mosaics of ivory, bone, or precious wood. The Dantesca was heavy, with only back and front semicircular X's and with a connecting bar as a back. The Savonarola, lighter and more graceful, had interlaced staves, and was so designed that it could be folded readily and put out of sight when not in use.

Figure 388 dates at about A.D. 1450 also, but shows a totally different influence. In England, only notables had seats, and the first of those were Gothic canopied forms, with square seats and straight backs (see Fig. 3). Backs were solid and thick (no man knew when a "faithful" retainer or unbidden guest would choose to creep up behind with a dagger), but the seats were well cushioned, and the austerity of the back was relieved with high-relief tracery (called *orbevoies*). Some double or triple seats were made, planned to serve both as seats and as couches or beds.

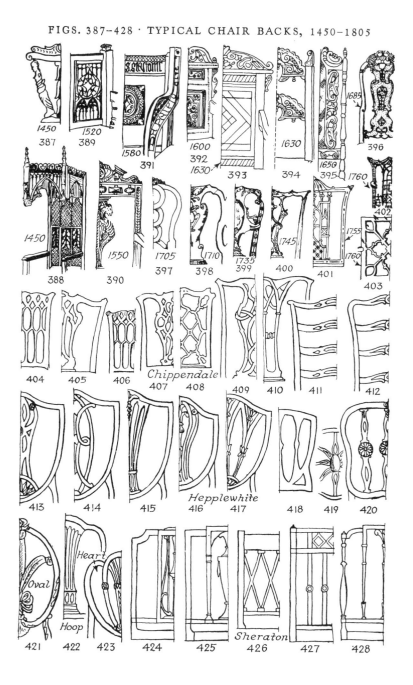

Later forms of the Gothic chair had elaborate pierced backs, the fear of the dagger from behind apparently having been removed. Next the chair lost its canopy. Figure 389 shows such a box-shaped seat. Its correct Gothic detail was probably produced by an arkwright, because the woodcarvers who knew Gothic design were employed by the clergy, and this is a layman's seat.

Figure 390 is sketched from a "fine chair" of the time of Henri II (1547–1559) in France, when a charmingly grotesque style flowered. The splats of these chairs usually had grotesque ornaments, and motifs in general were Tuscan rather than French (because Henri's wife was Catherine de' Medici).

Famous as the ancestor of the wainscot chair, the Glastonbury, really an elaborately carved folding chair, is sketched in Fig. 391. It is said to have been made for the abbots of Glastonbury (where Joseph of Arimathea was supposed to have settled when he came to England). It was a clerical seat, as contrasted with the wainscot chairs of Figs. 392 and 393, made for the laity. One of the latter was the principal seat in the manorial hall—the common man still had only a stool. "Wainscot" itself comes from the old Dutch *wagenschott*, meaning carriage-panel wood (because of the quality of the wood from which the chairs were made). Spelling not being an art in those days, the word was soon corrupted to *weynscott* and then to *weinscot*. In any case, it replaced the Gothic *chayére* during the second half of the sixteenth century.

All these chairs were English oak, but now begins the use of finer woods, like walnut, and more elaborate carving. Figure 394 is a so-called "Yorkshire" chair of 1630, complete with double crosspieces, elaborately carved, and including acorn pendants. Figure 395 is an unusual caned Stuart (late Jacobean) chair showing Flemish and Dutch influence in the scrollwork. Figure 396 is an example of the ultraelaborate William and Mary style, illustrated also by Fig. 13. Note the elaborate cresting and detailed scrollwork down the splat.

The early Georgian (1705) interlacing-circle splat chair of Fig. 397 is much like the Swiss chair back of Fig. 145, except that this back adds a detailed crest on the toprail. It dates from about the same time. Figure 398 is an early Georgian splat back also, but in this case is a solid, low-relief carved section. It is sketched from a double chair-back settee. The ultimate in the "decorated Queen Anne" style is the mirror back of Fig. 399, incorporating in the toprail the eagle's head which comes from the princely Italian house of Modena Este.

Figure 400 shows the back of one of the earliest English mahogany chairs. Its intricate carving is indicative of the hopelessness of trying to carve such designs in walnut, the earlier available "fine" wood. Mahogany began to come into England about 1720, but was first used only for very expensive furniture because of a prohibitive duty of $40 per ton. When this duty was removed in 1745, mahogany rapidly gained the ascendancy, although country carvers, less well off than their city fellows, continued to use walnut until 1760.

Because of the variety of Chippendale chair backs, I have shown 15 typical designs. Above everything else, Chippendale (1705–1779) was a master carver of great daring and originality, and has often been called "most famous of English cabinetmakers." He was without a peer as a carver in his own time, and such a strong stylist that he simply took over existing styles and adapted them for his own use. He made seven distinct types of chair backs —splat, square hoop, ribband, Gothic or tracery, fret, ladder, and square—and I have tried to show some of each.

Figures 401 to 403 are three examples from Chippendale's Chinese style, showing elaborate fretwork and typical motifs (see also Figs. 312, 317, and 322). Figures 404 to 406 are Gothic fret backs (see also Figs. 316 and 318); Fig. 405 has a Cupid's-bow toprail combined with the Gothic splat. Figure 407 shows a Gothic variation; Fig. 408, a pierced strapwork splat. Figure 409 is a more prominent interlaced strapwork splat (see also Fig. 146); Fig. 410 is a pillared splat. Two ladder-back designs are shown in Figs. 411 and 412, the first a simple design with Cupid's-bow toprail, the second a more elaborate scrolled-center design with hooped toprail.

Hepplewhite, like Chippendale, was at his best working with curved lines, while Sheraton, who followed, did better with rectilinear ones. His chair backs were of six general shapes: shield, round, square, oval, hoop, and heart. Figures 413 to 418 are all variations of the shield design, showing pierced-splat motifs. Hepplewhite customarily made splats in his shield-back chairs in lyre or urn shape (Fig. 416). His most famous oval or hoop form is the "honeysuckle," in which a series of narrow single scrolls radiate from the base, arching over the entire back.

Figure 418 is a simple form modeled directly from a Crusader's shield. Figure 419 is a rarer hoop-back design, with a wheel center replacing the usual bars or splat. Figure 420 is one of Hepplewhite's occasional tries at a square back, with bars replacing the splat. Figure 421 is typical of the subtle flattery indulged in by both Hepplewhite and Sheraton for the Prince of Wales; it shows his characteristic three feathers replacing the usual splat (Sheraton has the same motif in Fig. 428). The hoop designs of Fig. 422 and the interlaced heart of Fig. 423 are typically Hepplewhite.

Sheraton (1750–1806) was a designer, not a cabinetmaker. Only one piece of furniture has ever been claimed to have been made by him, and there is little real evidence that he made that. (Had he been a carver, he'd have been less poverty-stricken.) He characteristically used a square form on his chairs, as indicated in Figs. 424 to 428. A common form of splat was an elongated or bottle urn, shown in the splats of Figs. 424 and 425. Figure 425 is from his earliest, and best, period.

Sheraton was the last of the great English furniture makers. His work also marked the end, at least for the time, of the use of the pierced back. Later pieces usually had elaborate surface decoration and upholstered backs, as did the French pieces of an even earlier date. The days of the great carvers were over.

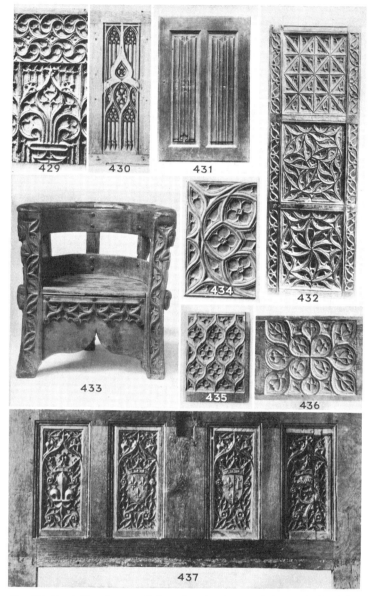

FIG. 429 · *French fifteenth-century Gothic walnut chest-front motif, showing the fleur-de-lis.* FIG. 430 · *A better executed chest front, also French fifteenth-century Gothic.* FIG. 431 · *The linen fold, a late fifteenth- or early sixteenth-century example from France.* FIG. 432 · *Another late French Gothic series of panels showing full cusping and the whirling cross.* FIG. 433 · *A North-Italian Gothic chair, circa 1450–1500.* FIGS. 434–436 · *Late fifteenth-century French Gothic panels showing foreign influence.* FIG. 437 · *A French oak chest front of the same period. All photographs courtesy Metropolitan Museum of Art.*

CHAPTER VI

GOUGE WITH KNIFE OR FIRMER

GOTHIC traceries and other forms of pierced patterns begin to utilize the third dimension available to the woodcarver. They begin to show the depth common to wood and stone sculpture which a painter can only imitate by shadowing or applying surface paint patterns with a palette knife. When the knife or firmer and the gouge are used together, it is possible to mold or model the surface, and we are carving in relief.

Modeled patterns can be raised from surrounding surfaces in *relief*, can be sunk or *incised* below the surface so that the design is surrounded by solid wood, or can be reversed in *intaglio* so that a plaster cast of the carving would form a true relief pattern (see Chaps. XIX and XX, *Whittling and Woodcarving*).

Several examples of Gothic tracery against wooden panels, in most cases created by grounding the panel so that the design is in true relief, are shown in Figs. 429 to 437. The combination of the French fleur-de-lis with the Gothic cusped motifs in Fig. 429 is repeated four times on the front of a fifteenth-century walnut chest. Figure 430 is a more conventional pattern, being one of nine panels forming the front of a chest of about the same period. The linen and parchment folds were also commonly used as panel designs at this time. Figure 431 is a French linen-fold panel (these folds and their origin are described on page 210 and shown in Fig. 309, *Whittling and Woodcarving*) in which the carver apparently forgot to finish the bottom of the right-hand fold, although he meticulously stamped the edges of each piece with a double row of circular punch marks to imitate the stitching.

Typical later Gothic panel and border motifs are shown in Fig. 432. The chair of Fig. 433 is also particularly interesting, both because it is one of the earliest examples of a movable chair (made for the clergy of the Piedmontese Church of San Orso Val d'Aosta between 1450 and 1500) and because it combines a relief design on the uprights with an appliquéd tracery across the stretcher. Figures 434 to 436 are late Gothic French panels showing final Gothic quatrefoil forms and (particularly Fig. 436) the beginnings of the change to the Renaissance style.

An excellent example of incised modeling is the oak chest front of Fig. 437, with four Gothic panels, two carrying shields, one a fleur-de-lis, and the fourth a heraldic fish, but all showing further evidences of the impending change in style.

So much for Gothic modeling. Later photographs and sketches will show modeled elements of other styles, but let us pause for the moment to discuss simple applications and motifs involving both the gouge and the firmer or knife. And to be sure the scratch is not forgotten, let us start with examples most easily produced with the aid of the scratch or scratch stock (Fig. 231, *Whittling and Woodcarving*). The scratch is usually a homemade tool, of simple L shape, into which a series of shaped cutters can be clamped. Cutters are usually ground to shape from pieces of broken hacksaw blades or similar pieces of tool steel. The tool is particularly useful for cutting continuous border or edge grooves that are semicircular or reeded. In use, the shaped blade is clamped in the long arm of the L so that the short arm, forming a shoulder, can be pressed against the edge of the piece to bring the tool to the proper position. Then the tool is moved back and forth to scrape in the desired groove. Obviously, such a tool is suited to the making of incised borders, as in Figs. 438 to 447.

The old Greek dot-and-dash moldings of Figs. 438 to 440 and 447 are shaped from a half-round relief or incised molding, the ends being formed with the gouge of an appropriate cross section and then rounded off with the skew firmer or knife. Figures 441 to 443 start with the same molding, but involve spiral shaping. The first is the familiar rope pattern, the second a large scroll wrapped about a smaller one (or a shaft), and the third a varying-length rope pattern. My drawing of it is intentionally left un-shaded because the pattern may be executed in half a dozen ways. The diagonal cuts can be rounded off to look like a rope with a wide strand; the narrow spirals can be made to appear to wrap around a bar by reducing the diameter of the wide section slightly; or the narrow spirals can be beaded, figured, or otherwise shaped.

Also stemming from a half-round molding are the ancient Greek foils of Figs. 454 to 457, in which one or two disks replace the smaller element. All are very suitable as moldings. Figure 457 is a leaf-and-dart variation from the Erechtheum. Figures 444 to 447, similarly based on the half-round molding, are more modern variations. Figure 444 is simply periodic notching of the half round with a knife. Figure 446 is a periodic gouge cut against a flat gouge, half-round gouge, or knife-stop cut. If gouge cuts are made from both directions against a shaped center ball, the pattern of Fig. 445 results. A knife or skew chisel will form the ball, or a half-round gouge of proper diameter may be used.

The six borders beginning with Fig. 448 are intended to be carved on a flat surface. The first involves a vertical gouge cut and removal of the angular chip with a knife or firmer. The center punch mark can be put in or left out as desired. Figure 449 is a repeated pattern of squares, in which one corner is cut down slightly until it appears to be caught under the adjacent square. A scratch stock can round the surface of this pattern slightly or make stop cuts at each side. Figure 450 is the same design executed with the gouge, the center punch marks being optional as before.

The alternating loops of Fig. 451 are susceptible to many variations. As pictured, the design can be executed by making the rounded edges with a flat gouge pushed straight down into the wood, outlining the border with knife or firmer, then wasting away the ground with a small gouge, knife, or skew chisel. The center diamond can be chip-carved out, stamped, or not removed at all. The diamond can be replaced also with any other shape—a triangle, stamped circle, etc. The same design can be done on a

half-round molding by cutting the black portions down to the surface of the piece.

The motif of Fig. 452 is similarly susceptible to variation. As shown, it is executed with the gouge and firmer making vertical stop cuts, then wasting away the ground as before. The small center is cored with a tiny half-round gouge, stamped, or chip-carved. As before, the scratch stock will be found valuable to scrape in edges for the design. The molding may be widened slightly and half circles executed on the opposite side, either so that they match those shown (leaving a grounded diamond between) or offset half a diameter (so that they leave a grounded triangle). Alternation of circle sizes between a small and a large produces another variation.

All these comments apply to the border of Fig. 453, the individual motif being produced by outlining with a flat gouge and removing a short groove with a small half-round gouge or incising a triangle with the firmer or knife.

Three more ancient Greek designs are pictured in Figs. 458 to 460. The easiest way to prepare the ground for the motif of Fig. 458 is to grind a scratch-stock cutter so that it will scrape in three parallel half-round moldings. Then cross this at regular or irregular intervals with a knife or firmer stop cut and gouge out the center or two outside half rounds alternately until the finished molding looks like small sections of dowel rod have been tacked into an incised groove. The same molding can be in relief, of course, as can the other two; Fig. 459 is another variation of the Greek fret, as are Figs. 476 and 479. The latter can be simply a surface fret or cut in so deeply that it looks like a ribbon on edge or a ruff collar.

For centuries, the sun has been an object of worship, and consequently dozens of variants showing the sun and emanating rays occur in Indian, Greek, Roman, and various primitive carved pieces. The Assyrian pattern of Fig. 461 is one example. The sun appears as a hemisphere or flattened hemisphere, the rays either concave or convex curves, with or without a surface *land* or crescent.

Figure 462 is a Swedish pattern from Skône, in which the pattern can be incised or in relief. In the latter case, the gouge is essential for grounding. Figure 463, which looks like another Greek fret, is actually a Mayan pattern from Uxmal temple, as are Figs. 468 and 470. Figure 468 is the familiar scale pattern which appears on Portuguese pillars (see Fig. 523), and Fig. 470 is the Mayan imperial standard, with relief or incised rays, and a relief or incised lantern-shaped hilt.

Another of the dozens of ribbon variations is sketched in Fig. 464. The design may be simple and relatively flat as shown, or the ribbon may be elaborately shaped and knotted, swirling in full relief from the surface. The dots can be incised, in relief, or left out entirely. From far-off Australia comes Fig. 465, a pattern of hexagons outlined with half-round molding and a series of gouged incisions to set off the rough center "gear." Figure 466 is a characteristically Jacobean border, the shield of the central motif being set off with a series of fins of triangular cross section.

Now for some more nonborder motifs. These are used as central elements in panels, as corner decorations, and so on. The familiar French fleur-de-lis of Fig. 467 actually came from Italy and is an early Renaissance motif. The apparently modernistic motif of Fig. 469 actually came from an old, old building in Philadelphia, as did the half-flower motif of Fig. 477 [directly below it]. This latter unit can be modified slightly to become another of the familiar sun designs, with its rays extending to fill a space of any shape. The petals can be concave or convex, as desired, or just outlined and left flat. The four-petaled flower of Fig. 471 is another familiar space-filling motif, used regularly for 2,000 years to fit everything from a circle to a long rectangle, in the latter case with petals elongated and pulled into pairs. The center element may be a complete flower or just a button.

Tibet contributes the circular motif of Fig. 472, apparently derived from our comma, and surprisingly similar to many of the variations of the comma design shown in Figs. 668 to 707. And in Fig. 473 is the fleur-de-lis again, in crude form to be sure, but antedating even the Renaissance. This one is sketched from the

Temple of Artemis in Magnesia, ancient Greece! The new Department of Justice Building in Washington contributes the familiar flower motif of Fig. 474, and modern Guatemala the motifs of Figs. 475 and 480. The complicated border of Fig. 478 comes from the ancient Indian temple of Muktesvara and is dated before the Christian era, although the beaded molding, reeded section, and flowered spiral didn't reach the Western world until the 1700's!

Typical applications of these and other motifs are shown in Figs. 481 to 483. The American press cupboard of Fig. 481, dating from 1660–1680, shows no less than 15 simple motifs of the period, all the way from the four-petaled flower to the simple notched border. All patterns are produced by incising into the surface of the panel.

Albert Wood's modern chair of Fig. 482 uses a tapered flat spiral, the lower element curving around a four-petaled flower which is repeated in the back and seat rails. A heraldic emblem— that of the family of the chair purchaser—is incised at each end of the seat rail. Done in primavera (the so-called white mahogany), the chair is typical of modern simple, flowing lines and low-relief carving with simple motifs.

That simplicity and flow of motif are not strictly modern characteristics is demonstrated by the Egypto-Arabic panel of Fig. 483. This stylized palmette design dates back to the ninth century. This particular panel also demonstrates the sharpening of the land between concave surfaces mentioned in connection with the spiral fluting of Fig. 548. The additional shadows created by this V grooving give a sharpness to the motif not otherwise obtainable.

A modern totem pole, the work of the boys of Boy Scout Troop 425 of Walnut Park, Los Angeles, Calif., is illustrated in Fig. 484. The wood is white pine, coming from the lowly cheese box. Tools are a narrow chisel and a knife, with a shallow gouge for grounding. Each panel is a squared-up cheese-box end, about $3\frac{1}{2}$ in. by $3\frac{1}{2}$ in. originally (which squares up to about 3 in. when the dovetail is removed), and the design is grounded about $\frac{1}{8}$ in.

FIG. 481 · *American oak press cupboard, dating from 1660–1680. Courtesy Metropolitan Museum of Art.* FIG. 482 · *Armchair in prima vera designed by Albert Wood.* FIG. 483 · *Ninth-century Egypto-Arabic door panel, stylized palmette design. Courtesy Metropolitan Museum of Art.* FIG. 484 · *Boy Scout merit-badge totem pole from Los Angeles. Courtesy "Scouting" magazine.*

Some 27 more elaborate motifs and complete panels, selected from typical pieces of a wide variety of styles, appear on page 80. All except Figs. 492 and 509 are modeled in relief and include considerable detail. Figure 485 is an alternating pattern of four- and eight-petaled flowers, separated by a conventionalized leaf, and comes from the island of Trinidad. Figure 486, included here to typify the hundreds of face and mask variations incorporated in woodcarving of all styles, is a Romanesque ornament from a Spanish church.

Figures 487 and 488 are repetitive leaf motifs, the first a Romanesque ornament from a French cloister and the second a Gothic molding from Stratford Church, England. The first is a very severe outline with gouge-hollowed centers; the second is completely modeled, even to the veins of the leaves.

The bird-and-flower motif of Fig. 489 is taken from a pool wall in a Mexico City park. It combines modern low-relief model-ing with almost pen-drawn outlines to represent the curling feathers on the bird's back and the flower tendrils. These can be put in with the knife or skew firmer, or more easily with the vee tool or veiner.

Another old Roman pattern, possibly the ancestor of our whit-tled ball-in-a-cage, is shown in Fig. 490. The interlacing ribbons surrounding the balls are often fully modeled, and in some Gothic examples were elaborately rippled, with the upper crossing full in relief, exactly as if two ribbon spirals had been laid in a trough of semicircular cross section. The ball is modeled on a pillar so that it appears to be loose within the ribbon cage.

Figures 491 and 495 are dogwood blossom and leaf patterns which I combined with the rope molding around a front-door frame (see Chap. II); Fig. 491, made right- and left-hand, is the pedestal for the rope; Fig. 495, the upper-corner filler element.

Selected from an old Russian gospel text, the strapwork of Fig. 492 makes an exceptionally interesting design as well as forming a capital T. The triangular motifs of Figs. 493 and 494 are representative of many such units, the first being a completely modeled leaf in William and Mary style, the second a modern

nine-petaled flower with leaves as corner fillers. The background for such a pattern may be smoothed off, but looks better if left fairly rough in a pebbled or pyramided surface.

Going back halfway to the dawn of recorded time, Fig. 496 is one element of a closed-lotus capital from the Ptolemaic epoch in Egypt, around 200 B.C. Figure 497 shows the same motif alternating with an open lotus in a border. It is copied from a paving slab in ancient Nineveh, probably laid about 700 B.C. Figure 498 shows half of a variation of the Greek anthemion motif, from the Temple of Artemis, Magnesia. Figure 499 is a crude branching pattern reminiscent of the design of Fig. 487 and also dating back to Romanesque. The gadroon (from the French *godron*, a plait or ruffle) edging of Fig. 502 is similarly carved.

Figures 500 and 501 are relatively modern, being taken from old Philadelphia buildings, although they obviously stem from ancient Greek motifs. The queer foliage repeat of Fig. 503 is from a Balinese temple. Figure 504, apparently a combination of the Egyptian lotus, a drape, and a trefoil, is very modern, coming from the South Tower of the Palace of Mines, Metals, and Machinery, at the Golden Gate International Exposition, San Francisco (1939). Only slightly different is the sun pattern variation of Fig. 508, which comes from ancient China.

The Renaissance was particularly prolific of carvings showing queer beasts, birds, and fish. Many carvings also incorporated medallions with more or less crude faces or busts. Figure 505 is a typical example, taken from a bench end at Somerset Church, England. Figure 506, from the same church, is definitely Gothic, while Fig. 507 again shows a complicated Renaissance floral motif. Figure 511, stemming back to Gothic oak-leaf and acorn motifs, occurs on a Philadelphia building, as does Fig. 510, a modern floral design. Figure 509, shown here as a strapwork pattern worked out with the gouge and firmer, is one of those basic designs which can be executed in a wide variety of ways. The ribbons may be converted to half rounds, not interlacing, or the center ribbon can be made a modeled heart instead of simply an outline. The whole design can, of course, be either in full relief

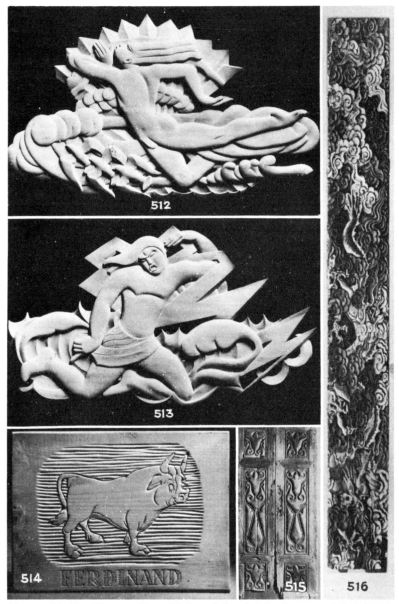

Fig. 512 · "Air," and Fig. 513 · "Storm." Both panels from the Main Restaurant, C Deck, R.M.S. "Queen Mary." By Bainbridge Copnall. Courtesy Cunard White Star Lines. Fig. 514 · Ferdinand, from Walt Disney's conception. By the author. Fig. 515 · Arabic ninth-century teak door panel. Courtesy Metropolitan Museum of Art. Fig. 516 · Korean panel, dragon motif. Courtesy Metropolitan Museum of Art.

or incised—and as are so many other of these patterns, the design is suitable for punching of the background or veiner outlining.

Further to contrast—or really, compare—the very ancient and the very modern in design, let us look at the photographs of Figs. 512 to 516. Bainbridge Copnall is responsible for the panels "Air," (Fig. 512) and "Storm," (Fig. 513), both in the Main Restaurant on C Deck of R.M.S. "Queen Mary" (see also Figs. 422 to 429, *Whittling and Woodcarving*). The strong planes of these panels make detail unnecessary for strength; in fact, any details would weaken rather than strengthen the design.

Figure 514 is submitted not as an outstanding example, but as indicative of the treatment of modern subjects in low-relief panels done with the knife and gouge. Ferdinand, from Walt Disney's Technicolor production of the same name, is simply outlined with the knife, then the background is produced with parallel gouge cuts. The wood is white pine, and formerly did duty as a protecting board for an advertising plate.

For comparison, the ninth-century Arabic teak door of Fig. 515 is interesting. It again has the flowing lines and simple planes which characterize modern work. So does the Korean panel of Fig. 516. Though detailed, its effects are obtained with planes. It also shows the effectiveness of color on certain designs.

In the early days of architecture and decoration, the Greeks used round pillars and columns. These usually showed so little artistic interest (because of their monotonous regularity) that the stone cutters added increasingly elaborate capitals and pedestals, and finally began to carve the surfaces of the shafts themselves. Figures 454 to 457, 560, and 562 to 566 show some of the motifs the Romans used about column pedestals and capitals. Figures 438 to 443, 458 to 460, 479, and 490 are similar Greek motifs. Figures 560 and 566 are pedestals from the Villa of Cardinal Alexander Albani in Rome; Fig. 562 is from the pedestal in the Temple of Quatuor Corovatorum in Rome; and Figs. 563 to 565 are from the Temple of Nero in Rome. Note the wide variety of motifs—all the way from the frilled collar or ruff (Fig. 562) which we have learned to associate with the Tudors in England, to the Portuguese wreath (Fig. 563), the modern fish net (Fig. 560), and the Scandinavian braid (Fig. 566)! The Greeks themselves used many variations of the acanthus, as in Fig. 534.

In the early centuries of the Christian era, all sorts of modifica' tions were made of the simple Greek fluted column. For example, Fig. 517 shows a twisted German Gothic pillar from the fifteenth' century St. Blasius Cathedral in Brunswick. Figure 518, resem' bling nothing so much as a taffy twist, is from the Italian Palazzo Municipale in Perusa. Figures 519 and 523 are mid-fourteenth' century Portuguese and show Renaissance influence, which manifested itself in England two centuries later at Charlton-on' Otmoor Cathedral (Figs. 520, 524, and 525). Charlton also has the motif of Fig. 523, but turned upside down. Colebrooke Church, Devonshire, dating at about the same period, had supports like those in Figs. 521 and 526 for its parclose screen.

In France, Chartres Cathedral, in the twelfth century, had pillars with the boxed-jewel design of Fig. 556, a cross between a diaper pattern (see *Whittling and Woodcarving*, Chap. XIX) and a square trough outlet. The Norwegian Church at Wal, showing Romanesque influence, had the modified garlands of Fig. 557. Menardt Church in Hungary boasted the spiral collar of Fig. 558 on a Gothic goblet executed by Johannes von Novavilla in 1484.

But let us pause a moment to recall the development of the application of circular carving to wood, using the work in England as an example. As has been mentioned previously, the carpenter was the important woodworker in fifteenth-century England. He built the roofs, the houses, the cathedrals, and similar important structures. The building of plebeian articles of furniture such as stools, tables, chests, and cupboards was left to the "arkwright" (coming from "ark," the early term for all chests, and "wright," meaning worker or maker). His earliest chairs were Gothic types, really a box or ark with a back (Chap. V). Later ones, in the Tudor period (1485–1603), were "turneyed" or "thrown" (medieval terms for wood turning). These gradually grew to be assembled entirely of turned spindles. Though earliest examples had spindled backs and arms atop a box seat, later ones had spindled legs with stretchers as well. These chairs are now almost nonexistent, but we know them from the faithful seventeenth-century copies.

Earliest tables were likewise simple, being just trestles of wood. But about the end of Elizabeth's reign (1603), tables with bulbous legs came into fashion. Though these persisted until the end of the Stuart period (1689), shortly after the Restoration (1660) the baluster or vase turning began to be used on large tables, and the spiral on small ones. The spiral, copied from chairs, was apparently first used on tables in England about 1665.

Even at an early date, however, the arkwright, or his patron, began to find something lacking in simple turned elements. Their turned finials, balusters, uprights, stretchers, chair arms (before the hoopskirt outlawed them), and legs were too regular—they lacked interest. So the arkwright began to carve them. Elizabethan and Jacobean refectory tables often had acanthus or similar leaf and foliage motifs carved on the bulbous legs which characterized them (Figs. 528 to 531), or were fluted or reeded.

In furniture of the William and Mary style the trumpet-turned leg replaced the bulbous one but the carving was increased. Even later, during the period of the great English furniture makers, Sheraton's chairs may be distinguished from some of Hepplewhite's because Sheraton used a turned, reeded, or fluted leg, while Hepplewhite preferred the square. On other articles of furniture, their preferences were just the opposite, witness Figs. 522 and 527, from a Hepplewhite bed.

It is perhaps advisable to define reeding, fluting, and spiraling before attempting an explanation of their applications. Reeding is the carving of the surface of a turned shaft or pillar to create semicircular, molded projections parallel to the axis of the shaft (Fig. 522). Fluting is just the opposite, a series of hollow, rounded furrows or channels around a shaft or pillar, or on a frieze or decorative band. It is simply a series of parallel gouge cuts. The wood ridge between cuts is called the land. Spiraling is the carving of a design in a band around a shaft or pillar so that the band seems to rise, as does the screw thread, or more commonly, the stripes on a barber pole (Fig. 547). Obviously, a spiral can be either a

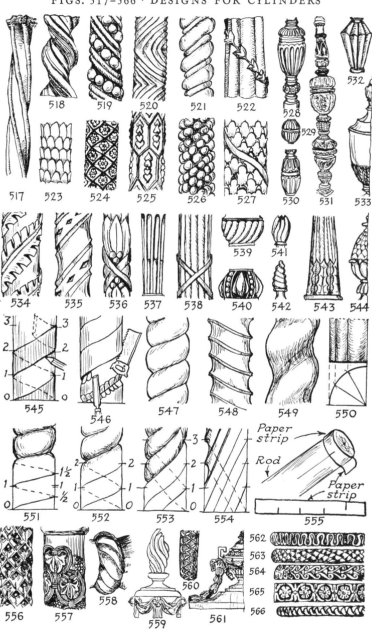

right- or left-hand spiral, being called right-hand (Fig. 547) if it rises toward the right, left-hand (Fig. 548) if toward the left. The old Greek rule was to have the spiral rising away from any opening which it frames—thus a spiral design at the right of a door or window would be a right-hand one; at the left, it would be a left-hand one. The two spirals were carried over the door to meet at the center in some sort of stop design like a cartouche or shell.

Fluting is done quite simply with the gouge by cutting a series of parallel grooves, semicircular in form and each about half as deep as it is wide. Unless it ends against a molding, cartouche, or similar element, the end of the flute should be carefully rounded, the top of the flute forming a half circle at the surface of the piece. From this half circle, the flute does not taper into the piece gradually, but enters in a sharp quarter circle, so that the end of each flute looks like a ball had been rolled through sand, then abruptly lifted away.

The only real problem is laying out the circular member so that the flutes run parallel with the axis and are spaced evenly around its circumference. A simple method of doing this is shown in Fig. 550. The end of the piece is divided up by evenly spaced "pie" dividing into the number of flutes desired. Then parallel lines are drawn on the turned sides of the piece to the opposite end, which is subsequently laid out to match the first end. This permits a check on the parallelism of the lines. To get the lines parallel with the axis of a piece of uniform diameter, simply put the piece on the table and lay a ruler against it so that the ruler forms a little shed roof from table to piece, then draw along the ruler's upper edge. Or clamp the piece in a vise, and draw diameters at each end with a plumb bob and line.

To divide up the end of a piece uniformly, use a protractor, or with the dividers space out even distances around the circumference. Dividers with an opening equal to that of the radius of the end of the piece will go around the circumference in just six steps. Dividers with an opening equal to the diameter of the piece will step around the circumference in three steps. Other divisions can readily be approximated from these.

A simple method for laying out, particularly irregular-shaped objects, is illustrated in Fig. 555. Just wrap a paper strip around the piece end and mark the amount of paper it takes to go all the way around (circumference). Then divide this paper strip up into the desired number of equal lengths, wrap it around the wood again, and mark the proper points. This method is particularly applicable when the piece being fluted is tapered or bulbous. For such lay-outs (Fig. 539, for example), use three strips, one at the greatest diameter of the bulge, and one at each end.

Reeding can be laid out similarly to fluting, except that in reeding the lines are cut away, not the spaces between them, and the job is done largely with the firmer instead of the gouge. In fluting, the gouge removes a semicircular section of wood; in reeding, a semicircular section is left, largely by cutting away parallel V's of wood with the firmer or knife.

Reeding is often combined with fluting in the "stop-reed" design (Fig. 537), in which a reed runs up part way of the height of the flute, then rounds off to end while a flute carries on. This element was commonly used in Louis XVI's day, but likewise now forms an important element. Reeding is also commonly bound with a simulated series of tapes or ribbons to make it appear like a bundle of rods (Fig. 538). A short section of such reeding becomes the familiar Italian fasces. When the reeding is shaped into berries or leaves, this becomes the laurel or bay garland (Fig. 536).

Either reeding or fluting can be spiraled around a piece, as well as any flower garland, leaf pattern, swag, etc. Figure 522 shows a continuing vine pattern spiraled about straight reeding; Fig. 534, two continuous spirals of acanthus leaves; Fig. 535, alternating spirals of concave bamboo sections and repeated diamond patterns on a flat ground; and Fig. 524, two sets of four spirals crossing each other to create the diaper background for the flower pattern. The simple spiraled reed pattern in Fig. 551 is, of course, the equivalent of a single section of spaghetti wound around a circular core. However, most spiral patterns have "faster" spirals, that is, they are the equivalent of two or more parallel spaghetti sections wound simultaneously. Thus Fig. 552 shows a double-section spiral; Fig. 553, a four-section; and Fig. 554, an eight-section. Note the increasing "pitch" or distance between the appearances of any single flute or reed. (Double spirals are shown applied in Figs. 90 and 312, *Whittling and Woodcarving;* a single Flemish spiral, in Fig. 376.)

Reeding and fluting, straight or spiral, are now commonly done by machine, but pieces so done are so regular they lose interest. If you are making a piece involving spiral sections, you can turn them up on a wood lathe, or order them turned for you, but your finished job will look better if you carve it by hand. You can of course have the blank turned, with or without capitals. Let us make a simple spiral design, choosing the most commonly used— the double-reed spiral. This is the equivalent of two cords or spaghetti sections twisted together (Fig. 547). Begin as shown in Fig. 545 by drawing parallel lines the length of the piece and on opposite sides. On these lines lay out distances equal to half the diameter. Thus, assuming my drawing shows a 2-in. diameter bar, the divisions up the sides are 1 in. apart. Then spiral a 1-in. strip of paper around the bar so that its upper edge starts at the base on one side, passes through the 1-in. mark on the other, through the 2-in. mark on the original side, and so on. Hold it tightly and draw lines along its edge top and bottom, and your layout is complete.

Shaping likewise is relatively simple. I prefer to saw along the spiral with a hand saw or back saw to a predetermined depth (in this case $\frac{1}{4}$ to $\frac{3}{8}$ in.), then take out chips from each side with the knife or firmer, as shown in Fig. 546. Following these roughing cuts, it is a simple matter to smooth up the continuous spiral.

If a fluting similar to Fig. 548 is preferred, you of course use the gouge exclusively, cutting to the desired depth between lines. For a spiral of this width, it is easiest to rough out the flute first with a smaller gouge, then smooth up the spiral by running along it with a 1-in. half-round gouge. A slight variation of the design may be created by carving the upstanding land between flutes with a vee tool.

The Jacobean spiral is about half-and-half flute and reed. As shown in Fig. 549, it is practically a reed and a flute wound together. It is done simply by widening the usual V groove in spiral reeding until its bottom can be rounded, and the reeded portion of the design is equivalent in size to the fluted portion.

Spiraling is said to have originated in the Far East, probably in India. It was brought to Europe by the Moors, who began to use it in Spain in the fifteenth century. It was later taken to Portugal, Italy, and Germany, and about 1665 began to be used in England, as evidenced by the pillars at Charlton (Figs. 520, 524, and 525). Several specialized forms of the reed should be mentioned. One is the gadroon pattern of Fig. 539, simply a series of tapered reeds spiraled around a bulb. Another is the egg-and-bead pattern of Fig. 540, in which the beads are created by rounding them out of a reed. They are flanked by narrow reeds as well, and the egg is shaped from a still wider reed. The third is the flame finial, illustrated in Figs. 541, 542, and 559. Figures 541 and 542 are Chippendale motifs; Fig. 559 is from the top of a Greek vase or urn in Independence Hall, Philadelphia. Figures 541 and 559 are spirals of very fast pitch; Fig. 542 is a single spiral. The two Chippendale motifs were commonly used for finials on four-poster beds.

Other common rounded forms were the vases or urns which are identifying elements of the Adam, American Empire, and Louis XVI styles. Figure 533 shows a typical Adam vase with an acanthus motif around its base. Figure 561 is a Louis XVI motif from a Paris hotel of the time, and includes the ribbons, flower, and leaf swags and general overdecoration of the style. Figure 544 is typical of the pineapple finial which was developed in America in the Empire style. (See also Fig. 1, *Whittling and Woodcarving*, for Grinling Gibbons' pineapple finial.) The pineapple finial in the Empire style is simply the old Portuguese scale motif of Fig. 523 put on to a tapered section, with leaf motifs added.

Figures 528 to 530 should also be noted as examples of Jacobean use of the tapered flute, the two latter being typical melon-bulb forms later replaced by the tapered-flute trumpet-turned leg of William and Mary style (Fig. 532).

Reeding, fluting, and spiraling, particularly in combination with the acanthus motif, are commonly used on many carved pieces even today. Candlesticks, powder boxes, fruit bowls, wooden bases, and similar circular pieces lend themselves to such treatment. If you use these motifs, remember the importance of the irregular curve in creating interest and of an occasional unexpected element to break the normal line of the design. Thus, you will often find that the acanthus looks better if leaf tips curve outward from the piece instead of being plastered down as they appear in Fig. 534. Above all, be sure that your design is not overdone, judged by present standards. Practically all the designs of Figs. 517 to 544 are still usable (except in a frankly "period" piece), provided you make them in low relief, modify circular forms into flat domes, space flutes a little wider apart, etc. Interest can also be lent to a reeded or fluted section by using a base or cap design. Thus Duncan Phyfe used the holly leaf (Fig. 543) for a base motif on tapered reeded sections; Hepplewhite threw a spiral vine or ribbon around a reeded pattern (Figs. 522 and 527); and other carvers often filled alternate spiral flutes with flower swags, vines, continuous berry clusters, etc., or a simple border motif of the types shown in previous chapters, as well as in this. Some typical motifs are Figs. 41 to 65, 147 to 164, 173, 174, 193 to 219, and 309.

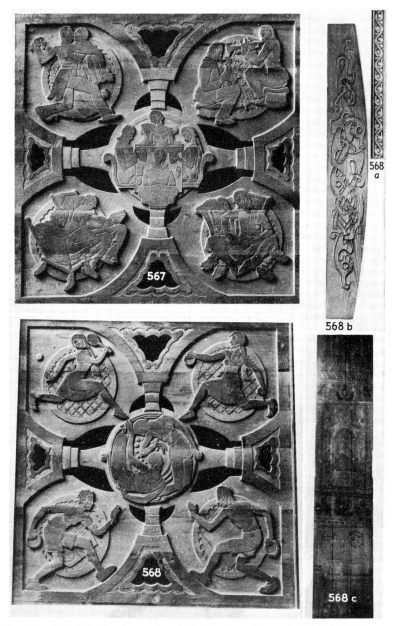

FIG. 567 and FIG. 568 · *Carved screens from the Smoking Room, Promenade Deck, R.M.S. "Queen Mary." Courtesy Cunard White Star Lines. (See also Figs. 708–711.)* FIG. 568a · *Molding, and* FIG. 568b · *Runic design on settee back, from Iceland.* FIG. 568c · *Part of traditional-style heroic panel by Bróz, native Czechoslovakian (before 1938).*

CHAPTER VII

VEINER AND VEE TOOL · *Outlining*

PREHISTORIC man scratched crude pictures and designs on the walls of his caves; the ancient Egyptian cuneiform and the more modern Chinese brushed characters are simply variations. Both come very close in application to veiner and vee-tool carving, for the veiner and vee tool are primarily *outlining* tools. With them, you can draw a simple line drawing just as surely as you can with ruling pen or drawing pencil.

Modern furniture and decoration, stressing areas and simple line design, is particularly susceptible to this form of carving, which fortunately happens to be the simplest to learn and to do. In fact, except for the greater difficulty of keeping these tools sharp (as well as of sharpening them in the first place), anyone who can copy a line drawing, even with carbon paper, can carve with the veiner. To make things even easier, veneered woods are commonly being used now, thus offering the required contrast at the base of the cut and automatically governing cut thickness. Several forms of veneers actually have contrasting second layers so that a veiner or knife cut down to that layer will unveil a second color. A queer kind of combination carving and peeling school of design has grown up in which even figures may be drawn in silhouette, outlined with the knife, then given strength and body by peeling away the top layer of veneer within the cut lines.

Most of these designs are composed of simple curves and straight lines, the motifs being conventionalized floral patterns— often conventionalized out of all recognition. Square flowers and round leaves stand atop stems which have boxes at their lower ends. However, done in moderation, they often provide relief in an otherwise severe and uninteresting panel.

Such patterns, as well as many of those shown in this chapter, lend themselves to use on two-color, three-ply plastics as well.

[93]

For example, I have a plastic-resinoid name plate in which white letters (produced by exposing a core stratum) stand out against the surface black.

Other methods of treating veiner designs include filling the line with paint or enamel, tinting or toning the outlined design (in various colors if floral), or stamping it or the background with a punch. The veiner has for centuries also been commonly used to outline a surface pattern or to indicate lines of a surface design. Two modern examples of such technique are shown in Figs. 567 and 568, carved lime-wood screens by James Woodford, from the R.M.S. "Queen Mary," which also are unusual in that the surfaces are intentionally roughed with the gouge to give the appearance of hammered copper or infinitely patient "whittling" out of the design with a gouge. Note also that all lines are very sharp and incisive and that three definite carving planes are created, often with outlining on each and relatively little modeling on any.

Because the veiner is much easier to sharpen and to use, as well as more commonly used by carvers, the remainder of this chapter will mention the veiner almost exclusively. In every case, however, the vee tool may be used instead, and will give a sharp-bottomed groove, instead of the rounded groove of the veiner. With either tool, you will soon learn the trick of "rocking" the tool as you push it, and the timesaving procedure of making all cuts in the same direction at the same time, thus avoiding troubles with grain and with position.

Even the ultrasimple veiner outline has its uses in design. In Figs. 569, 570, and 571 I have sketched three that are well-suited to modern decorations, although all date back to the ancient Greeks. The first is the sine curve so familiar to mathematicians and electrical engineers. It is, of course, susceptible to a number of variations just by varying the height and width of the nodes, by adding another sine curve 180 degrees out of phase or slightly out of phase, or by tinting or punching one side of the design. The two other outlines may be varied similarly by changing the semicircles into hyperbolas or even triangles.

〖 94 〗

Figure 572 combines a continued veiner line with a small punch design. As before, changing the shape of the triangle changes the design decidedly. Figure 573 is a conventional ladder or railing design, depending on whether laid horizontally or placed vertically. Or the verticals (as shown) may be made diagonals, thus forming a lattice border or an allover pattern.

Two common Tudor borders are shown in Figs. 574 and 577 and a modification of the Flemish scroll in Fig. 575. The latter may be modified by standing the scrolls side by side or by placing them at an angle. Figure 576, shown here as a border, may also be used as an edging. Figure 578 is one of dozens of triangle motifs. Though Fig. 579 looks like a Greek fret, it is actually a prehistoric design from ancient Styria! Figure 580 is a single braid motif.

To illustrate further variations of the triangle of Fig. 572, I have drawn the variations of Figs. 581 to 583. The first is an equilateral triangle, the second modifies this with small veiner lines, the third doubles the V element of the design (and incidentally comes from the tomb of the modern Chinese, Wu Ting Fang). A further modification of Fig. 582 is shown in Fig. 590, and still another in Fig. 593, the latter approaching the acanthus motif.

Three curve motifs are sketched in Figs. 584 to 586. That of Fig. 585 is a prehistoric pattern from Lourdes, and that of Fig. 586 is from Bosnia. All show the "curves within curves" that characterize many of these designs. A similar modification of a straight-line design of Fig. 581 is shown in Fig. 589.

The remainder of this plate is devoted to distinctive national and "period" motifs. Figures 587 and 588 are Jacobean; Fig. 591, Mayan border from Uxmal; Fig. 592, an Islamic strapwork design from the Alhambra; and Fig. 594, half of an Indo-Chinese motif. Several interesting early Italian motifs suitable for veiner carving are shown in Fig. 11.

Parenthetically, I might say here that any of these designs lend themselves to line inlay (see Chap. X), to coloring of enclosed areas, pattern punching, or even to inlay or marquetry of these same areas. In fact, Fig. 588, as originally used on the seat rail of a Jacobean chair, was outlined with the veiner, then filled inside

with a punched pattern. I have also seen Fig. 589 with the dia-
monds in contrasting colors.

The flowing single-line design of Fig. 595 comes from Turkey,
that of Fig. 596 from Oberammergau, Germany. Figure 597
comes from Indo-China, while that of Fig. 598 is a Jacobean
conventionalized floral motif. Figure 599 is taken from a second-
century Roman chariot, Fig. 600 from a mural in the tomb of the
Arab, Beni Hassan. An ancient Persian design is sketched in
Fig. 612. That of Fig. 613 comes from the tenth-century gateway
of Tiahuanaca, Bolivia; Figs. 614 and 615 are fifteenth-century
Aztec designs.

Various furniture styles give us the designs of Figs. 601 to
611. Figures 601 and 602 are variations of the tulip motif appearing
on an early American chest dated about 1650. The holly motif of
Fig. 603 was a favorite of Duncan Phyfe. All may be used with
stained or punched backgrounds. Figures 604, 605, and 610 are
designs by the Adam brothers; Fig. 606 is Gothic (one side is
marked to show punching); Figs. 607, 608, and 609 are by Chippendale himself. Figure 611 has been for centuries the emblem of the
chief warder of the Tower of London, England.

Modified acanthus designs lend themselves readily to veiner
execution. Figures 616 and 617 show two panel forms commonly
used on eighteenth-century furniture, the first with simple slots
only, and the second showing the characteristic acanthus "eyes."
Surfaces can, of course, be modeled if desired, with everything
from a concave to a convex surface or individually modeled leaflets.
Figure 624, which could readily be mistaken for a complex acanthus
motif, is really an Oriental motif from a Javanese tomb outside
Jidda.

Strapwork, executed either with single veiner cuts stopping
just short of the point at which they are supposed to dip under
an adjacent strap, or with double parallel cuts outlining the
supposed strap, are shown in Figs. 618, 621, and 622. Each pen
line may be considered a separate veiner cut, or the parallels may
be considered as outlining a single cut. Though all these are strapwork, they come from widely separated sources. Figure 618 is

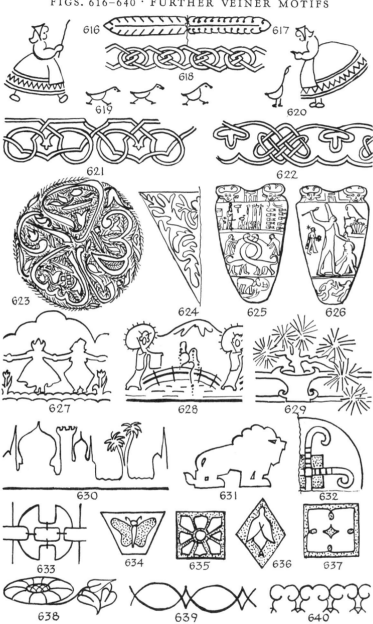

from a Moorish gate at Fez, Morocco; Fig. 621 is an old Persian running design; and Fig. 622 is based on a Mexican embroidery pattern. Compare these with Fig. 639, which comes from Ashley Hall, Charleston, S. C. This design was quite commonly used on eighteenth-century furniture, and is really prehistoric Greek. Compare them also with Fig. 640, an Indo-Chinese design.

Figures 619, 620, 627, 628, and 630 show veiner-executed frieze designs planned for paneling in a children's library or in a playroom. Figures 619 and 620 show a Bohemian girl with her geese; Fig. 627, a Dutch boy and girl; Fig. 628, a conventional Japanese motif with two kimonoed girls on clogs, the arched bridge, and Mount Fujiyama in the background. The tree leaves or fruit can be done with a series of punches. Figure 630 is an Arabian or Mohammedan silhouette, showing the bulging domes, the tower of the muezzin, and the leaning palms that character-ize the outline of many of these desert oasis cities. Figure 629 is a similar frieze design, but purely floral in motif.

Byzantine ornament in general is characterized by the working of Arabic script letters into the design. Often such elements are highly elaborate and illustrate some verse from the Koran. Such a motif is sketched in Fig. 623, the outlined portions being Arabic characters, with a sort of fernery filling the remaining areas of the circle.

The palette of King Narmer of Egypt, shown in Figs. 625 and 626, is an interesting ancient example of outline picture writing, and is included here as indicative of how nearly alike the drawn and veiner outlines really are. Made about 3000 B.C., this palette commemorates some victory. The center panel of Fig. 626 shows Narmer clutching a fallen enemy by the hair, preparing to smite him with his uplifted mace. Below, the two running figures repre-sent the fleeing enemy army. The other side, sketched in Fig. 625, is divided into four zones. The upper center zone shows the name of the king, with the goddess Hathor's head at each side (also shown on reverse). In the second zone, the king, followed by his sandal bearer and preceded by his prime minister and four stand-ard-bearers, looks at two rows of decapitated enemies (heads

641

642

643

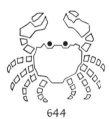

644

645

646

647

648

649

650

651

652

653   654   655   656   657   658

659   660   661   662   663   664

shown between their legs). In the third zone, the angry heads of two long-necked animals (strangely like our reproductions of dinosaurs) are kept apart by men pulling at neck ropes. In the lowest zone, a bull (representing the king) is battering down an enemy town and trampling his foes underfoot.

To come back to less warlike things, Fig. 631 is a lion's silhouette, the trademark of Loewe's, Berlin. Note its massive strength and also how readily such a design may be converted into an inlay or a tinted silhouette. Figure 632, which is slightly more than a quarter of an Aztec round shield, and Figs. 634 to 637 show further examples of the use of the veiner and punch in combination to produce elements to fit areas of various shapes. From a ceiling frieze in the Gibbs Art Gallery, Charleston, S. C., comes the design of Fig. 633. Figure 638 is simply another floral design, showing how readily such units may be produced to fill any desired space.

To provide some typical patterns of wall panels suitable for veiner execution, I have included Figs. 641 to 652, all square panels depicting the signs of the zodiac in a slightly facetious modern vein. All were designed by Béla Z. Reiter. Figure 641 is of Aries, the Ram (Mar. 21–Apr. 19); Fig. 642 of Taurus, the Bull (Apr. 20–May 20); Fig. 643, Gemini, the Twins (May 21–June 20); Fig. 644, Cancer, the Crab (June 21–July 22); Fig. 645, Leo, the Lion (July 23–Aug. 22); Fig. 646, Virgo, the Virgin (Aug. 23–Sept. 22); Fig. 647, Libra, the Balance, (Sept. 23–Oct. 22); Fig. 648, Scorpio, the Scorpion (Oct. 23–Nov. 22); Fig. 649, Sagittarius, the Archer (Nov. 23–Dec. 21); Fig. 650, Capricornus, the Goat (Dec. 22–Jan. 19); Fig. 651, Aquarius, the Water Carrier (Jan. 20–Feb. 18); Fig. 652, Pisces, the Fishes (Feb. 19–Mar. 20). Figures 653 to 664 show the symbols for these signs of the zodiac, in the same order (see also Figs. 818 to 830, Chap. IX). The panels, with the symbol worked into a convenient corner, make a novel frieze for library or game room.

This chapter would not be complete without mention of the Chinese scratch carvings which suggest similar veiner work— outlining the motif and then filling in the background with a

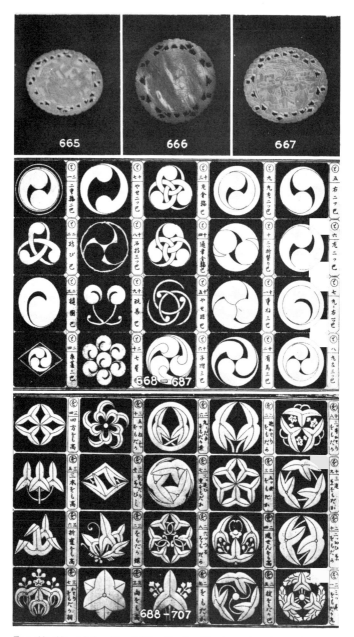

FIGS. 665–667 · Mother-of-pearl disks with pierced borders and scenic scratch carving. Chinese. Three of a set of six fitting the ivory box of Fig. 8. Courtesy Mary Quist. FIGS. 668–687 · Twenty designs conventionalized from the comma, and FIGS. 688–707 · Twenty designs from the arrowroot. Japanese. Figs. 668–707 courtesy American Museum of Natural History, New York.

close pattern of parallel veiner lines. Examples of Chinese scratch-work on ivory are shown in Figs. 9 and 300, and other examples, this time on mother-of-pearl, in Figs. 665 to 667. These scenic disks are half a set of six originally included in the round box of Fig. 8.

Veiner patterns are literally everywhere around you, or can easily be conventionalized from familiar objects. As examples, I have included Figs. 668 to 707, showing 20 designs conven-tionalized from the comma, and 20 more from the familiar water plant, the arrowroot. Both sets were produced by Japanese designers, and are on exhibit in the American Museum of Natural History, New York. They serve only to typify what can be done with a little imagination. Incidentally, to determine whether any picture or design can be made bisymmetric (see Chap. I) simply stand a mirror on edge over its center. Move the mirror along until the result is pleasing. To create an entirely symmetrical design, use two mirrors at right angles.

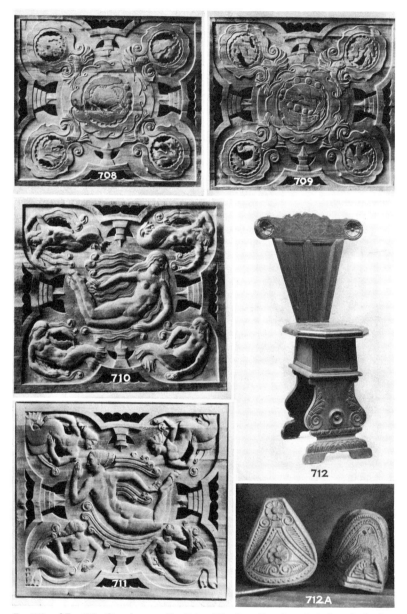

Fig. 708 and Fig. 709 · Carved screens. Fig. 710 and Fig. 711 · Pierced panels flanking the fireplace. All in the Smoking Room, Promenade Deck, R.M.S. "Queen Mary." All of lime wood by James Woodford. Courtesy Cunard White Star Lines. Fig. 712 · Italian early-sixteenth century sgabello in walnut. Courtesy Metropolitan Museum of Art. Fig. 712a · Box stirrups carved by "Huasos," or native Chilean cowboys.

CHAPTER VIII

VEINER AND GOUGE · *Modeling*

SAID Dr. Charles Eliot of Harvard, "We have lately become convinced that accurate work with . . . tools . . . trains well the same nerves and ganglia with which we do what is ordinarily called thinking."

Undoubtedly, Dr. Eliot had felt the same urge to *shape* things that comes to every worker in wood. Mere surface patterns are not enough; we want to see a design in relief, so that it begins to resemble the thing from which it was taken. Next, we want to see something created in the round, so that it has the third dimension of depth. When the desire to carve in relief gets the best of you, the gouge becomes indispensable. We have already seen what the firmer and gouge can produce when used together; now let us pause a moment to combine the cutting powers of the veiner and the gouge.

Some indication of the possibilities of panel treatments principally with these two tools is shown in Figs. 708 to 712. The upper two panels (Figs. 708 and 709) are companion carved screens to Figs. 567 and 568 in the Smoking Room on the Promenade Deck, R.M.S. "Queen Mary." Note particularly the use of the veiner to outline the loops in the circular wave motif at the center and in delineating the details of the fish and seaweed elements. Again, the surface is covered with a fine pattern of gouge lines, parts of the panel are pierced, and the carving is done on at least three distinct levels.

Carved by James Woodford, these panels are interesting to compare with those of Figs. 710 and 711, where Mr. Woodford has used the human figure, with considerably more modeling, against the same general background shape. Particularly noteworthy here is the use of the veiner on the hair of the figures and

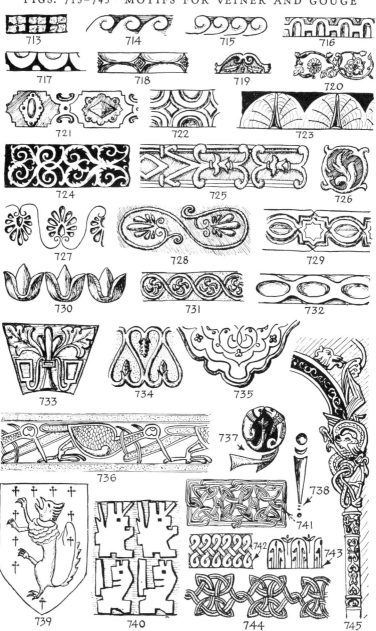

the curving of the figures themselves to create harmonious designs within the desired areas. Lime wood was used for all the panels.

Just by way of contrast, I have pictured in Fig. 712 an early sixteenth-century Italian *sgabello*, or panel chair. The fine-line relief carving of the toprail is almost indistinguishable in the photograph, but the carved rosettes and the designs on the front panel can be seen easily. Note the veiner work on both.

To serve as bases for designs using the veiner and gouge, I have chosen 33 motifs, varying widely in source, "period," and treatment, but each suggesting many others. Figure 713, for example, is a running border made up of the familiar four-petaled flower motif. Primary variations can be created by bringing the flowers closer together or by moving them farther apart. Secondary variations are endless by varying petal shape or position, removing the center entirely or making it so large that it becomes a floweret or boss itself, or by changing the number of petals.

Many Persian patterns are readily rendered with these two tools. The repeated wave motifs of Figs. 714 and 715, considered characteristically Greek and Roman, in these cases come from Persia (although undoubtedly a result of Greco-Roman influence). The background is cut down with a veiner, while the outer wave surfaces are shaped with the gouge to create concave surfaces. Another Persian pattern is sketched in Fig. 735, with veiner tracery supplemented by a gouge-shaped convex border. Other Near-East motifs include the Byzantine capital of Fig. 733, dated at around A.D. 530. Here is the familiar acanthus in an Eastern version (see Chap. IX).

Taking the sketches in numerical rather than chronological order, the next group are Jacobean motifs, including Figs. 716, 717, 721 to 723, 731, 734, and 738. The first is a familiar border with the characteristic vertical concave gouge cuts. Figure 717 is made by veiner outlining of the half circles, with a gouged quarter sphere for each core. This motif is often doubled, with a complete-circle motif, or half circles facing each border. Figure 722 shows one of the variations, although this one is also Italian. Figure 721 is a more elaborate Jacobean design from a cupboard dated 1665. It combines label, lozenge, and diamond elements. Figure 723 is again a familiar Jacobean unit, the repeated conventionalized semicircular leaf. The stem of each leaf is a rounded cone with an incised triangle at its center, and each lobe of the leaf is a convex curve dropping to a deep-cut veiner line representing the vein. Figure 731 is a guilloche variation from a frieze. The double-heart motif of Fig. 734 has been commonly used as a decoration around a cone on Jacobean bedsteads. It can be made to fit perfectly by reducing the size of the upper heart so that the continued design forms an arc instead of a straight band. (In laying out a cone for such a motif, divide its circumference top and bottom into an even number of parts by the paper-strip method detailed in Chap. VI.) Figure 738 comes from the uprights on a cupboard.

Chippendale used the two "Chinese" motifs of Figs. 718 and 725. The first has a floweret at the intersection of the gouge depressions, and the second has relief scrolls set completely above the background.

An oak-leaf motif from a canopy at Pilton, Devonshire, is shown in Fig. 719. Done in the early sixteenth century, it is one of the earlier Renaissance units. Figure 720 is another, this being a relief panel at Mary's Church, Cambridge. For contrast, I have included Fig. 724, a Norwegian seventeenth-century Renaissance motif. Figure 726 is a familiar English plant unit, and Fig. 732 a gouge-cut band from a 1745 English chair.

Two familiar Greek patterns, dated at somewhere between 1100 and 800 B.C., are sketched in Figs. 727 and 728. Here is the basic antefix pattern, with connecting scrolls, in one case done with the veiner, and in the other with the gouge upside down. The petals of the antefix are simple gouge cuts. The originals of these two patterns were on a water jar. Another familiar Greek motif is that of Fig. 730, taken from the Temple of Artemis at Magnesia.

I have shown only one Moorish motif, that of Fig. 729, taken from the gate of Fez, Morocco. There is also only one South American motif, that of Fig. 740, taken from the gateway of Tiahuanaca, Bolivia, and dated at about the tenth century.

The Celts in Ireland developed designs that were all their own, for they, among all the peoples of Europe, were among the last to be influenced by Greek and Roman ideas. Two of the early Celtic designs are shown, both converted for woodcarving from an eighth-century manuscript. They are the bird border of Fig. 736 and the fish motif of Fig. 737.

The strapwork motif is particularly successful when executed with the veiner and gouge, the strap itself being made either slightly concave with the gouge or grooved and convexed with the veiner. Sketched are four examples of such work, all Romanesque, yet coming from widely separated sources. Figure 741 is a socle from the church at Wal, Norway, and shows a triplex cord inter-lacing. Quite similar is the Lombardic border motif of Fig. 744 from the portal of San Ambrogio in Milan. This one, however, is only a duplex cord. A single strap design is shown in Fig. 742, taken from the pulpit in Bitanto Cathedral, Italy. And lastly, we have the queer half-Roman, half-Celtic tenth- or eleventh-century Norwe-gian portal of Fig. 745, showing the dragon motif, the Flemish scroll, and the Roman strapwork, all together.

Also Roman in origin is the delicate little veiner pattern of Fig. 743, from a Pompeian mural fresco. The leaves are made with the veiner and gouge in a sort of "flattened S-curve" shape. Show-ing some Italian influence is the Renaissance heraldic desk end of Fig. 739, carved in Manchester Cathedral, England.

When supplemented with the firmer, the knife, and the specialized carving tools, the veiner and the gouge can produce quite elaborate motifs. Let us now pass on to them.

FIG. 746 · *Egyptian ship panel, showing king, slaves, slavedriver, etc.* FIG. 747 · *Greek and Roman boats, with slaves and members of ruling class.* FIG. 748 · *Cinque Ports boats and the Santa Maria, with the Queen of Portugal and her attendants. All from the Main Restaurant, C Deck, R.M.S. "Queen Mary." Courtesy Cunard White Star Line.*

CHAPTER IX

ALL TOOLS · *Relief, In-the-Round*

"**Y**OU have to have a good disposition to work in wood." This statement of the old woodcarver who replied in the negative to a reporter's question about labor troubles in his department is never truer than when you begin to try high-relief and in-the-round carving. You have to have a good disposition, or you'll emulate some disappointed golfers and throw piece and tools out of the window. As Earnest Elmo Calkins says, "You have it—or you get it!"

Why? Well, wood in itself is such a charming, warming, reasonable material that it forces you to settle down and enjoy yourself. That is, it does if you've stayed within your powers of execution and don't try to be the first man to carve the Lord's Prayer on a piece of ironwood or to do detail work across a knot. Equivalent problems begin to plague you when you work in relief and in the round, because there the design must go on, though it take all summer. You can't just move over to a clear section of wood and carve the panel there.

Problems of shaping and working wood under all sorts of conditions have made many specialized tools necessary. You undoubtedly have some of them—back-bent gouges and firmers, front-bent gouges, macaroni tools, fluters, and fishtail tools are typical ones. And certainly, some of the photographs (berries, for example) in preceding chapters have suggested the need for such tools. More pictures of designs requiring them are shown in this and subsequent chapters, particularly in figure carving. It is not our purpose, however, here to explain how these tools are used except in unusual applications, for basic instructions have already been given (see *Whittling and Woodcarving*, Chap. XVII on tools, Chap. XIX on low relief, Chap. XX on high relief, and Chap. XXI on in-the-round carving).

FIG. 749 · "*Sovereign of the Seas*" with Charles I (reigned 1625–1649), and boats and sailors of Lord Nelson's time (1785). FIG. 750 · The first iron Cunarder, "*Persia*," with Victorian people. FIG. 751 · The "*Wm. Fawcett*" and building a future Cunarder. All from the Main Restaurant, C Deck, R.M.S. "*Queen Mary*" and, like Figs. 746–748, executed by Bainbridge Copnall. Courtesy Cunard White Star Line.

Just a few general hints may be in order before we begin any detailed discussion of the examples shown here. I have already said that everything rises to plague in modeling. Grain becomes a serious problem, because it is advisable and essential to make long, unbroken sweeping cuts in most cases. Just as everything is going well, and your longest sweeping cut is smooth and regular, the wood suddenly begins to "fur" and the tool to dig. Grain has tripped you up again. That means making the rest of the cut from the opposite direction, then carefully cleaning up the furred spot with a riffler or wire brush.

Many relief patterns are foliage motifs, bringing up problems with thin leaves, vines, tendrils, and flowers. Particularly in finishing up details, it is essential for you to "nibble" away the wood to avoid splitting or breaking off an unsupported section or a delicate detail. The saw will help in any last-minute removal of large masses of waste wood. And where details are particularly delicate, it is advisable to be sure they are supported by tendrils, vines, or leaf masses. Make them *look* thin and delicate, but don't *carve* them that way.

The veiner is particularly handy in starting a high-relief carving, as well as in finishing it. A preliminary veiner cut serves to outline the carving, as a stop cut, and as an accent around a finished carved element (because it creates a deeper shadow). Also use the veiner as a roughing tool for the vee tool—it saves sharpening time on the latter.

Now for a general rule or two about carving. Usually, a plane is better than a curved surface. It gives stronger shadows and sharper outlines and serves to accentuate the carving. Clean, long cuts are normally better than short ones. They create long, smooth lines and the desired planes and produce a finished piece that doesn't require ruinous sandpapering. Professionals differentiate, in relief carving, between such pieces as the R.M.S. "Queen Mary" panels at the beginning of this chapter, which stand out from the background, and *incising*, which is the process of cutting a design so that its highest element is at the level of the surrounding wood, as in the chest of Fig. 785. There is little difference in execution—in one case the margins are cut away or reduced to the level of the ground, in the other the margins are untouched.

In working with particularly involved details, it may help you to model the details first in clay, then work out the carving to match.

Most modern carving contrasts sharply with older examples. Pictures in this chapter are chosen to show both. Note particularly the plain (and plane) surfaces of the modern examples in comparison with the elaborate detail of an early day. Also, relief in modern pieces is much lower—gone is all the high-relief carving with dust-catching pockets. Many once-elaborate elements are now merely suggested with a veiner line or two. Thus the texture of the driver's loincloth in Fig. 746, and many similar details in Fig. 748, are just veiner lines. Faces may not be defined at all, or shown just with a vee-tool line defining an eyebrow or a firmer cut to show the eyebrow-nose curve. Draping is essentially simple, yet entirely natural.

I like the modern pieces better; you may not. In case you don't, or are planning a period piece, I've sketched a number of details beginning with Fig. 752, the famed Greek antefix, this particular one from the Parthenon in Athens. It is carved with both fluted and reeded "petals." Figures 753 and 754 are two typical Gothic round motifs suitable for "squints" in doors of proper style, or as ornamental motifs in proper surroundings.

Cartouches, supposed to have originated from curling-edged parchments, have become at various times fearful and wonderful things. Reproduced in wood, stone, and metal, the edges have been made to curl outward and inward, to interlace, and to form weird designs. A good example of elaborateness is Fig. 755, a cartouche from the Renaissance pulpit of St. George's Church, Wismar, Germany. Figure 760 is a more restrained Baroque example, executed for the Berlin Armory early in the eighteenth century by Andreas Schlüter. A Dutch example of the same style and of about the same time is sketched in Fig. 767. Notice the curving feather at the side, the hanging tassel, the tendrils, the leaf, the shield. Figure 765 shows a typical Louis XV cartouche, which is asymmetrical, as compared with the symmetrical ones of Louis XIV and the Regency. In fact, asymmetry is one sure way of distinguishing Louis XV from the two other styles. Figures 831 to 839 show halves of nine simple cartouches in later Renaissance Baroque style, readily carved and plain enough for modern use.

Used like the cartouche, but normally not nearly so elaborate, is the shield, examples of which are shown in Figs. 756, 757, and 758. The very simple Rococo example of Fig. 756 is from the Royal Castle at Dresden, Germany (see also Fig. 816). The edged shield of Fig. 757 is a Renaissance motif, and bears the triple fleur-de-lis. Another Renaissance example, a simple pointed oval bearing an eagle rampant over a boar- or wolf-headed dragon, is shown in Fig. 758. It comes from the Palazzo Ferroni in Florence.

Associated with the cartouche and the shield is the shell or *coquille* motif, developed from the shell-like crown that pagan grotesques wore in early Renaissance carving. It reached its peak in France as the "motif *par excellence*" of the Louis XIV style, and was used everywhere, on chair aprons or valances, arm ends, corners above the legs, in cresting, in tapestry borders—even on architectural tombstones. Louis XIV pieces seldom occurred without it.

In England the shell was also used, particularly on "Decorated Queen Anne" pieces. Chippendale and his disciple, the very skilled American cabinetmaker, William Savery of Philadelphia, used it in the French manner. Probably America's most perfect furniture craftsman was John Goddard of Rhode Island. He used the Queen Anne convex shell at each side of a piece, with an intaglio one in the middle. On highboys and secretary-cupboards, he carved the shell in relief at each side, bringing the "reeds" down to the surface around the arc, but extending the high body of the shell as a raised panel all the way down the front of the piece. Correspondingly, the intaglio shell was fluted from the surface down to a flat base channeled out all the way down the front of the piece. Such shells were straight across the bottom, in contrast to the elaborately shaped one made by one of his followers on a commode and sketched in Fig. 764.

To illustrate the variations, I have shown seven shell types. Figure 773 is an early Georgian example; Figs. 766 and 770 show Louis XIV examples; Fig. 768 is a Louis XVI example from a sofa cresting; Fig. 774 is "Decorated Queen Anne"; Fig. 763 is from a Savery lowboy; and Fig. 764, after John Goddard.

Perhaps at this point we had best stop and discuss the elaborate chair legs of Figs. 774 to 782. The first five are Queen Anne examples, although why they should be so-called no one has ever been able to explain exactly. Anne was a simple, unpretentious Stuart ruler, who avoided all the display and ceremony she possibly could. Further, the first of the Queen Anne styles didn't come into fashion until after her death in 1714. Really, all are Early Georgian examples. Anyway, Fig. 774 shows a leg of "Decorated Queen Anne" style, with cockle shells, pendant husks, and claw-and-ball feet. This style lasted from about 1714 to 1725, and was succeeded by the "Lion" style, lasting from 1720 to 1735, illustrated by Fig. 775. This in turn was succeeded by the "Satyr-Masque" style of Fig. 777, derived from German sources and stressing Grecian border motifs with the acanthus and grotesque masks at the knee. Final Queen Anne style is the "Cabochon and Leaf" (1735–1749) of Fig. 776, which gradually became a "translation style" from which Chippendale was derived. (A "cabochon" is an oval boss surrounded by carving.) To show the extent to which carving elaboration can go, I have sketched in Fig. 778 another Queen Anne example, combining shell, acanthus, scroll, bead, mask, and pendant husks. To top it all off, this leg was finished by gilding!

Although Chippendale derived his leg style from the motifs of Fig. 776, they underwent many changes during the translation period. Disregarding for the moment the Gothic and Chinese examples he later used, Figs. 779 and 780 show two typical Chippendale legs, both using only the leaf, in both cases modified forms of the acanthus.

During the Louis XVI period in France, legs, seat rails, and back edgings of the highly upholstered chairs were carved all over. Two examples from this style (1774–1793), both from examples in

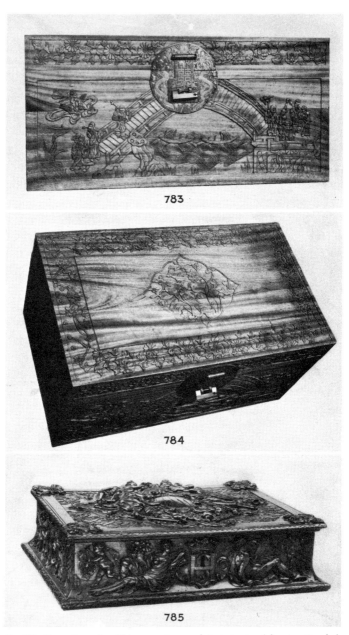

783

784

785

FIG. 783 · *Front of a modern Chinese camphor-wood chest, showing elaborate antique lock. Courtesy Faith Bisson.* FIG. 784 · *Top of same chest.* FIG. 785 · *French seventeenth-century walnut chest with figures symbolizing elements and arms of Henri, Duc de la Ferté Senneterre, Marshal of France. Courtesy Metropolitan Museum of Art.*

the Metropolitan Museum of Art, are sketched in Figs. 781 and 782.

One more example of the elaborate—Fig. 762, a Jacobean chair with a cornucopia of fruits, a crown cresting, simple acanthus elements below, and turned spindles for uprights—and then to simpler things. Figure 761 is an interesting portal from a farm-house at Kirkebös, Norway, an old Norse example from the time of Leif Ericson (A.D. 1000). It combines pure pagan and Christian motifs without qualm or fear of criticism.

An interesting little circular motif is the full-relief boss or knot of Fig. 759, which comes from Guatemala. Another is Fig. 769, a modern treatment of the old laurel garland of Greece and Rome, taken from the first platinum medal, struck a few years ago.

Perhaps it should be mentioned in passing that the half panel of Fig. 770 illustrates very well the ornateness of carving during the Louis XIV "period." Scrolls, volutes, floral garlands, and the shell are all used. While Louis XIV volutes were single curves, curled in at the ends, the Louis XV ones were double parallel curves joined together with bars modeled to form O-shaped holes between each pair. These connecting bars were called *bretelles* in France (meaning braces). From the volute (which is the sectional view of the cockle shell) too came indirectly the word "Rococo," a corruption or combination of two French words, *rocaille* mean-ing rockery and *coquille* meaning shell (in the volute form). The word thus expresses two leading characteristics of the style of the Regency and Louis XV. It was first used about 1718.

We have wandered far afield, but there are still two sketches on the panel of page 116 which we have not mentioned. One is Fig. 772, an interesting ribbon variation taken from a mosaic in a Turkish mosque. The other is Fig. 771, a medallion in Renaissance style by Della Robbia. It is an unusual foliage fleur-de-lis in a petaled, almost egg-shaped panel.

From China comes the camphor-wood modern chest of Figs. 783 and 784. The front view portrays the Bridge of Life, with a top border of flowers (Fig. 783). The top has the cock and a floral motif for a center medallion, with a floral border symbolizing

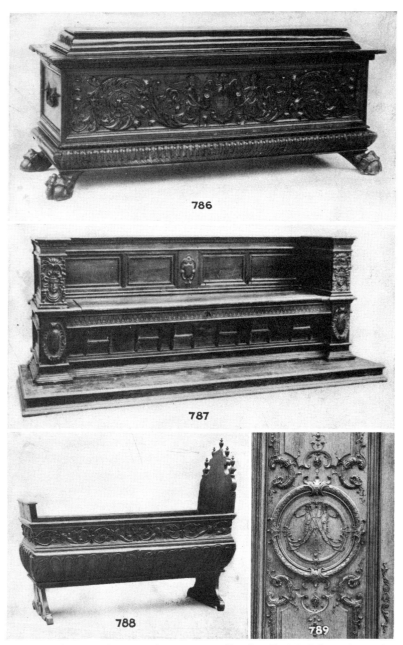

FIG. 786 · Italian sixteenth-century walnut cassone or wedding chest. FIG. 787 · Italian mid-sixteenth-century Florence bench in walnut, showing panels, masks, and cartouches. FIG. 788 · Late sixteenth-century Florentine cradle. FIG. 789 · French eighteenth-century (Regency) armoire detail. All courtesy Metropolitan Museum of Art.

the flowers of the seasons (Fig. 784). Every element has a symbolic significance. Carving is shallow relief, with plain smooth backgrounds, many details indicated by shallow veiner grooves (for example, the water in Fig. 783) or sloping planes created with the firmer. This is a good object lesson in simplicity, giving maximum attractiveness without ostentation.

Now compare with the Chinese chest the French high-relief walnut chest of Fig. 785. Dated at 1651–1661, it carries figures symbolizing the elements and arms of Henri, Duc de-la Ferté Senneterre, marshal of France. Its detailed carving is almost incredible in walnut.

The Italian *cassone* of Fig. 786 is another example. It likewise is carved in walnut and dates at about the sixteenth century. Here, however, the acanthus rinceau is much simpler. Also look at Fig. 11, another Italian example of the same period, which uses the scroll almost exclusively as a motif. These *cassoni* were wedding chests—the "hope" chests of their day—and were highly prized, particularly in Italy. They served the double purpose of a storage place and a seat, and often depicted the arms of the intermarrying families, or elaborate and finely executed paintings or sculpture.

An Italian mid-sixteenth-century Florence bench, with panels, masks, and cartouches carved in walnut, is pictured in Fig. 787. It is unusually simple for the period. Note that it too includes a chest compartment under the seat. Of about the same time is the Florentine cradle of Fig. 788, with an acanthus border around the top and acanthus corners and center motif below.

A beautiful example of detailed Regency carving is the armoire detail of Fig. 789, a French piece. It is unusually delicate, even for its period, and much less ornate than many contemporary pieces.

Probably most popular of all motifs is the acanthus. This more or less conventionalized motif became common in Greek ornament during the fifth century b.c., its first use being as a mask for the bases of the branching scrolls on the anthemion. Whether the ornament was copied from the acanthus, a South European plant

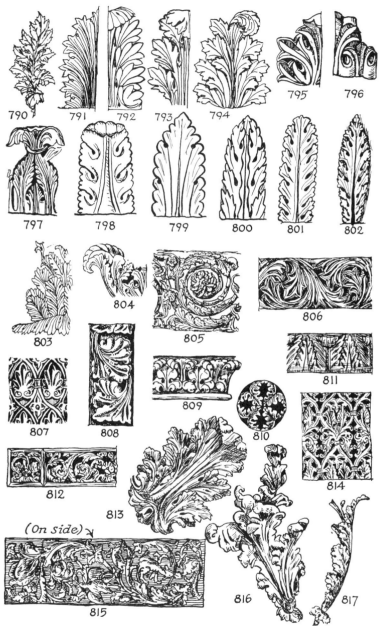

790 791 792 793 794 795 796

797 798 799 800 801 802

803 804 805 806

807 808 809 810 811

812 813 814

(On side) ↘

815 816 817

related to the burdock, or whether a conventional scroll or leaf shape was gradually elaborated and fluted until it looked like the acanthus, no one seems to know. Early examples could be almost any leaf, and some later ones could just as well be oak, poppy, thistle, or any other deeply indented leaf. It is certain, however, that the Greeks and Romans eventually copied both *Acanthus spinosus* (Fig. 790), with narrow leaves composed of lobes terminating in spines, and *Acanthus mollis*, a broader, blunt-tipped leaf. The first looks much like our common red oak, the second more like the white oak.

Vitruvius, to explain the origin of the Corinthian capital (which has the acanthus leaf as its essential characteristic), tells an interesting, but unlikely, story about a basket of funerary offerings set in the heart of an acanthus plant. The Romans used this capital, as well as the Composite (derived from it), much more commonly than did the Greeks, so varied its shape and arrangement. Other styles made other variations, so that we now identify them by the conception and treatment of the margin and shape of the leaf. I have endeavored to trace this variation in the sketches of Figs. 791 to 802, using as my sources two excellent texts, Meyer's *Handbook of Ornament* (1888) and *The Acanthus Motive in Decoration* (1934), the latter a pamphlet by the Metropolitan Museum of Art.

The Greek acanthus had pointed leaves (Fig. 791); the Roman (Figs. 792 and 793) was broader, rounder, to some extent more vigorous, heavier, and more drooping. The acanthus rinceau, or scroll (Fig. 805), became a favorite Roman continuous design, with the leaves masking successive branchings much more elaborately than in the Greek. It was the Romans, too, who began to combine the acanthus extensively with figures, flowers, vines, and rosettes, although the classic Greek acanthus plant of Fig. 803 was originally flanked by two human figures.

Spreading eastward with Greco-Roman culture, the acanthus motif became common in the Near East during the Roman, early Christian, and Byzantine periods. Its eventual flat, stiff, sharp-edged, less delicate, characteristic Byzantine form is shown in

See also Figs. 641-664.

the half leaf of Fig. 795, from the Church of Santa Sopha, and the running border of Fig. 806, from the Church of St. Sergius, both in Constantinople. Meanwhile, in Italy, the acanthus had become even more richly developed, as indicated in Fig. 794, from a pilaster in the Uffizi, Florence.

During the late Romanesque and early Gothic periods, the acanthus, both as a leaf and as a rinceau, was popular throughout western Europe, in some cases having an almost Byzantine form. Figure 796 is a Romanesque leaf from St. Denis, France, as is Fig. 797, the latter a twelfth-century capital. The more conventional leaves of Figs. 798 and 799 come from the capitals of pilasters at St-Guilhelm-le-Désert, and are late twelfth-century French. Probably because it was Roman influence that carried the acanthus into Europe, it was often combined there with grotesques, flowers, and fruit; and the Roman rinceau, or scroll, became the heavier, higher-relief whorl. Early Gothic carvers preferred the round, bulbous forms of the acanthus; later ones preferred bizarre, long-extended, thistlelike foliage. Both used naturalistic foliage, with highly idealized details. Except in Italy, however, the acanthus eventually fell into comparative disuse, being superseded by local foliage forms.

But when the Renaissance spread from Italy to the other countries of Western Europe, it brought with it the acanthus (Fig. 800, an Italian A.D. 1500 capital), which had been persisting stubbornly on its native soil, just as had the classic tradition. The Renaissance developed the acanthus to its highest point, but at the same time began extensive use of the tendril, which later almost swallowed up the leaf itself (Fig. 817). Its repeated rinceau and foliated termination of figures also spread to many other kinds of materials, and it is at this time that we first find the acanthus done in wood and in metal, where it became much more detailed (Figs. 815 and 816). Thus it was used on Louis XVI armchairs in the low-relief form shown in Fig. 801, curved to fit the arm support or leg.

Throughout the seventeenth century, the acanthus was common, although often in an elaborately executed and heavy style like the Baroque examples of Figs. 812, 813, and 816. Early in the eighteenth century, such popular Rococo motifs as the shell supplanted it to some extent, but during the second half of the century, the classic revival brought the acanthus back again, both as a leaf (Fig. 802) and as a scroll or spray. Figure 802 shows the tapered design favored by Wedgwood in his urn-shaped, blue jasper-ware vases. Many acanthus motifs at this time were subordinated, the sprays being lighter in scale and more like a garland, hence earning for themselves the name "artificial foliage," but showing acanthus derivation nevertheless.

Today, the acanthus is used principally in work of the classic or Renaissance styles, but in modified form appears in many unexpected places. In fact, "acanthus" has become a general term identifying heavy foliated scrolls, sprays, and spiny leaves, even though they stem from some other source.

In the acanthus applications in Figs. 803 to 817, Fig. 803 is half of an acanthus plant in the classic style, while Fig. 804 is half of a full-relief spray from the Villa Poniatowsky, Rome. The rinceau of Fig. 805 is from the Villa Aldobrandini, Rome. Variations in Romanesque ornament in Germany are indicated by Figs. 807 and 811, the first being a portion of a twelfth-century column decoration at Buchenberg, near Gothar; the second, a section of the frieze from the Burg at Münzenburg, Hesse. Figure 808, which comes from the Abbey at Larchant, France, and Fig. 809, a section of a pillar capital at Notre Dame de Paris (A.D. 1180) provide good examples of early Gothic treatment. The medallion of Fig. 810 is from the roof of the fourteenth-century church at Cunault, France. Figure 814 is a sixteenth-century Renaissance design from a Russian door. The table panel of Fig. 815 is another Renaissance example, combining the acanthus scroll with bird and animal motifs. It comes from Oudenarde, Belgium.

A carved openwork Baroque panel from St. Mary's Church, London, using the acanthus scroll, is sketched in Fig. 812. The single leaf in Baroque style is sketched in Fig. 813. After 1725, the Rococo in fantastic form held sway in South Germany. Figure 816 is an example of the acanthus treatment there, being a spray from the pavilion of the royal castle in Dresden, the most original building of the period. When the classic ornament returned during the time of the great English furniture carvers, it often assumed the shape of the spray of Fig. 817, designed by Thomas Sheraton.

Other examples of the acanthus in use can be found in Figs. 278, 298, and 411 of *Whittling and Woodcarving*, with a particularly good example of Gibbons' treatment of this motif in Fig. 2, described on page 222.

Thus far, I have said little about intaglio, the inverting of a carving so that when finished it will form a cast like a relief carving (see Chap. XXII, *Whittling and Woodcarving*). However, this technique is probably as old as relief carving, for the rulers of ancient Egypt were already using intaglio seals to identify state proclamations and government orders before the dawn of history. Any relief carving can readily be duplicated as an intaglio, and vice versa. Thus, for example, I have sketched the zodiac figures (see also Figs. 641–664) of Figs. 818 to 830 as relief figures, although Sidney Waugh designed and etched them in Steuben glass in intaglio. They appear around the rim of the famous Zodiac Bowl, copies of which are now in the Metropolitan and Victoria and Albert Museums. Assume that the light is coming from the lower left instead of the upper right, and the designs then will appear to be in intaglio as is the original, with every relief convex curve becoming an intaglio concave one. Figure 827 shows half of the center sun element of the same bowl, while the symbols corresponding with each sign are sketched near it as simple block outlines.

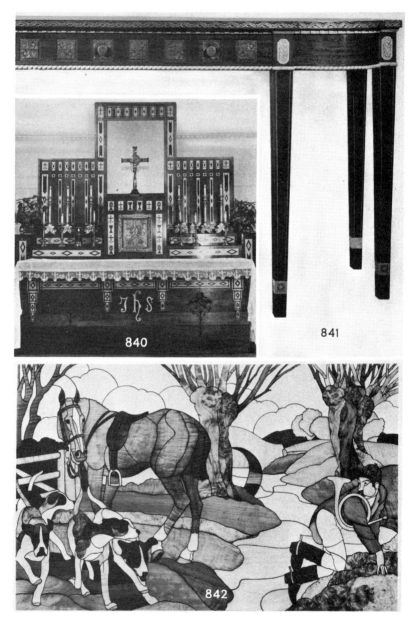

FIG. 840 · Inlaid altar from Boys' Town, Neb. Courtesy Rev. E. J. Flanagan. FIG. 841 · Half of a
mahogany table designed and executed by Albert Wood & Five Sons; it combines carving with holly
inlay. FIG. 842 · A marquetry panel by C. Cameron Baillie from the third-class Smoking Room, R.M.S.
"Queen Mary." Courtesy Cunard White Star Lines.

CHAPTER X

INLAY AND MARQUETRY

NO thoroughgoing discussion of carving and associated decorative techniques would be complete without some mention of inlay and marquetry, those arts of inserting ivory, gold, silver, tortoise shell, mother-of-pearl, and various precious woods into a base (and sometimes baser) wood. For several hundred years, whenever inlay and marquetry have risen in favor, carving has declined, and vice versa.

During the time of William and Mary in England, inlay and marquetry probably reached their highest peak. Work of that time (1689–1703) is almost amazingly delicate, detailed, and yet in most cases unpretentious (Fig. 883). Before and since, the urge to combine all the known varieties of wood, or to show a skill at permanent jigsaw puzzles, has led inlayers and marqueteurs to dizzy heights. Their productions are almost kaleidoscopic in color and variety, thus usually gaudy. The recurrence and prevalence of certain familiar motifs, made up with rainbow-colored woods, have created disdain for the whole art. Yet these two techniques, properly handled, alone or combined with carving, can be used to produce really artistic pieces.

There is no need here to discuss methods of inlaying or marquetry. (For complete details, see Chap. XXII, *Whittling and Woodcarving*.) But let us look at a few ancient and modern examples, plus a few worth-while simple motifs that, sensibly applied, may aid in regaining this 4,000-year-old art its rightful place.

Figures 840 to 842 are three modern examples. The first is the altar at Boys' Town, Father Flanagan's home for homeless boys just outside Omaha, Neb. It includes several good simple motifs, although the boys who designed and built it apparently were

844 845 846 847 848 849 850 851 852 853 843 854 855 856 857 858 860 861 859 862 863 864 865 867 866 868 869 870 871 872 873 874 875 876 877 878 879 881 880 882

carried away somewhat by the urge to cover the surface with them. Figure 841 is half of an inlaid table, designed and built by Albert Wood & Five Sons, which shows a combination of carv-ing, inlay, and overlay which is unusually pleasing. Not only are carved motifs used in the base wood (mahogany), but inlaid panels and overlays are carved likewise. The rope motif and fasces design of the overlaid molding are sketched in Figs. 861 and 862; the floral motifs of the leg inlays are shown in Figs. 856 and 874. Carved in holly, the inlays contrast beautifully with the base wood, and the proportions of plain wood and decoration are such that there is no feeling whatsoever of dressiness or gaudiness. Used as a decorative wall piece in a large hall, the table stands under a huge old tapestry—and blends beautifully with it.

Perhaps we should not leave this table without further mention of the narrow holly outlining on the legs. This serves to accentu-ate their slenderness, as well as to set off their taper and to tie the lower and upper inlays together. Although these are flush with the surface, such narrow lines are capable of infinite variation. Two, for example, are: *raised inlay*, in which the inlaid piece is cut a little higher than the base and allowed to project and create a shadow (used almost entirely in borders); and *lined inlay*, in which the inlaid piece is cut a little narrow, so that thin outlining strips of contrasting wood, precious metal, ivory, celluloid, or some other material can be pressed in with it. If this technique is used with an inlaid or marquetry scene, the result is almost like that of leaded glass.

Third of the modern examples is Fig. 842, a marquetry panel in the Third-Class Smoking Room, R.M.S. "Queen Mary." Designed by C. Cameron Baillie, it is an unusually effective treat-ment of a humorous subject. Its colors do not clash at all, and it resembles nothing so much as a cross between a well-done poster and a capably executed leaded-glass window. Elaborately figured veneers are used to represent textures, and do so without ostenta-tion or the slightest hint of gaudiness.

Now to some typical examples of inlay, overlay, and marquetry patterns down through the ages. In the panel of page 130, 40 different ones are shown. Figures 843, 853, 855, 870, 878, and 880 are Jacobean examples. The first combines a number of charac-teristic patterns—the guilloche, checkerboard, floral panel, decorated rope molding, and various bandings. Figure 855 is a floral motif; Fig. 853, a combination of the Flemish S with the four-petaled flower and leaf elements. Figure 870 is the common Jacobean zigzag border; Fig. 880, a conventionalized Jacobean tulip; and Fig. 878, a quartered-tulip motif.

An interesting group of simple Aztec border patterns is shown in Figs. 844 to 851. The first is an outline square with a square center inlay. Figure 845 is one of the common triangular motifs, and may be made as shown, without the rule borders (which might be metal, celluloid, or some other material contrasting in texture as well as color), or in the form shown in Fig. 847. Figure 848, like Fig. 844, is a combination of rule or line and mass inlay. So is the design of Fig. 850, which looks much like beads or shells strung on a cord. Figures 849 and 851 are dentil patterns, also capable of the variations mentioned for Figs. 845 and 847. They, like Fig. 841, make suitable raised inlays.

The ribbon motif has long been a favorite one for inlaid borders. Figures 852, 858, and 859 are typical motifs, in these cases created with two colors of wood which contrast with the background. They are simpler, and often more attractive, if the borders are left off and the design is made in a single color of wood, ivory, or metal. Figures 854 and 863 are simple, single-color inlay borders, the first taken from the Syrian chest of Fig. 888, the second a common design since the days of the Greeks or before. Figure 864 is a slight variation of the motif of Fig. 863, in which the intro-duction of a parallelogram of wood of contrasting shade makes the border look like a series of boxes side by side.

The Albert Wood motifs used on the table of Fig. 841 are sketched in Figs. 856, 861, 862, and 874. The first is another simple variation of the four-petaled flower (see Fig. 853), and is actually carved in the larger square, which in turn is inlaid. Such a piece must be of $\frac{1}{8}$-in. wood, as compared with the usual $\frac{1}{28}$-in. veneers used for inlaying. Figures 861 and 862 are overlay designs. Figure 874 is again a carved inlay in ⅛-in. white holly. See also Fig. 910, Chap. XI.

The exquisite shell motif of Fig. 860 was made in ivory on an English highboy dated at about 1740. Other ivory inlays are the floral patterns of Figs. 875–877; Fig. 876 simply provides an alternate head for the thistle of Fig. 877. Contrast these with the heavier, rougher Jacobean tulip motif of Fig. 880.

Next are several William and Mary (around 1700) motifs, among them Figs. 866, 868, and 869. The first two are geometric line inlays, the third a portion of an elaborate floral marquetry panel on a chest. Contrast their simplicity with the seaweed marquetry on the walnut cabinet of Fig. 883, dated at about the same time. The peculiar name of "seaweed" was derived in an interesting way. "Marquetry" itself comes from anglicizing the French *marqueterie*, which in turn came from *marqueter* (pro-nounced marktay), meaning to variegate. The seventeenth-century Dutchmen who used it first were flower lovers, so their marquetry panels likewise were floral designs—naturalistic tulips and carnations in loose bunches. When marquetry came to England about 1680, all English gardens were very formal, so that the naturalistic Dutch floral motifs were mingled with con-ventionalized scrolls at the base of each bunch and the whole panel made bisymmetrical. This gradually grew into a detailed and brilliant scrollwork of conventionalized foliage, so fine in pattern and workmanship that it was called "seaweed mar-quetry." Toward the end of Queen Anne's reign, the seaweed motifs became complicated arabesques, and marquetry, thus degenerating, died out.

Marquetry, essentially, is just inlaying into the surface veneer of a piece, and probably occurred spasmodically from the time veneering itself was developed. Veneering, in turn, is supposed to have been invented about the time of Solomon, although Arthur DeBles of the Metropolitan Museum thinks that the idea may have sprung from the phrase in the Bible, "And he covered the walls on the inside with wood, and covered the floor of the house with fir," describing the building of Solomon's Temple.

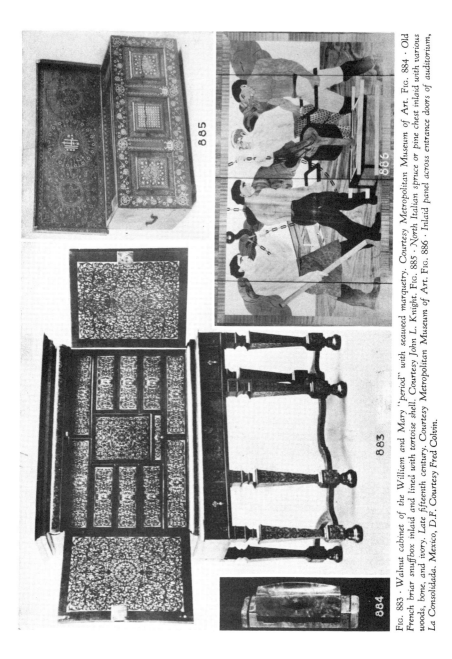

Fig. 883 · Walnut cabinet of the William and Mary "period" with seaweed marquetry. Courtesy Metropolitan Museum of Art. Fig. 884 · Old French briar snuffbox inlaid and lined with tortoise shell. Courtesy John L. Knight. Fig. 885 · North Italian spruce or pine chest inlaid with various woods, bone, and ivory. Late fifteenth century. Courtesy Metropolitan Museum of Art. Fig. 886 · Inlaid panel across entrance doors of auditorium, La Consolidada. Mexico, D.F. Courtesy Fred Colvin.

But let's get back to our inlaying. The rest of the designs sketched in the panel of page 130 come from a wide variety of sources. Figure 857 illustrates a four-petaled flower commonly used in Italian certosina work of the late fifteenth century, and usually done in ivory, mother-of-pearl, or metal. It can be seen in the chair of Fig. 890. (*Certosina* is pronounced chairto'seena, and means "a very delicate and beautifully executed inlay of triangular pieces of bone or ivory designed in set geometric patterns"—Arthur DeBles. It derives its name from "Certosa," Italian for a Monastery of the Order of Carthusians, in whose famed Certosa di Pavia, in Lombardy, it was first used.)

Figures 865 and 867 are Bedouin designs, usable for inlaying with any material, or for overlays. These would of course also make good gouge-dot designs—and therein show the same adapta- bility to technique of execution as have so many of the preceding patterns in other chapters.

A German Romanesque repeat pattern from the ninth-century Lorsch basilica is sketched in Fig. 871. It makes a good border or even an allover pattern.

Two spot inlay patterns are sketched in Figs. 872 and 873, both from Amusgos, Mexico, and imitating woven designs in textiles. The inlay work of Fig. 881 is a Swiss pattern, imitating a balus- trade, and comes from Lower Engadine, Switzerland. A marble inlay dating from A.D. 1200, but entirely applicable to strapwork inlay in wood, is sketched in Fig. 882. It comes from Cosmati (named after the brothers of that name who did it) work in the pulpit of a church in Ravello, Italy. Figure 879 is a pattern from the marble pavement of the Baptistery in Florence, Italy. Like Fig. 882, it is only a quarter of the complete pattern.

So back to our photographs. Figure 883 pictures a walnut cabinet covered inside and out with the elaborate seaweed marquetry of the William and Mary style (late seventeenth century.) At its right is a North Italian spruce or pine chest inlaid with various woods, bone, and ivory, and dating from the late fifteenth century. Below that is a very modern marquetry panel, from the wood-paneled double doors to the auditorium in

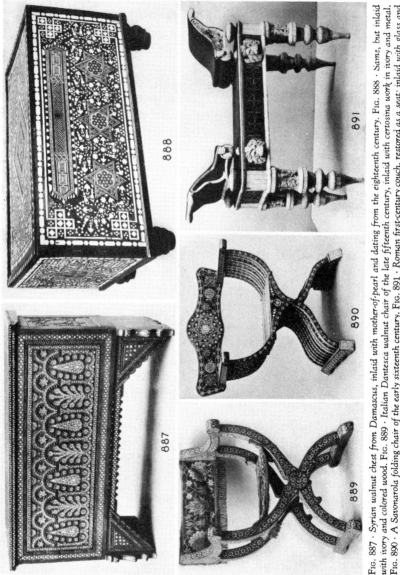

FIG. 887 · Syrian walnut chest from Damascus, inlaid with mother-of-pearl and dating from the eighteenth century. FIG. 888 · Same, but inlaid with ivory and colored wood. FIG. 889 · Italian Dantesca walnut chair of the late fifteenth century, inlaid with certosina work in ivory and metal. FIG. 890 · A Savonarola folding chair of the early sixteenth century. FIG. 891 · Roman first-century couch, restored as a seat; inlaid with glass and bone carvings. All courtesy Metropolitan Museum of Art.

the Administration Building of La Consolidada, Mexico City, D.F. At lower left in the same group is Fig. 884, an old inlaid briar snuffbox, dating back about a hundred years. The inlay, and incidentally the lining of the box, is tortoise shell, applied by the technique developed by Boulle, famed French marqueteur.

Very elaborate geometric inlays are shown in Figs. 887 to 891, all dating back several hundred years. Figures 887 and 888 are eighteenth-century Syrian inlaid chests from Damascus; Fig. 888 is inlaid with ivory and colored wood, Fig. 887 with mother-of-pearl. Below them are three ancient pieces of seating equipment (see Chap. V). Figures 889 and 890 are Italian (Lombardy) chairs, the first from the late fifteenth century, the second from the early sixteenth. Both are inlaid with certosina work of ivory and metal. Figure 889 is the earlier Dantesca type; Fig. 890, a folding Savonarola chair, is later. Figure 891 is a Roman couch reconstructed as a seat and dating from the first century A.D. Here glass inlay and bone carvings (really high-relief overlays) are skillfully combined.

Probably this lengthy discussion of inlay and marquetry, intermingled with carving of various types, has been so confusing that it is advisable to tabulate the outstanding characteristics of the various "periods." This has been done in the next chapter.

FIG. 892 · *Door to a home in Washington, D.C., carved by mountain boys and girls trained by Eleanor Vance and Charlotte Yale of the Tryon Craft School, Tryon, N.C. Illustrations from "Handicrafts of the Southern Highlands" by Allen H. Eaton. By permission of the publisher, the Russell Sage Foundation.*

CHAPTER XI

STYLES · *Identification*

THE fair Florentine measured the breadth of the Venetian's shoulders, palpitated as his brown eyes smiled. Nudging a lady-in-waiting, she whispered: "Yonder Romeo sends the shivers racing down my spine. He has the manner of a prince, so dashing, so intriguing, so handsome! Ah, my heart! Would that I might meet him!"

Horror blanched the face of the lady-in-waiting. "My fair mistress!" she cried, "Thou art truly but little versed in the ways of Venice! Yon swaggering impostor is not what he seems. Cease thy unfortunate yearnings, for he is not for thee! Yon regal-appearing young fop is naught but a two-shelf fellow!"

Two-shelf fellow? Renaissance slang for the station in society of the young man in question. By placing his furniture, the lady-in-waiting placed the man. Renaissance etiquette dictated that the commoner might have but two shelves to his dresser, the nobility three, royalty four or five.

Such an incident is but one of many which characterize the ability of furniture and of architecture to reflect individuality. The moods of nations, the peculiarities of rulers, the atmosphere of an era, all have left their marks on the work of master crafts-men since the dawn of civilization.

In the effort to correlate and identify the various decorative styles, I have compiled here three tables: Table I lists the rulers of France and England and the furniture styles during the years of the great furniture makers. Table II indicates characteristics of the carving or other decoration and the woods used during these "periods." Table III lists the styles of architecture, and tabulates typical motifs for each. Table IV answers many of the questions about finishing methods of these craftsmen (see also *Whittling and Woodcarving*, Chap. XXV).

Seams sewn in his first crude skin garments undoubtedly suggested such geometric motifs as the cross and the zigzag line to primitive man, which, after the animal outlines of the Reindeer Age (10000 B.C.), became his first decorative motifs. Woven work suggested reticulated (network) patterns, braided hair suggested the braid and plait. A tree fork revolved in the sand makes a circle or a series of dots suggesting the polygon. Simple lines drawn across a polygon produce the star; a shell suggests the spiral. It is easy to determine that geometric patterns must be continuous bands, panels, or area repeats—no amount of scratching in sand will produce any additional ones. Here are completed all the preliminary steps which lead to such geometric art forms as are found in Moorish paneled ceilings, Gothic tracery, and the guilloche. When one stops to consider that the Egyptians developed geometry into a science, their additional use of the ellipse as an important element in design is far more readily understandable.

Man's increasing intellectual development brought deeper understanding and more technical skill; he began to copy animals, plants, and finally the human figure itself. Beauty of form, as evidenced in outline of leaf, delicacy of spray, curves of the form, etc., undoubtedly had to do with ancient man's preferences for certain floral and leaf patterns. The other vital fact is that certain selected floral elements, figures, and shapes had religious or symbolic significance.

Thus, the laurel and olive both played an important part in the tree worship of the prehistoric Greeks. The laurel, sacred to Apollo, signified atonement, victory (as shown by crowns woven of it), glory. The olive branch, sacred to Athene, meant peace, success. Vines were representative of Dionysus; grape and ivy, sometimes combined with laurel, were decorative motifs for drinking cups, paintings of bacchantes, etc. (By contrast, ecclesiastical art of the Middle Ages combined the vine and the ear of wheat to symbolize Christ!) Another famed Greek motif, the acanthus, has already been described in detail, and its development traced (see Chap. X).

The lotus and papyrus are as important to the Egyptian and Assyrian civilizations as is the acanthus to the Greek. Papyrus stalks provided ancient Egypt's mats, baskets, and fuel; papyrus pith made wicks for lamps; its roots were edible; it provided the first crude paper. Inevitably, both papyrus and lotus gained religious significance and were incorporated in the art of the peoples, which deified the only art patron—the king. Thus the lotus was sacred to Osiris and Isis as the symbol of immortality, signifying as a water plant the recurring fertilization of the land by the Nile. This explains the spoons and other utensils decorated with lotus flowers and calyxes, the column capitals imitating lotus buds or flowers, the shafts resembling a bound bundle of stalks, the bases appearing like root leaves. These two water plants occur again and again in Egyptian art, in everything from mural painting to sculpture.

The palm likewise soon attained religious significance—which even to this day it has not lost. Palm leaves first symbolized victorious peace, leading Egyptian processions to Osiris, Hebrew kings into Jerusalem, Olympian athletes to the Greek games, and Roman victors returning home. The Christmas tree is only a northern version of the palms carried at the midwinter solstice feast of Osiris (later adopted by compromise as Jesus' birthday), and the palm still signifies peace in church rituals. Hence, from late Renaissance right down to the present day, the palm motif has signified peace (on tombs, memorial plaques, and the like, eternal peace).

European ivy, an evergreen climbing vine, was formerly sacred to Dionysus, hence was used freely in decorating drinking cups and vases, as well as being twined around the thyrsus which bacchantes waved in dances to the god. It also symbolized the friendship of a weaker with a stronger person. Ancients used the young leaf, a heart-shaped, lancelike motif, much more than they did the mature five-lobed leaf.

Other plants commonly used as motifs, and deriving religious significance as the staff of life, are the "corns,"—wheat, oats, rye, barley, and spelt. The hop, so vital in making beer, thus became

893

894

Fig. 893 · A Gothic-style door embodying linen and parchment folds, Flemish I and a heraldic panel with quatrefoil and trefoil in transom above. Fig. 894 · Carved door combining gouge-cut and chip-carved simple borders, running borders of acanthus, wave and varied floral motifs. Executed by the Adam Dabrowski Studio, as was Fig. 893.

a motif for drinking cups and tavern or inn decorations. The oak, symbol of power and strength as well as of Jupiter, appears time and again in various art styles. Oak foliage and acorns, as well as maple foliage and seeds, occur in early Gothic friezes, cornices, and column decorations. In Italian Renaissance, the oak appears frequently too, but for another reason—it was the crest of the della Rovere family, two members of which became Popes Sixtus IV and Julius II.

The floral festoon and single floral motifs undoubtedly come down to us as a result of the custom of strewing flowers before victors or religious processions; the fruit festoon as a result of the Roman custom of hanging such festoons on temple friezes alter-nating with the skulls of slaughtered sacrificial animals. Such sacrificial instruments as the candelabra and tripod were also combined with this decoration, and sooner or later the whole thing was reproduced in wood or stone. The open space over the center of the festoon was filled by the Romans with masks, figures, or rosettes; during the Italian Renaissance, angel heads were substituted there, particularly on tomb and ecclesiastical-building decoration.

But let us get back to the principle of using living things in decoration. A living thing can be employed in ornament in two ways: as formed by nature, called *naturalistic;* or as influenced by political, religious, or other influences, called *stylistic.* First and strongest is the naturalistic ornament, in which the artist is simply imitating nature as he sees it. As this becomes more and more elaborate, is worked into shapes to suit a design, space, or artist's notion, it becomes more and more stylistic, and usually more decadent.

It is basic in design that ornament should conform with the object upon which it is placed, not conflict with it; should be subordinated, not stifling; and should be influenced by both the material and the style. As more elaborate styles are developed, they obscure the decorated object, hence lead to their own decadence. This process can be traced time and time again through the known history of art.

[143]

After all, the history of art is a relatively recent thing. You have already seen in *Whittling and Woodcarving* (Introduction) how little we know of the history of these arts. Only a little over a hundred years ago, we knew nothing of the art of Egypt, Greece, or even of the Middle Ages. Of course, men stumbled upon examples, but these were variously thrown to one side, disregarded, destroyed, or thrown into the sea as heathen. Archaeology didn't become popular until the latter part of the nineteenth century. Then, as is usual in such circumstances, everyone wanted to be a great archaeologist.

It was with extreme skepticism that the authorities greeted the announcement of the Marquis de Sautuola that his little daughter had found some prehistoric paintings in the cave of Altamira in Spain. That was as recently as 1879. But examination showed the red of these cave paintings to be iron oxide, the blue manganese oxide, the yellows and oranges iron carbonates, the black burnt bone, all mixed with fat to make them stick. The artists had evidently used hollow bones for paint tubes, flat stones for palettes. Now, if the Marquis had gone, as some claimed, and hired a Madrid artist to paint the pictures for him, he certainly wouldn't have gone to all that trouble. But promptly, similar paintings began to be discovered in caves all over France and Spain—and cave painting was added to our history of art.

Why wasn't it found earlier? Principally because these paintings were in dark, inaccessible sections of caves where the first searchers never thought to go. Why were they where they were? We don't know, but we suspect it was because they were used in religious exercises to assure success in the chase (all of the paintings are of animals commonly sought for food), and that the exercises had to be held where the animals couldn't conceiv, ably find out about them, even if their spirits did travel around at night.

The same relative youth appertains to our "discovery" of the Egyptian civilization. It resulted directly from Napoleon's con, quest of Egypt in 1798 and the accompanying discovery of the Rosetta Stone, which gave the key to the riddle of Egypt.

Previous paragraphs have pointed out two things—that ornament derived from living things varies with local fauna and flora, and that it varies in treatment with various epochs. For example, the Egyptians used the lotus and papyrus, the Greeks the acanthus —but the acanthus was at certain epochs used decoratively in countries where it couldn't possibly grow. The style or treatment varied with the epoch—and thus permitted a given time to be traced through a series of countries, because preferences for certain living things and certain treatments permit that style to be identified wherever it appears. It is for this basic reason that art of all kinds is customarily classified by style rather than by motif. It is variation in the *treatment* of the acanthus motif which distinguishes the early Greek from the later, the Roman from the Renaissance, even the early primitive cave paintings from the later ones. (Later ones became stereotyped and stiff, like the saints of Russian and Byzantine icon makers.)

Undoubtedly, it was an effort to secure success in the chase, or to placate the gods of things he did not understand, that inspired man's first efforts at art. We don't know a great deal about them even now, but we do know that they go far back beyond recorded history, back 6,000 years at least. And roughly, they correspond with man's civilization. Even a little civilizing apparently begins to bring out the artist in a man.

Even though we know so little about this prehistoric time, we can divide it into four more or less obvious parts, usually called the Wooden Age, Stone Age, Metal Age, and the Primitive. Along the Mediterranean, the Wooden Age flourished about 6,000 years ago; in New Zealand it flourished as recently as 100 years ago when the first white man came. The Maori tribesmen there had never seen metal of any kind until then, but still had done surpassingly beautiful and craftsmanlike sculpture in both wood and stone—an elaborate version of prehistoric art.

It was probably during the Stone Age that man began to carve, for stone provided a material hard enough to mark wood and ivory in southern countries or reindeer horn and bone in northern ones. Also, about the same time he learned how to form crude dishes, and began to decorate them with scratched patterns of game animals, usually colored with reds, browns, and yellows.

Perhaps it was his discovery of fire and its control that began man's climb in civilization and culture, that literally raised him from the ground, first to a bed of boughs, then to a stone couch padded with skins, then to a higher stone slab for a table on which he placed those first crude dishes of clay.

The Metal Age brought first bronze, then iron in rapid succession, and such repeated motifs as concentric circles, spirals, the zigzag spiral, nested squares, triangles, and various crude geometric figures. The Primitive Period elaborated these into more detailed designs, plus chip carving, runic patterns, symbolic figure carving, and simple depiction of flora and animals. Here, before the beginning of recorded history, is the dawn of wood-carving—or more properly, whittling—in decorated paddles, figureheads, gods, stools, simple jewelry—first probably having deep religious significance, later merely a way of beautifying an otherwise purely utilitarian object.

The climate and terrain of Egypt make wood relatively scarce, and then the thousands and thousands of years of life it supported soon used up what little there was. (Before the Pharaohs, all Egyptian architecture was in wood—and there was lots of it.) So woodcarving in Egypt was limited to statuary, furniture for the king, and religious utensils. But the rigid and systematic, hence cold and stiff designs developed there are now coming back in modified form, as well as the shallow, angular, low-relief carving there used on wood, stone, and plaster. Egyptian, as well as primitive and other Oriental art, was without perspective. (In fact, the principles of perspective were not discovered until the fifteenth century.) But portraiture was already of a high order, and fair likenesses were obtained, although in most cases the portrait was undoubtedly more attractive than the subject, owing to the Egyptian desire to deify the ruling classes—who were the only subjects. Colors at first were only red and black ink, though yellow, green, blue, and a sort of red-orange were added later. Motifs included the papyrus, palm, reed, lotus, animals, and men.

Egyptian civilization is customarily divided into "kingdoms." First came the Ancient Kingdom (4000–2200 B.C.), centered in lower Egypt at Memphis. Under King Chafre, first king of the tenth dynasty, it reached its cultural peak. The Middle Kingdom (2200–1550 B.C.) began with the conquering of Egypt by the Hyksos, a Semitic race, and moved up the Nile to middle and upper Egypt, with the capital at Thebes. (All civilizations seem to start along some life-giving river.) Here decoration and design began to play an important part, for it was these groups of Egyptians which fashioned such incredibly beautiful altars for their temples, some in stone, some in wood (ebony, redwood, cinnamon, kheyst), the latter inlaid with colored bits of stone and glass as well as precious metals. At this time too were developed wood sculptures and the ancestors of our present chairs,[1] first as

[1] It is perhaps of interest to detail several of the outstanding examples of Egyptian work in wood. The famed Sheikh el-Beled (IV Dynasty, 2900–2750 B.C.), is a free carving of a middle-class overseer. The figure was apparently covered with linen and painted, and eyes of crystal were inserted. The figure is so-named from the exclamations of the excavation laborers, who recognized in it the counterpart of the chief of their present-day village.

The Egyptian sense of design was far superior to that of other peoples of their time. Excellent proof of this is the detailed low-relief panel of Hesire (about 3800 B.C.), with its single figure off center, yet balanced by the staff and writing utensils held in the left hand. Though main lines are vertical, the horizontals of feet, baton, girdle, and shoulders provide the necessary breaks. The figure, though conventionalized, still has tremendous life and vigor, the face is highly individualized and carefully modeled, with high cheekbones, firm mouth, and noble bearing. Modeling is exceptional also about the neck, shoulders, and knees.

Woodcarving was really quite advanced in Egypt—one of the best evidences being cosmetic jars. A "perfume spoon" (now in the Louvre) is shaped to represent a girl swimming and pushing along a duck whose body forms a cosmetic box, with the opening between the slightly parted wings. (The figure of the girl is sketched in Fig. 929.) Another is a cosmetic jar of the XVIII Dynasty (1580–1350 B.C.) representing a slave stooped under a huge jar he is carrying. Modeling of face, figure, and jar are all exceptionally well detailed, the adaptation of the pose is fine, and the figure and its elements are as good as any modern pieces I've seen.

The Egyptian cabinetmaker was skilled too, combining with skill in design and workmanship the crafts of the ivory carver, goldsmith, and lapidary. Thus an ebony jewel casket of the XII Dynasty (2000–1788 B.C.) is inlaid with ivory, gold, blue glaze, and carnelian. The color harmony accentuates the "quiet richness" of the design, laid out in carefully proportioned panels that follow the structural lines of the casket. Alternate narrow panels are decorated with gold ornaments and strips of blue faïence topped with a red carnelian square, and an undecorated ivory rectangle runs the length of the casket above that. The

FIG. 895 · An old carved-oak mantel from Southampton, N.Y. The original is about 8 ft. high by 12 ft. wide. Courtesy J. A. Lucas. FIGS. 896–901 · Various carved elements for incorporation in "period" rooms include three floral and bird elements in florid Renaissance style, a low-relief incised panel of a piper, and a knife-cut doorknob. FIG. 902 · Simple diapers and two veiner borders decorating an early-Renaissance door by the Adam Dabrowski Studio.

purely royal or ecclesiastical seats to elevate rulers and priests above the "common herd." These had four legs, shaped backs, and vertical slats—a design that reached Europe about 3,000 years later!

At Thebes, too, was the capital of the Modern Kingdom (1550–663 B.C.), including the reigns of Ramses and Leti, and declining after 1220 B.C. The so-called Later Period (663–31 B.C.) likewise was at its peak at first, but began its decline with the Persian conquest in 525 B.C. Alexander the Great captured Egypt in 332 B.C., the Ptolemies took over at his death in 323, Rome in 31 B.C.—the great Egyptian civilization was at an end. It survived in Alexandria for a thousand years longer and developed Coptic art—mainly textiles and small carvings distributed over the Western world by the Crusaders, but the great days of Egypt were over.

The Chaldean, Sumerian, and Babylonian-Assyrian styles all had their inception along the Tigris and Euphrates rivers in "holy Mesopotamia," just as the Egyptian began along the Nile. The time was about the same, too, about 6,000 years ago. From 4000 to 2000 B.C., the Sumerian civilization developed there. Then suddenly, about 2000 B.C., Babylon under King Hammurabi (who wrote the famous code of laws from which Moses "borrowed so heavily" in preparing the Ten Commandments about a

---

base curves in harmony with the hollow cornice and curved lid, the latter inlaid with gold, blue faïence, and carnelian heads of Hathor. Other examples include ivory and semiprecious stone jars shaped as lotus buds or partially opened flowers, an ideal receptacle for cosmetics.

The excellence of Egyptian chairs has been mentioned several times previously. One from the tomb of a noble of the XVIII Dynasty (1580–1350 B.C.) is of redwood, with decoration of gold leaf on plaster. Front legs are cabrioled with upstanding carved goddess' heads at the knee. Leg shape is feline. Side arms curve up to a solid shaped and braced back and incorporate elaborate carved panels. The seat was plaited string. The tomb of Tut-ankh-amen provides a similar, though more slender, chair of wood covered with gold. The intertwined lotus and papyrus that symbolized the union of upper and lower Egypt were executed in openwork gold in the span between leg brace and seat. The arms are serpents wearing the double crown of the union and having partly opened wings to form the body of the arm and enfold the royal cartouche filling the curve at the front. The back panel is a domestic scene showing lotus and papyrus columns in the background. This panel is inlaid with gold, silver, and colored insets.

thousand years later) blossomed into an important city. Shortly after his death the city was overrun by the Hyksos who also passed on to end the Middle Kingdom in Egypt. Along about 1400 B.C., the Hittites (mentioned in the Bible as the sons of Heth) were controlling all Chaldea, only to lose it a hundred years later to the Phrygians or Free Men (who devised the French liberty cap). About 1200 B.C., Nineveh and the Assyrians rose to power, and in 1000 B.C. Babylon was reborn as a great and influential city (to last 500 years—it was in ruins when Alexander died there in 323 B.C., on the eve of planning its rebuilding).

This latter period was that of the great artistic development. Because of the scarcity of wood, architecture was mostly air-dried bricks or stone covered with terra cotta, plaster, or asphalt and decorated with colored mosaics. Typical motifs were the Babylonian lion and winged globe (ancestors, believe it or not, of our angels and cherubim!), rosettes, and various geometric patterns. Egyptian influence, undoubtedly introduced by the traders (probably Phoenicians) of that day, brought the lotus and the palmetto motifs, probably also the four-legged chair, which in Assyria gained the animal-foot shape later rediscovered in Europe. Here, too, we find the first "stump" figures with heads larger than bodies, and such grotesques as the human-headed, bird-winged steer. Elevating their rulers almost to the deity level, these peoples also developed marvelous inlay, embossed leather, carved woods, and precious metal in fashioning furniture for their kings.

Median-Persian art developed from Egyptian, Assyrian, and Hebraic beginnings. Though the Medes apparently existed in 1500 B.C. or earlier, their real culture began with their conquest of the Elamites in 700 B.C. The Persians under Cyrus conquered the Medes in turn 150 years later, and art in all forms prospered under such kings as Darius and Xerxes. Alexander the Great defeated the Persians in 330 B.C., bringing with him some Greek influence. But Persian art lived on—in fact is living today. Centered about Bagdad, Persian art survived the Moslem conquest—in fact, absorbed the conquerors culturally, to serve as a great art clearinghouse in medieval times. Early motifs include winged lions and bulls and various geometric figures, mostly in low relief, as well as mosaics and inlays in royal furniture. Later motifs are principally involved floral and geometric interlacing.

Egyptian and Assyrian influences also predominated in Phoenician-Hebraic art, which originated about 2000 B.C. The Hebrews, learning from their rivals, the Phoenicians, reached a high peak of artistic skill during the reigns of David and Solomon (about 1000 B.C.). They made inlays in precious stones and metal, and were skilled in carving, as recorded in the Bible (see *Whittling and Woodcarving*, pages 3 and 4). Hebraic art began its decline with the capture of Jerusalem by Nebuchadnezzar in 586 B.C.

Another early, but tremendously advanced, civilization was that of Crete and the other islands of the Aegean Sea. Running from about 3000 B.C. to the conquering of the capital city Cnossus by the raiding Greeks in 1100 B.C., it developed such motifs as the chevron, spiral, rosette, palmette, dentils, and interlacing spirals, some of which we now consider as Greek inventions. Workers of Cnossus did exceptionally detailed carving of ivory trimmed with gold, enamel work, and inlay with colored (particularly blue) glass.

At first subject to Oriental and Aegean influences, Grecian art soon developed the originality which has made succeeding styles but poor imitations. More genial and pleasing than the Egyptian, it included such familiar motifs as the anthemion and antefix, circles, cyma curves, scrolls, flowers (principally woodbine and lotus), leaves (principally the acanthus), feathers, animals, birds, fish, human beings, and such geometric repeats as the Greek fret. The earliest Greek art was in wood, hence circumscribed by the shape of the block. Stone sculpture at first imitated this rigidity. The Greeks were also great architects, and their first wooden structures so inspired the later stone ones that essential wooden structural elements appeared in stone structures where they were totally unnecessary. Although we customarily consider Greek art as simple, it was really (as Van Loon says) "gaudy" in appearance—highly colored and having elements of carved ebony, ivory, and gold.

〚 151 〛

Greek art is usually divided into four periods: the Mythical (to 1104 B.C.); the Archaean (1104 to 470 B.C.), during which the Doric column was developed; the Ionic (470–338 B.C.), marked by development of the Ionic column; and the Hellenic (338–146 B.C.), marked by development of the Corinthian column and ended by the Roman conquest of Greece.

Subject to Chaldean influence was Etruscan art (in Etruria or Tuscany), with the principal motifs animal and human figures. It lasted from about 1000 B.C. to 400 B.C., when the Romans conquered the country. Etruscan art was not so charming as that of the Greeks; it was more primordial and primitive. The "archaic smile" (really an attempt to depict sadness) lingered in Etruscan sculpture long after the Greeks had learned better. The Etruscans were, however, among the greatest workers in terra cotta.

Roman art was really a composite both in its beginnings and in its later development. Rome itself was influenced in its art by Greece and Etruria, though it deserves great credit for the perfection of its sculptures and mosaics. As is so often true in adapted and conventionalized art, later Roman decoration hid the objects it covered, being pure overornamentation. An "offshoot" style was that of Pompeii, featuring colored stucco, metal, and elaborately decorated small articles. It ended sharply with the burial of that city by Mount Vesuvius in A.D. 63.

And now, to keep our story straight chronologically, let us go to Asia, where China and India both developed decoration to a high plane, particularly in wood, jade, and ivory. Chinese art, which had its crude beginnings back about 3000 B.C., is said to have had its real beginnings during the Han period (206 B.C.–A.D. 220). In any case, it reached its peak during the Sung period (960–1279). It was rigidly isolated, hence original. (A few Chinese geometric motifs are quite similar to those of other countries, but they were undoubtedly independently developed.) Though the intensive Chinese culture developed no architecture, it did develop a wide variety of ornament. This, combined with the Chinese attributes of patience and thoroughness, often turned the artistic into the artificial; carefully detailed ornament into overdecoration. We must admire the amazing detail and the care in execution of much of this carving, although it is often so complicated and overdone that it is difficult to determine what lies under it.

Common Chinese motifs were based on flowers and leaves, animals, the human figure, and such mythological or religious figures as dragons. Almost every motif has more than a decorative significance; it either assists in telling a story—as do primitive carvings elsewhere—or has some religious importance. Almost all motifs are highly conventionalized. Materials included available woods, such as ebony, camphor, and teak, as well as ivory, mother-of-pearl, even local hard-shelled nuts and soft stone. Carving was often in high relief, traceried, or in the round, and painting, lacquering, and gilding were employed in finishing.

Japanese art, derived from China through Korea, was never so conventional, probably because it was originally an adaptation, and later was more frequently subjected to outside influences. It can readily be divided into epochs corresponding with normal historical changes. First was the Heroic Age (960 B.C.–A.D. 278), during which the Daimios, with their feudal lords, the Samurai, reigned over Japan, until finally the empire was united under the Mikado. The Second Epoch (278–1108) saw the introduction of Buddhism (constituted the state religion in A.D. 624), with consequent introduction of Chinese and Indian influences, and weakening of the Mikado's power by the Shogun (Imperial Chancellor). During the Third Epoch (1108–1549), three families controlled the Shogunate, consequently the nation, and art was more circumscribed. The Fourth Epoch (1549–1868) was begun by the Portuguese introduction of Catholicism, marked by its destruction (in 1638) by the Dutch, and ended by the re-establishment of the Mikado's power and introduction of European civilization in 1868.

Indian art has often been called very old, for did not the Aryans drive the older inhabitants out and establish a civilization there almost 4,000 years ago? Again, this is a result of the Oriental desire to establish great age, for, although this civilization began

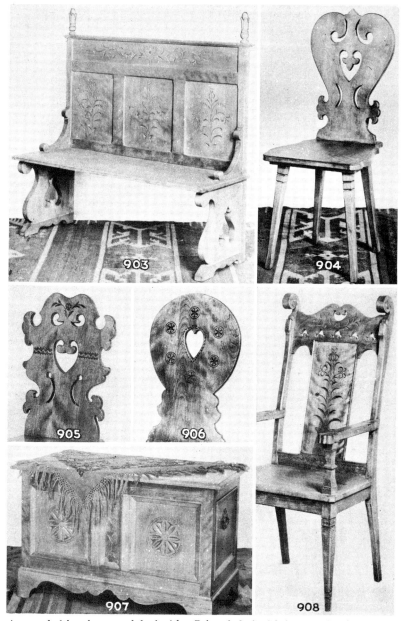

A group of solid-wood pieces made by the Adam Dabrowski Studio. Much open work and modernized chip-carving motifs characterize the pieces, simple in outline and treatment.

about 1700 B.C., there was no architecture until 600 B.C., or sculpture until Alexander the Great made his conquering march. Further, India is not one tribe or people, but many, each with its own civilization. The first general period of Indian civilization is usually considered as the Vedic Period (1700–256 B.C.). The great King Asoka (ruling 264–227 B.C.) was converted to Buddhism in 256 B.C., and began the Buddha Epoch (256 B.C.–A.D. 647), during which all the arts prospered. Greatest portion of this Epoch is the Gupta Period (A.D. 320–647), golden age of Hindu culture, lasting until the Tatar invasion and return of the country to Brahminism. It brought forth many elaborate wood and ivory carvings of all sorts.

The New Brahmin period (A.D. 647–1250) developed fantastic, bizarre, almost hateful (to our Western eyes) ornament, over the entire surface of an object. With the completion of the Islamic conquest in 1250, a new phase of Indian art began, called the Mogul Period (1250–1818), during which Shah Jehan built the lovely Taj Mahal (1632–1653) for his dead wife, Mumtaz-i-Mahal. Delicate, graceful, suppressed, low-relief ornament of the Taj contrasts sharply with usual Indian ornament. It used the lotus motif principally, combined with other floral designs, showing Hellenic, as well as Islamic influence.

Indian art first showed Persian influence, then Hellenic, and finally Islamic, although it has never been superseded by any. Even after the Mohammedan conquest, India kept on with its Hindu custom of placing tortured, weird figures depicting the Buddha, mounted horsemen, elephants, animals, winged griffins, many-armed gods, grotesques, and monsters all over the surfaces of its temples from foundation to topmost gable, all in violation of the Koran, of course. It also has always used geometric and floral patterns, in exuberant, unrestrained ornament.

North of Greece and Rome, the Germanic tribes had been developing an art all their own, almost all having religious significance and expressed in motifs on weapons and useful articles. Such units as circles, pierced loops, geometric patterns, and the sine curve, as well as crude scratch carvings of animals and warriors, were the forerunners of the Celtic art which flourished in England and Ireland, in the latter country for a much longer time because it was uninfluenced by Roman conquest. To this, when Christianity was introduced into Central Europe by the Romans, were added strap and ribbon patterns, knots, twists, braids, the acanthus, and various foliage elements. Much of this later art was based on the Byzantine, an influence from which it was not freed until A.D. 900.

Celtic art itself was based on ornamental tracery, with the bodies of birds and animals (many fantastic) skillfully interlaced with foliage (the latter a result of Roman influence after the ninth century). Roman influence, by way of Ireland, caused the end of the Archaic Period of Scandinavian art (A.D. 1150) and the development of the Roman, or more properly Romanesque (1150–1250). This in turn yielded to the Gothic. North Norway is particularly worth mention here, because it was there that wooden architecture began real development about 1075. (It is from Scandinavia also that the finer modern furniture designs have stemmed.)

Byzantine art originated in A.D. 330 when Emperor Constantine made Byzantium (or Constantinople) on the Bosporus his capital. It reached its peak under Emperor Justinian (527–563) and died in 1453 when the Turks finally captured the city. Its principal products were finely carved ivory and painting. Although the leading characteristics of its art were a lifeless formality and a continued, hopeless repetition, it exercised a tremendous influence upon the design of later countries and peoples which embraced the Byzantine, or Greek Catholic, faith.

Beginning about A.D. 1000, under Byzantine influence, Russian art was modified by Tartar rule from 1237–1480 into a distinct style. Half Oriental, half Occidental, it was so isolated it suffered little change until Italian artists were imported during the later Renaissance. Even then, they were so influenced by it that their pure Renaissance style was considerably modified. Wood was the preferred material because of the shortage of stone, and necessitated smaller, square structures and more rigid sculpture—principally of saintly, but stilted, images called icons.

Islamic or Moslem art began about A.D. 622 as a result of Mohammed's uniting of the Arab peoples throughout the East. It includes bits of all the other contemporary styles, except that no animal or human figures were incorporated because of the ban against such depictions in the Koran, Principal motifs were geometric and vegetable, often highly involved, and worked into elaborate traceries and trellises, mosaics, and screens. Geometric inlay was also practiced in Islam. Wood was the preferred basic material, usually worked into pulpits, doors, and screens, with inlays of bits of mother-of-pearl, glass, colored stones, and tortoise shell.

The Moorish subtype, developed by those Moslem conquerors who named a captured Spanish rock "Jeb el Tariq" (or Gibraltar) after their commander-in-chief, Tariq, often used letters or complete mottoes in ornament, working them around with elaborate tracery apparently derived from the Persian. The Saracen subtype was a stronger, more virile, more simple art, mainly used for decorating weapons of war, tents, personal jewelry, rugs, etc. Ottoman artists particularly favored such motifs as the pea tendril, the watermelon, pomegranate, canary-bird flower, gourd, and amarynth. Arabian-Persian artists were more distinguished for the rich coloring of their designs, Arabian-Indian ones (eleventh century) for their naturalistic plants. The latter group also defied the Koran proscription by using animals as design motifs.

We should not neglect, in discussing the development of ornament, the purely American art forms of the Mayans, the Aztecs, and the Incas. The Mayan civilization, apparently flourishing during the sixth century A.D., was dead and gone before the first white man ever saw Guatemala. But Cortez, seeking only gold, destroyed the "heathen" records of a great civilization in Mexico when he destroyed the Aztec gods and temples and forced Christianity upon the people. Even then, their civilization was decadent, however, for archaeologists place its peak at around A.D. 1000 to 1100. Pizarro, likewise seeking only the precious yellow metal, similarly destroyed the remnants of a great civilization in Peru—that of the Incas, or children of the sun. Their civilization was flourishing at about the same time the Gothic was weakly beginning—A.D. 1200. All three of these great nations produced great architecture and great sculpture, the Inca particularly to be remembered for its delicate detail. Some of the motifs have been shown earlier.

It is from such diverse beginnings that our arts of wood decoration have come. The more familiar art styles, as delineated in Table II, sprang from such divergent peoples and ideas that the foregoing outline is essential to understand them. Undoubtedly, I should also point out again here that all preceding ornament epochs were closely tied in with royalty or the clergy—ornament seldom appeared anywhere except on objects destined for the ruling or ecclesiastical classes. It wasn't until the rise of Christianity that the common man was afforded the luxury of furniture. Even then, his pieces were the simplest of tools, benches, cots, and trestle tables. The Dark Ages inspired no outstanding improvements—in fact, only the barest essentials graced homes. But in the Romanesque style there was forecast a new period of development.

Romanesque was an art style, predominantly religious, which developed out of the old Roman art as the empire fell apart. It covered the great span of time from A.D. 476, when the Roman Empire became nothing but a name, until the beginning of the thirteenth century, when the Gothic style replaced it. Its development was exceedingly slow and painful, for the northern peoples were especially suspicious of anything Roman. It might never have developed at all had it not been for the Benedictine monks, who made their abbeys centers of learning and of art. Essentially simple at first, Romanesque art began to take on an Oriental note after Charlemagne and Harun-al-Raschid, famous Caliph of Bagdad, made their exchange of gifts which permitted a certain subsequent influx of Persian art into western Europe.

Seeing these barbaric tapestries, rugs, chessmen, and carved ivory pieces, Europe began to take a new interest in art. By the middle of the ninth century, Oriental elements began to be combined with older Romanesque motifs in churches. William the Conqueror carried the new style to England in 1066, where it was fittingly called "Norman" style.

All things considered, we owe much to Romanesque for providing a base upon which the great Gothic style could be built. It was at best ostentatious and overdone, except in architecture and sculpture, and even there it exhibited a certain grotesqueness and "nervousness," perhaps at attempting to combine the old Roman, itself a decadent composite of styles, with the newer Oriental. But for a childlike people, rising from the yoke of Roman masters, it was good. It provided a fitting horizontal note from which the vertical Gothic could rise.

"Gothic" is really a term applied by the Italians to anything from the North, hence barbaric. Gothic art sprang from Romanesque art at its peak, but was freer and more intellectual, though saturated with religious mysticism and emotionalism. It began in Italy about A.D. 1200 but soon lost ground to the Renaissance there, though it persisted much longer in northern Europe. At first, the wide traveling of artists and apprentices kept it uniform, but when the Black Plague killed a quarter of Europe's population and discouraged travel, each area developed a specialized type.

Gothic ornament never concealed the form of the object. The principal motif was the leaf molding from native flora, although the cusped patterns are much more familiar nowadays. It is customarily divided into three periods, Early, Middle, and Late, the first characterized by naturalistic leaf motifs, the second by more forceful and energetic patterns, though stylized, and this third by entirely stylistic motifs, hollow, stiff, and rigid, giving sharp contrasts of light and shadow (often due to piercing) which resulted in an unsteady, unsettled appearance. We are indebted to the Gothic, however, for the real beginnings of the application of wood in architecture as well as the much commoner use of furniture—hence the beginnings of wide application of woodcarving.

With the end of feudalism in the fourteenth century, the Renaissance spread northward from Italy. It brought cushioned

Fig. 909 and Fig 911 are a matching desk and chair, both in French walnut. Center motif of desk end-panel is repeated in stretcher center and on leg top. Fig. 910 is a chess table in teak, with stylized chess-piece motifs in low relief on stretcher and end panel and monogram-letter motif and Greek-fret details. The board itself is inlaid with rosewood. All by Albert Wood & Five Sons. See also Chap. III. Fig. 912 · Stylized group from the Swiss State Woodcarving School at Brienz.

beds and benches, wall hangings of linen and tapestry, chests raised on legs, shelves moved out from the wall and set on legs (giving rise to the social distinctions mentioned earlier), and a general return to comfort in the home. It began in Italy as early as 1420, with Brunelleschi a moving factor. In France, it couldn't displace the Gothic, so it simply combined with it. More profane than the ecclesiastical Gothic, Renaissance art reached castles, manors, and finally French homes. German Renaissance was in general more bizarre. Introduced by such masters as Dürer, Burkmair, and Holbein, it was not monumental, but was noteworthy for artistic grouping and ornamental treatment of single parts, particularly in building construction. Though first evidences in Germany were castle portals made as early as 1492, the Renaissance did not come into full flower until 1525 or thereabouts.

In Sweden and Norway, the Renaissance came in the sixteenth century, adding Dutch and Flemish motifs to the already well-established wood architecture of those countries. Sweden, during the later Renaissance (1630–1720), was under direct Italian influence. Russia and Poland likewise invited in Italian artists, but found the visitors affected by the Oriental northern art. However, Russian Renaissance woodwork architecture reached an extremely high state of perfection.

In England, the first evidence of the Renaissance was in 1519, when the Italian artist, Pietro Torrigiano, was commissioned to design a monument in Westminster Abbey to Henry II and his wife. For some time Renaissance art was limited to the Abbey, but eventually it spread to castles, country houses, and finally to middle-class homes, "Elizabethan" being a transition style. With James I, English Renaissance entered the more classic stage, free of Flemish influence and preparing the way for the so-called "Later Renaissance," which in reality was Baroque.

The joyousness and frivolity of the Renaissance were reflected in the carved decorations of furniture. Beautiful cabinets, chests, tables, chairs, and couches appeared in profusion, many serving no practical purpose except that craftsmen enjoyed making them and nobles and commoners alike appreciated them. Heavy-duty furniture, except for the highboy, did not exist. This time-honored piece, however, was a by-product of increased travel. Originally designed to accompany its owner on voyages, it eventually sprouted short legs to become the lowboy, then was doubled up to become the chest-on-chest, and finally grew into the highboy.

In England, Queen Elizabeth had fostered home furniture making by forbidding Flemish importations. The English industry resulting from this edict began designing furniture whose style, shape, utility, and general appearance varied with the traditional change in national temperament, as has been detailed earlier. The crude, sturdy, but much-ornamented pieces of the Jacobean era were followed by the austerity of Cromwell. When Charles II ascended the throne in 1660, a gayer note crept into English life and was at once reflected in furniture design. This period of comparative luxury was in turn submerged under the wet blanket of Queen Anne's influence, when the somber, homely, strictly utilitarian pieces in vogue were relieved only by painted tapestry upholstering. With the Georgian period (1714–1830), however, furniture bloomed again into its golden day. Royalty began to encourage craftsmen in making furniture and decorations of all sorts. The cabinetmaker found himself a personage of considerable importance—the Master Carver in Wood to George I, for example, received the then princely salary of 18 pence a day!

At the same time that furniture was undergoing these vicissitudes, architecture was undergoing the degeneration or stylizing of the Renaissance which produced first the Baroque and then the Rococo. Decoration became more important than the decorated object. Led by such artists as Michelangelo and Palladio in Italy, the Baroque (from barroco, a huge irregular, hence grotesque, pearl) style spread throughout Europe. In France it was called the style of Louis XIV, in the Netherlands the style of Rubens (early seventeenth century), and in England the style of Inigo Jones and Sir Christopher Wren (who deserve much credit for freeing English architecture of Gothic influences), but basically it was the same as the Baroque style developed in Germany immediately after the Thirty Years' War (1618–1648).

The Rococo style likewise was so-called only in Germany, al-though it is difficult to differentiate from the style of Louis XV in France and of Chippendale in England, both having the same florid ornament. Rococo lasted only a short time (France disposed of it in 35 years), losing out to the Empire style except in Germany, where it persisted until the end of the eighteenth century.

But let us return to England and the Golden Age of furniture making. Over the horizon in 1738 came Master Craftsman Thomas Chippendale, bringing with him the weighty importance of the first furniture catalog. Lovers of his delicate designs, provided they had $16 or its equivalent in English currency, could thumb through page after page with delight. Chippendale, Hepplewhite, Sheraton (who incidentally invented twin beds and the roll-top desk), and the Adam Brothers followed in rapid succession—the outstanding cabinetmakers and furniture designers of all time.

Meanwhile in France, an ultrafeminine touch was applied to everything. Soft elegance and elaborate curves characterized every piece. Such magnificence, of course, sooner or later must give way. Under Marie Antoinette (1774–1793), a few of the curves were straightened out. Under Napoleon, the feminine influence virtually lost itself completely in a Napoleonic edict that created a mad transition calling for bombastic, militaristic furniture. Here, bursting like a bomb over Europe, was the Empire style.

From this kaleidoscopic Old-Country background, the Ameri-can colonies were hard put to find any stable design trend either in architecture or in furniture. So they chose the best of each style. And because life in the new country was rough, even primitive, house furnishings in particular developed an individuality which we now know as the Colonial style (monumental after 1775). California and Florida meanwhile were developing the Spanish Renaissance style. The greater range of native woods gave greater scope to the cabinetmakers' individuality, and we developed such master craftsmen as John Elliott, James Gillingham, John God-dard, Jonathan Gostelowe, Samuel McIntire (famed principally for decorative carvings and excellent architectural details), Benjamin Randolph, and Thomas Tufft, as well as the much better-known William Savery and Duncan Phyfe. The latter was primarily responsible for development of the American Empire style, taken almost exclusively from the late Sheraton. He had many imitators, but was outstanding for his selection of fine, straight-grained, dark Cuban mahogany, which he carved with a method almost akin to sculpture.

Let us talk a little more about this latter style, Empire, of which the more extravagant elements fortunately survived only about as long as their inspiration, Napoleon. It rose in France with his rise, showing first classical Greek and Roman motifs. After his Egyptian campaign, carved sphinxes and grotesque griffons began to appear everywhere. Then Bonaparte announced his preference for the industrious bee (or B, which, of course, was most fortunately his own initial), and the bee motif became common. With the growth of imperial ambitions, the more regal N (for Napoleon I) and the eagle replaced the earlier motifs. The style constantly increased in ostentation and in bombastic, militaristic feeling as well. Then came Waterloo. American Empire's cycle was similar, but simpler.

Subsequent American "periods" have been: Gothic (during the nineteenth century—still some, but now purely functional), Queen Anne, Italian Renaissance, Spanish Mission (remember the fumed oak and square outlines?) and Neo-Classic, in that order. The last produced the incentive for many of the transplanted (and rather out-of-place) Greek edifices that make up modern official Washington, as well as for other similar buildings throughout the country. A building designed for a hilltop thus finds itself far from the heights and from the sea.

More recently, we have evolved a hopeless confusion of "periods" mixed with the modern (really simple Classic) and the modernistic, but the rebuilding of Williamsburg at least indicates one healthy trend back to a type of architecture more suited to our landscape and to our seeming preference for Colonial interiors. Or perhaps it is time for a new order of architecture and decoration, based upon our knowledge of new building principles and materials, upon steel and its alloys, concrete, and plastics.

TABLE I.—THE AGE OF THE GREAT FURNITURE MAKERS

England		France		Style	
House of Tudor					
Henry VII	1485–1590	Louis XII	1498–1515	Gothic	1100–1500
Henry VIII	1509–1547	Francis I	1515–1547	English Renaissance	
					1519–1603
Edward VI	1547–1553	Henry II	1547–1559	French Renaissance	
					1500–1643
				Elizabethan	1558–1603
Mary	1553–1558	Francis II	1559–1560	Jacobean	1603–1649
Elizabeth	1558–1603	Charles IX	1560–1574	Louis XIV	1643–1715
House of Stuart		Henry III	1574–1589	Cromwellian	1649–1660
James I	1603–1625	Henry IV	1589–1610	Carolean	1660–1688
Charles I	1625–1649	Louis XIII	1610–1643	William and Mary	
					1688–1702
Protectorate		Louis XIV	1643–1715	Queen Anne	1702–1714
		Louis XV	1715–1774		
Cromwell	1649–1660	(Regency)	1715–1723	Georgian	1714–1760
Restoration (Stuart)					
Charles II	1660–1685	Louis XVI	1774–1793	Louis XV	1715–1774
James II	1685–1689	Revolution	1791	Chippendale	1705–1779
House of Orange					
William III and Mary		The Directory	1795–1799	Adam Brothers	1762–1792
	1688–1702				
Anne* (Stuart)		Napoleon	1799–1814	Hepplewhite	17? –1786
	1703–1714				
House of Brunswick		Louis XVIII	1814–1824	Louis XVI	1774–1793
George I	1714–1727	Charles X	1824–1830	Sheraton	1750–1806
George II	1727–1760	Louis Philippe	1830–1848	Empire	1793–1830
George III	1760–1820	Second Republic	1848–1870	American Empire	1795–1830
George IV	1820–1830				
William IV	1830–1837				
Victoria	1837–1901				

Prominent Early American Furniture Makers

John Elliott, Philadelphia	1713–1791	Thomas Tufft, Philadelphia	? –1793
William Savery, Philadelphia	1720–1787	Samuel McIntire, Salem, Mass.	1757–1811
John Goddard, Newport, R.I.	1723–1785	Thomas Nutt, Philadelphia	? – ?
John Townsend, Newport, R.I.	? – ?		
James Gillingham, Philadelphia	1736– ?	Benjamin Randolph, Philadelphia	
			? – ?
Jonathan Gostelowe, Philadelphia		Duncan Phyfe, New York	1768–1854
	1745–1793	John Brinner, New York	? – ?

* Calendar change makes either 1702 or 1703 correct here.

〖 165 〗

TABLE II.—DECORATION
(In England,

Style	Material*			Technique	
	When carved or painted	Inlay or marquetry	Veneer	Inlay or marquetry	Turning
Jacobean (1603–1649)	Oak, pine, pear, or lime when gilded or painted; occasionally chestnut, deal (fir or pine) for simple pieces.	Mahogany, holly, bog oak, silver, precious woods. Inlay only.	Walnut on oak.	Stiff, small, floral panels in inlay. No marquetry until time of William and Mary.	A favorite technique. Pear-shaped balusters, nulled or knobbed spindles and stretchers, balls, bulbs.
Cromwellian (1649–1660)	Oak, walnut, ebony, and as above.	Little.	Little.	Stiff, small panels.	Heavy, severe.
Carolean (1660–1688)	Oak, walnut, cedar, mahogany, cherry (after 1675)—, and as above.	Little.	Added "oystered" or whorled (transverse slices of small boughs).	Intricate, allover flowing patterns of birds, beasts, fish, flowers, leaves, chequering, cross banding, feather edging, herringboning. Late: Oblong panels, often with arced ends, filled with natural flower sprays or acanthus (usually spiky Dutch type).	Spiral (after 1665).
Colonial (1725–1775)	Oak, pine, pear, cherry, apple, ash, elm, all maples, cedar, walnut, hickory.	Contrasting-color woods. Occasionally ivory.	Rare, then usually bird's eye or curly maple, etc., on pine instead of oak, as in England.	Inlay of contrasting woods occasionally. Later pieces copy European designs.	Split balusters, finials, legs, bulb feet.

DURING THE GOLDEN AGE OF CARVING
France, and America)

Technique		Motifs
Applied ornament	Carving	
Rosettes. Geometric moldings in panel form.	Traditionally the favorite. Well-molded relief, with background lowered by gouge and chisel. Carving incised so that highest elements were level with panel surface. Designs flat, with sharply gouged-out ground. Scratch carving usually of simple foliage, with vigorous, sharp outlining.	Guilloche, frequently inclosing rosettes, paterae, or bosses. Diaperwork usually geometric, often interlaced circles. Strapwork, cabochons, and cartouches (latter alternating with decorated and bossed roundels). Lunettes or half circles, often elaborate or flowered. Tulip (frequently used) conventionalized and natural. Conventionalized heart. Rose, acanthus, foliated and floral scrolls, grapevines, laurel leaf, palmated chain, pomegranate, sunflower. Channeling (or fluting), reeding, gadroons, nulling (chiefly beading, cabling, and hollows), lozenge (after 1625). Human figures, masks (until 1660), dragons (in Welsh examples only).
Diamond panels.	Plain, severe, simple.	As above, but restrained in accordance with Puritan ideas.
Geometric mitred moldings appliquéd, often nested. Panels, oval bosses, pendants, oval split balusters.	As in Jacobean, but more elaborate and carving larger areas. Gibbons' elaborate style sets pace for others.	As in Jacobean, plus extravagant use of rose, acanthus, Flemish scroll, etc. Under James II in England, eagle motif added.
Split baluster moldings handles, bosses.	Varied from scratch carving to high relief, depending on skill of carver, etc.	All European, but usually with 25- to 30-year lag. Also simple geometric and chip-carving motifs, usually on maple and pine chests. Later pieces copy European in extreme detail. Considerable variation, depending upon "home country" of carver or settlement.

〖 167 〗

TABLE II.—DECORATION DURING
(In England,

Style	Material*			Technique	
	When carved or painted	Inlay or marquetry	Veneer	Inlay or marquetry	Turning
William and Mary (1688–1702)	Walnut (starting "Age of Walnut"), some olive and ebony for small mirror frames. Oak for country cabinetwork and base for veneer or marquetry, paneling, and wainscoting. Deal for paneling and heavy carving to be gilded. Pine, pear, lime, cedar, etc., for elaborate carving—usually gilded or painted.	Marquetry with all woods. Inlay with sycamore, laburnum, box, holly, apple, walnut, etc.	Walnut, plain or oystered, on oak or softwood.	Marquetry, just introduced, very elaborate. Mainly floral, although some birds, animals, and flowers. Acanthus design gradually supersedes all others, in turn superseded by elaborate "seaweed" design.	Appreciable increase—open-twist or spiral baluster, spindle, bun feet.
Queen Anne (1702–1714) Early Georgian (1714–1760)	Walnut still most important wood, but mahogany becomes common after 1720. Oak in England, but not much in America. Pine, lime, and chestnut when gilded or lacquered. Pear, beech, elm, and yew used by country joiners as above.	Walnut, etc., on flat surfaces, chair backs, etc. Later, mahogany over oak or soft wood was used on chair backs.	Walnut on oak, pine, lime, or chestnut.	Public taste for these techniques gradually dying out. common until 1740, as above.	Inverted cup and bun feet going out. Turned side stretchers and Windsor chair come in—not ornate. Principal motifs vase, ball, ring, and baluster.
Louis XIV (1643–1715) Louis XV (1715–1774)	Oak for carved paneling and large carved cabinets. Walnut, some mahogany (after Regency), ebony by Boulle and his imitators.	Walnut, box, violetwood, laburnum, kingwood, holly, sycamore, and many others. Tortoise shell with metal (Boulle). Brass and white metal.	Walnut, box, violetwood, laburnum, kingwood, holly, sycamore, and many others. Tortoise shell.	Return to intricate inlay in wide variety of woods. Marquetry common, usually pictorial. Veneering much used.	Overshadowed by carving and gilding, inlay and marquetry.

THE GOLDEN AGE OF CARVING.—(Continued)
France, and America)

Technique		Motifs
Applied ornament	Carving	
Used sparingly.	Elaborate, including very high-relief and in-the-round elements. Declined in favor with style trend to inlay.	Flemish and Spanish scrolls, Dutch scallop or cockle shell, some acanthus, pendant husks, in-the-round flowers, terminal figures, heads, goats' feet, laurel swags.
Little.	Elaborating, refining, and embellishing existing forms. Flowers, cyma-curve shapes. Curved bedsteads fashionable again after 1714 (slight carving of knees, earpieces, and feet before). Mirror frames, console, and sideboard tables heavily carved. Tables, chairs, and some cabinets elaborately carved after 1714. Bold, vigorous, and strongly religious until 1735.	Concave and convex shells were favorites, usually combined with pendant husks, of fuchsia flowers and honeysuckle. Bold claw-and-ball feet. Eagle-head terminals on chair arms. Also animal and bird motifs on mirror frames, consoles, sideboards, tables. Acanthus, floriated scrolls. Four chair-leg styles: Decorated Queen Anne (1714–1725), Lion (1720–1735), Satyr-Masque (1730–1740), Cabochon-and-Leaf (1735–rise of Chippendale). Lion style brought lions' heads and feet; Satyr-Masque (from Germany) supplanted cockles and eagle motifs with satyr masks and other grotesques. For details, see Chap. IX.
Tortoise shell, veneer overlays. Appliquéd carved units.	In-the-round and relief in elaborate and detailed forms.	Rococo rocks and shells, wisps of nondescript foliage scrolled all over in all shapes. Also wreaths, cupids, finialed busts, satyrs, doves, fountains. Acanthus, fruits and flowers, pendant husks and ribbons, trophies, musical-instrument shapes, and similar extravagant ornament. Diaperwork all over plane surfaces of panels during time of Louis XIV.

TABLE II.—DECORATION DURING

(In England,

Style	Material*			Technique	
	When carved or painted	Inlay or marquetry	Veneer	Inlay or marquetry	Turning
Chippendale (1705–1779)	Mahogany (principally San Domingan and Cuban). Pine for mirror frames and gilt pieces. Rosewood, amboyna, and walnut.	Minor use.	Some on "French-type" Furniture.	Rare.	To some extent, but purely mechanical.
Adam Brothers (1762–1792)	Mahogany most common. Much satinwood (called "Age of Satinwood"), natural or stained sycamore, amboyna, tulip, pine and lime if gilded.	Satinwood, holly, ebony, and other woods.	With grain arrangements in symmetrical patterns, often with painting.	Delicate decoration of flat surfaces. Wedgwood plaques. Elaborate paintings.	Only sparingly, on table, chair, and sofa legs.
Hepplewhite (17?–1786)	Mahogany in cabinets and chairs or other pieces to be carved. Satin if to be decorated by painting. Beech for chairs, tables, settees, and the like to be painted and parcel gilt. Pine, lime, sycamore if carved and gilt.	Amboyna for fine panel work. Thuya, kingwood, sycamore, harewood, tulip, holly, ebony, and rosewood for inlay.	Mahogany, amboyna, and other mellow-colored woods.	Inlay on table tops, console cabinets, chairs, sideboards, and bookcases. Marquetry usually in "French-type" work.	Almost always carved or painted afterward.
Louis XVI (1774–1793)	All woods, but principally mahogany. Cheaper woods if gilded or painted.	As in Louis XIV and XV.	As in Louis XIV and XV.	Tied in with carving.	Spiral, on chair and table legs.

THE GOLDEN AGE OF CARVING.—(Continued)
France, and America)

Technique		Motifs
Applied ornament	Carving	
Occasional carved units.	Chief decorative process. Very delicate, sometimes ornate. Much pierced fretwork on table edges, cabinet tops. Table and chair-leg carving usually on solid background.	Four styles: 1. English: Lions' heads on seat rails and table underframes, knees of chairs, and settee legs. Human and grotesque masks on elaborate pieces, wave pattern (called *evolute*) on early pieces, claw-and-ball feet, acanthus, egg-and-dart moldings on early pieces. 2. French: Shells and other Rococo motifs. 3. Chinese: Pagoda and other adapted motifs, including Chinese fret. 4. Gothic: Pointed circles, quatrefoils, trefoils, cusped motifs.
Composition for fine details. Small paintings held with moldings.	On mahogany, and on pine and lime objects to be gilded. The Adelphi were primarily designers—many carvers, including Hepplewhite and Sheraton, executed their designs.	Three styles: 1. Architectural: Floral and drapery swags, beading, guilloche, interlacings, paterae (both circular and oval), masques, Ionic capitals, anthemion or classic honeysuckle, many Pompeian details, spandrel fans, egg-and-dart moldings, riband designs. 2. Floral: Pendant husks, water-plant leaves, endives, roses, palmette, pineapple, acanthus, fuchsia drops, all conventionalized. 3. Animal: Lions' and rams' heads, goats' heads and feet, griffins, birds, human figures.
Some carved elements.	Great elaboration and delicacy of design in mahogany chairs, tables, and console cabinets.	Same as Adam. Floral swags, acanthus, pendant husks, round and oval paterae, water leaf, architectural details, rams' heads, fluting, reeding, pearling, spandrel fans, rosettes, ribbons, three feathers (Prince of Wales), ears of wheat and rye, lyre. Preferred concave curves, oval or round chair backs.
Broken panels, with paterae at breaks.	High and low relief, very elaborate and detailed.	Floral wreaths and ribbons, baskets of flowers, acanthus, celery, pastoral and musical emblems, laurel, acorns and oak leaves, guilloche, rosettes, chequering and diaper patterns, thistles, arabesques, myrtle, lyre, pendant husks, vases, urns, and other classical details. Also round medallions, paterae, ovals, heads, busts, and human figures. Fluting, reeding, pearling, and beading.

TABLE II.—DECORATION DURING
(In England,

Style	Material*			Technique	
	When carved or painted	Inlay or marquetry	Veneer	Inlay or marquetry	Turning
Sheraton (1750–1806)	Mahogany (dark) for chairs, cabinets, and other pieces to be carved. Satinwood if to be decorated by painting. Beech for chairs to be painted or japanned. Some sycamore and harewood. Rosewood for moldings.	Tulip, holly, and ebony as inlays and banding. Rosewood and kingwood for banding.	Light mahogany, amboyna, satinwood, thuya, kingwood, often over pine.	Preferred over painting.	Spirals, particularly tapered. Also plain.
Empire (1793–1830)	Mahogany, both solid and in veneer. Ebony and rosewood for special pieces. Cheaper woods if painted or gilded.	Extensively used on door panels and drawer fronts.	Mahogany over chestnut or other cheaper woods.	Little used. Some inlay of metals, some marquetry.	Legs of furniture, columns, pilasters of sideboard, bureau, and secretary fronts.
American Empire (1795–1830)	Mahogany, some walnut and rosewood, occasionally curly maple or other native woods. Cheaper woods if gilded.	As above.	Mahogany over pine.	Some inlay with brass. Occasional marquetry.	As above.

* See *Whittling and Woodcarving*, Chap. I, for details on wood characteristics, colors, etc.
Note: Dates given under Chippendale, Hepplewhite, and Sheraton are birth and death dates, rather than style limits.

THE GOLDEN AGE OF CARVING.—(*Continued*)
France, and America)

Technique		Motifs
Applied ornament	Carving	
Some carved elements.	Mainly low reliefs, reeding, fluting, openwork.	Swags, spandrel fans, floral wreaths, square, oval and round paterae, water leaf, oval, slender urn, conch shell, star, lyre (taken from Hepplewhite), Roman diamond lattice, fluting, and reeding. Preferred convex surface curves, square chair backs. Thomas Shearer, a little-known carver of the same period, is now credited with development of many so-called Sheraton designs.
Chief feature usually elaborate brass. Some small painted landscapes.	Heavy, deep-cut, bold, detail carefully worked out.	Classic: lions' and bears' claw feet, wings, cornucopias, classic honeysuckle (anthemion), acanthus, pineapple, plain and carved pillars. Chimerical beasts such as wyverns, bewreathed "N," Empire star, bees, Egyptian winged motif, fasces, shields, swords, and other warlike trophies.
Elaborate brass and occasional small paintings.	As above.	Bears' and lions' claws, wings, sphinx heads, griffins, acanthus, pineapple, melon, cornucopia with various fruits and flowers, spirals, reeding, classic honeysuckle.

American styles usually followed European by 25 to 30 years, were more crude, and used a wider variety of woods.

TABLE III.—TYPICAL MOTIFS OF VARIOUS ARCHITECTURAL STYLES

Period	Typical Motifs, as Shown in Figures Numbered:
Primitive 4000–100 B.C.	79–128, 132, 136–139, 141–144, 334, 335, 578–586, 589, 590, 593. (W & W)* 278.
(still common in remote areas)	
Egyptian 4000–525 B.C.	496, 625, 626. (W & W) 210, 278.
Coptic 31 B.C.–A.D. 1000.	483. (W & W) 367.
Chaldean:	
Sumerian 4000–2000 B.C.	
Babylonian-Assyrian 2000–500 B.C.	461, 497.
Median-Persian:	
Median 1500–550 B.C.	
Persian 550 B.C.	612, 621, 714, 715, 735.
Phoenician-Hebraic 2000–586 B.C.	
Aegean 3000–1100 B.C.	
Greek 3000–146 B.C.	54, 147, 183–219, 233, 234, 235, 248, 250–258, 438–447, 454–460, 469, 471, 473, 476, 477, 498, 500, 501, 559, 569–571, 575–577, 639, 727, 728, 730, 752, 791, 803, 863. (W. & W) 278.
Etruscan 1000–400 B.C.	
Roman 146 B.C.–A.D. 1150	450, 452, 454, 457, 464, 490, 534, 538, 560, 562–566, 572, 573, 599, 633, 792, 793, 804, 805, 852, 858, 859, 861, 862, 891. (W & W) 393.
Romanesque A.D. 476–1200	154–156, 182, 384, 486, 487, 499, 502, 509, 540, 556, 557, 741, 742, 744, 794, 796, 797, 798, 799, 807, 811, 871, 879, 882.
Pompeian 100 B.C.–A.D. 6	743.
Chinese 3000 B.C.	8, 300, 309–312, 324, 508, 535, 594, 597, 640, 665–667, 783, 784. (W & W) 98, 101, 102, 122, 182, 205, 206, 207, 209, 302, 313, 419.
Japanese 960 B.C.	308, 516, 668–707. (W & W) 180, 181, 183, 292, 430.
Indian 1700 B.C.	2, 302, 478, 624. (W & W) 204, 208, 212.
Mogul 1250–1818	(W & W) 366.
Celtic (combining with Roman) 2500 B.C. (?)–A.D. 1150	736, 737.
Byzantine A.D. 330–1453	492, 733, 795, 806.
Russian Byzantine 1000–1480	

* (W & W) indicates *Whittling and Woodcarving* illustrations.

NOTE: Limiting dates on architectural styles are in most cases only approximate, marking merely an outstanding event that pointed the new trend. Back-country areas normally continue a style for a much longer time, and variation in date of style change from country to country may be very wide. Many pieces, likewise, are neither all one style nor all another, being "transition pieces" just as Elizabethan was a transition style. These have been classified, within my abilities, as of the style showing predominance. Modern pieces of a given older style have been listed with that style. Substyles, evolved styles, details by country, and furniture styles within an architectural style period are indented.

TABLE IV.—SURFACE FINISHES
Jacobean (1603–1649) and Cromwellian (1649–1660)

Type.—Mostly unfinished, but some coated with oil or wax. Occasionally a "varnish" of gum copal dissolved in boiling oil. Two or three colors, particularly on armorial bearings, arabesques. Black over-all painting on cheaper woods, touched up with gilt.

Process.—Where oil-coated, first coat was nut or poppy oil to "feed" wood. "Sweat" (unabsorbed oil) wiped off, then piece was coated with beeswax absorbed in enough turpentine to form a thick paste. Rubbed and polished with woolen rag.

Carolean (1660–1688)

Type.—As in Jacobean, with japanning added after 1675. Much more paint and gilding.

Process.—As in Jacobean.

Colonial American (to 1725)

Type.—As in Jacobean, but some spindles painted black, cupboard moldings red-leaded. "Dutch-influence" pieces have heavily bunched flower and fruit paintings.

Process.—As in Jacobean.

William and Mary (1688–1702)

Type.—Oil finish on plain pieces. Marquetry shellacked. Many painted pieces, with gold Oriental decoration over black, blue, red, or green ground. Conventional painted borders or diapers. Gilt-touched painting on legs and stretchers of chairs, settees, stools Often gilding over entire surface.

Process.—Oil finish as in Jacobean, particularly on plain walnut. Marquetry was finished with white gum shellac dissolved in alcohol, brushed on in thin coats without previous oil coating. Final polish with a mixture of beeswax and turpentine, thus liable to worm attack (because of shellac). Walnut furniture unfinished, or finished only with wax, is nearest free of worm danger. Shellac and varnish are bad.

Queen Anne (1702–1714) and Early Georgian (1714–1760)

Type.—Sometimes oil and wax, sometimes white paint with parcel gilt, particularly on large pieces of "architectural" furniture. Gilding on elaborately carved wood, and to embellish turning or carving on mahogany or walnut. Lacquer in black, red, green, blue, and yellow in pictorial designs like those seen now on platters and plates.

Process.—On oak, usually traditional oil and wax finish, occasionally gum shellac in alcohol. Walnut was sometimes oiled and waxed, but usually shellacked as in preceding period. Mahogany likewise.

Louis XIV (1643–1715) and Louis XV (1715–1774)

Type.—Complete and parcel gilding much used, often over monotint grounds on softwood. Lacquering common. Boulle work (metal inlay in tortoise shell appliquéd to surface of wood) and counter-Boulle (tortoise inlay in metal) finished with lacquer.

Process.—Usually none because of gilt and painted finish.

Chippendale (1705–1779)

Type.—Gilding on mirror frames only. Some lacquering in Chinese-style pieces.

Process.—Same as Queen Anne at first; later same as Sheraton.

Adam Brothers (1762–1790)

Type.—Most effective use of painting. Delicate floral wreaths, ribbons and minute Pompeian motifs, small panels, plaques and cartoons painted by noted artists. Satinwood only partly painted. Greens, whites, other colors, form base for gilding over pine and lime.

Process.—Unchanged.

[[177]]

HEPPLEWHITE (17?–1786)

Type.—Painting preferred over inlay and done by first-class painters. Gilding on painted pieces. Japanned grounds for painting and lacquering as in previous styles.

Process.—As in Queen Anne and Sheraton.

LOUIS XVI (1774–1793)

Type.—Painting and lacquer, or French polish.

Process.—French polish (see *Whittling and Woodcarving*, Chap. XXV), with shellac.

SHERATON (1750–1806)

Type.—First-class lacquering. Other finishes, oil and wax, by processes below.

Process.—1. Beeswax dissolved in oil, as in Jacobean. Wax rubbed with cork to spread and work in. Final polish—brick dust sifted through stocking onto surface, then rubbed with cloth until dust removed wax clemmings. 2. Also used mixture of turpentine and beeswax, plus a little red oil to help wood color. Rubbed off with cloth. 3. On plain cabinetwork, used linseed oil (or with a little alkanet for color). Oil allowed to stand two days on softwood, week on hardwood. Plenty of brick dust sifted on through stocking, then rubbed with soft cloth. Mixture forms a polishing putty. Dust not added during polishing. When hard rubbing warms wood, it will polish. Surplus removed with bran of wheat flour. 4. Chair polish—hard wax on polishing brush. When grain was well impregnated, wax rubbed off with cloth—*no* dust or bran.

EMPIRE (1793–1830)

Type.—Painting and gilding on pretentious chairs, sofas, settees. Sometimes gilt picked out with black over colors.

Process.—French polish over heavy varnish. Older methods also commonly used. Red staining common also. Fuming oak done by hanging in stable. Can be done now by putting piece in tight box containing saucer of ammonia. Fumes react with wood acid and darken wood.

AMERICAN EMPIRE (1793–1830)

Type.—French polish, stain and varnish, or painted (often in black).

Process.—(As above for finishing. Worth recording probably is this old American wax polish: Dress wood with raw linseed oil. Then melt a lump of beeswax in turpentine over a slow fire—using enough beeswax to give a creamy mixture when cool. Suspend cheesecloth bag containing alkanet root in hot mixture to give desired color. Put on and polish with soft flannel, using only a little of the mixture at a time.

MODERN

For shellac and varnish finishes, see any furniture handbook. For oil or wax finishes, sand with progressively finer papers to extreme smoothness. Fill grain in porous woods, such as pin oak, to avoid later stickiness. Then sponge with a damp rag or sponge to lift grain; sand, responge, and resand. This surface is rubbed with a handful of shavings, then with the palm of the hand. Mix thin boiled linseed oil with turpentine and benzol to make a mixture which will penetrate and dry on your particular wood, testing with a spare piece. Then put the surface to be finished in a hot room, heat the oil mixture as hot as you can stand it, and brush or wipe on a thin coat. Rub it in with a soft cloth, then with the hands —the heat of rubbing helps penetration. Apply up to a dozen coats of the mixture at 1-day intervals, rubbing in each hard and long. This finish preserves the natural beauty of the wood, improves with age, is impervious to scratches and ordinary stains, and can be waxed. See also Chap. XXV, *Whittling and Woodcarving*.

CHAPTER XII

FIGURES · *Proportions, Variations*

BACK in the golden age of Greece and Rome, Pliny the Elder
advanced this rule of thumb[1]: "It has been observed that the
height of a man from the crown of the head to the sole of the foot
is equal to the distance between the tips of the middle fingers of
the two hands when extended in a straight line." (This obviously
leads to our present-day "shopper's yard"—from pit of throat to
tip of extended middle finger—giving a figure height of 2 yds., or
6 ft.) Down through the ages have come dozens of similar rules
of basic proportion, aiding us in our efforts to depict the "faultless
body" that goes with Homer's "blameless mind."[2]

Such factors as age, sex, race, and physical structure of the individual cause wide variations of proportion. Let us, as an example
of racial variation, compare the Greek standard of the "form
divine,"[3] the Venus de Milo, with a modern American, "Miss
Perfection," so named by McClelland Barclay, noted illustrator,
and a jury of other artists (see also Table V). Dorothy Belle Dugan,
Los Angeles socialite and newcomer to motion pictures, is the
modern standard. Her measurements are: height 5 ft. 6½ in.,
neck 12½ in., bust 34 in., waist 26 in., hips 34 in., thigh 20 in.,
calf 13 in., ankle 7½ in., upper arm 10 in., forearm 9 in., and wrist
6 in. If Venus' measurements are reduced in proportion (the
original was a heroic figure 80½ in. tall[4]), they are: neck 15.3 in.,
bust 42.5 in., waist 32.2 in., hips 42.1 in., upper arm 13.6 in.,
extremely generous proportions indeed, as judged by our modern
standards of perfection!

[1] *Natural History*, Book VII, Section 77.

[2] "A faultless body and a blameless mind"—Book III, Line 138, *The Odyssey of Homer*,
Pope's translation.

[3] *Ibid.*, Book X, Line 278.

[4] Complete measurements in *Whittling and Woodcarving*, pages 235–236.

〖 179 〗

Furthermore, Venus did not escape the sad fate allotted to most idols—or ideals—her feet are too large. Instead of being the ideal—the same length as her head, they're over 10 per cent longer. All in all, Venus hardly met the standards of our fathers' day either, for with proportions reduced to the legendary 5 ft. 2 in., her bust measurement is 39 in., instead of the "perfect 36."

To win admiration, the male body must imply the ability to accomplish superior muscular feats, while still retaining harmonious and graceful curves. Dr. Sargent of Harvard recently obtained average measurements from the 50 strongest men selected from 400 athletes who had excelled in all forms of sport. The resulting figure is 5 ft. 9 in. tall and weighs just under 159 lb. It is much more light and graceful than would be expected, with torso evenly proportioned to legs, strong wide shoulders, and broad chest. Girth of neck, knee, and calf are the same, with that of the upper arm $1\frac{1}{2}$ in. less. The 40-in. expanded chest is one-third greater in circumference than the 30-in. waist. Hip girth is almost the same as that of the unexpanded chest, while waist breadth is only slightly greater than foot length. The thigh is $\frac{1}{2}$ in. smaller in circumference than the head.

Dr. Sargent's averages very closely parallel those for men in the table developed by PHYSICAL CULTURE magazine, as given in Table V. The tabulated data are for mature persons, thus indicate slightly heavier figures and greater weights than those of the athlete. Inserted in the table are the average measurements of 1,000,000 recruits, made by the Medical Department of the United States Army in 1917–1918, giving a fair picture of the average American male—the measurements considerably under those considered ideal in most respects! Also included in the figures for women are the proportions of "Miss Perfection 1939" and of the Venus de Milo in comparative scale.

What are ideal proportions for any carved figure? The artist and the sculptor both measure them in "heads," the distance from the top of the skull to the tip of the chin, thus overcoming the primary variable of height. Of course, this measurement is still only an approximate one; no two of us have identical measurements or proportions. In fact, even the fabled bisymmetrical human body shows exterior variations—as well as interior ones—from side to side.

Many of the "head" proportions have already been given in *Whittling and Woodcarving* (Chaps. XIV and XXI), but will be repeated here for convenience. As indicated in Figs. 918 to 921, the average human being is 7½ heads tall and 2 heads wide at his widest. Individuals vary from 7 to 8 heads high; most caricatures are drawn as 6-head figures; so-called "stump" figures (those with enlarged heads used in many caricatures) are 3-head figures; and the common "fashion" figure is 9 or 10 heads tall. Even the statu-ettes of Figs. 931 to 934, from R.M.S. "Queen Mary," are 8-head figures, although they look quite normal.

The common 7½-head male figure has its greatest width just below the shoulders (between points 3 and 4, Fig. 918) where it is just over 2 heads wide. The hips are 1½ heads wide, the nip-ples 1 head apart, and the arms (from armpit) 3 heads long, from finger tips to elbow being 2 heads. See also Fig. 939, an excellent male figure.

Although, in Figs. 920 and 921, I have drawn the female figure the same height as the male for convenience, the average female is somewhat shorter, with narrower shoulders and a broader, shallower pelvis, hence wider hips. Female collarbones are shorter and straighter, too, which with the narrower shoulders, combines to make the neck longer and more graceful but to create more sloping shoulders. Thus the female neck customarily has a greater forward angle than the male. The female figure likewise has a shorter upper arm, hence a higher elbow and a shorter total arm length. The female torso is proportionally as long as the male, but the breastbone is shorter (making the abdomen deeper), and the legs are shorter. Leg length in females varies so widely also, that it is difficult to guess the over-all height of a woman seated or even kneeling. In Fig. 940 is a typical female figure, in Fig. 945 a kneeling one.

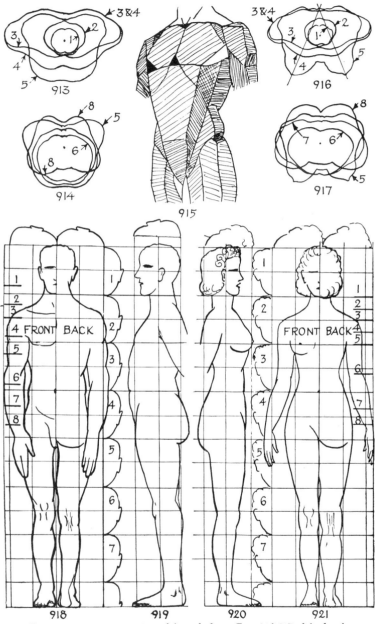

FIGS. 913–914 *are cross sections of the male figure;* FIGS. 916–917 *of the female.*

TABLE V.—AVERAGE IDEAL MEASUREMENTS FOR ADULTS

Height		Weight	Neck	Upper arm	Fore-arm	Chest	Waist	Hips	Thigh	Calf
Ft.	In.	Lb.	In.	In.	In.	In.	In.	In.	In.	In.
Men										
5	3	143	15.4	13.2	11.9	41.2	31.0	38.0	22.4	14.3
5	4	147	15.5	13.3	12.0	41.5	31.2	38.3	22.5	14.4
5	5	151	15.6	13.4	12.1	41.7	31.4	38.5	22.6	14.6
5	6	155	15.7	13.5	12.2	41.9	31.6	38.8	22.8	14.7
5	7	159	15.8	13.6	12.3	42.2	31.8	39.1	22.9	14.9
a5	7½	141.5	14.2	*	*	33.2	30.7	*	20.7	13.4
5	8	163	15.9	13.7	12.5	42.4	32.0	39.3	23.0	15.0
5	9	167	16.0	13.8	12.6	42.6	32.2	39.6	23.1	15.1
5	10	170	16.1	13.9	12.8	42.9	32.4	39.9	23.2	15.2
5	11	174	16.2	14.0	12.9	43.1	32.6	40.1	23.4	15.4
6	0	178	16.3	14.1	13.0	43.4	32.8	40.3	23.5	15.5
6	1	182	16.4	14.2	13.1	43.6	33.0	40.6	23.6	15.6
Women										
4	11	110	12.1	10.3	8.9	32.0	24.6	35.6	21.6	13.1
5	0	114	12.2	10.4	9.0	32.2	24.8	35.8	21.7	13.2
5	1	118	12.3	10.5	9.1	32.4	25.0	36.0	21.8	13.3
5	2	122	12.4	10.6	9.2	32.6	25.2	36.3	21.9	13.4
5	3	126	12.5	10.7	9.3	32.8	25.4	36.5	22.0	13.5
5	4	130	12.6	10.8	9.4	33.0	25.6	36.8	22.1	13.6
5	5	134	12.7	10.9	9.5	33.2	25.8	37.0	22.2	13.8
5	6	139	12.8	11.0	9.6	33.4	26.0	37.3	22.4	13.9
b5	6½	*	12.5	10.0	9.0	34.0	26.0	34.0	20.0	13.0
c5	6½	*	15.3	13.6	*	42.5	32.2	42.1	*	*
5	7	143	12.9	11.1	9.7	33.6	26.2	37.5	22.5	14.0
5	8	147	13.0	11.2	9.8	33.8	26.4	37.8	22.6	14.1
5	9	152	13.1	11.3	9.9	34.1	26.6	38.1	22.8	14.2

NOTE. All measurements in the table are from *Physical Culture* unless otherwise specified.

* Measurement not taken.

a Average figures for 1,000,000 U. S. Army recruits in 1917–1918.

b Measurements of "Miss Perfection 1939."

c Measurements of Venus de Milo reduced in proportion to height of "Miss Perfection 1939."

Study of Figs. 918 and 921 (drawn half front and half rear views) will soon acquaint you with the basic proportions. Note that the 7½ heads are divided thus: 1 head for the head, 2¾ heads

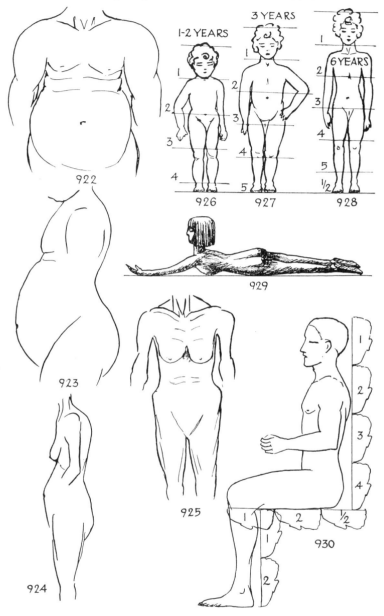

FIGS. 922–930 · FIGURE VARIATIONS

922

923

924

1-2 YEARS

926

3 YEARS

927

6 YEARS

928

929

925

930

for the neck and trunk, and 3¾ heads for the legs and feet. The foot is 1 head long by ½ head wide, the male neck ½ head long. The face is three-quarters the head height, and about the same length as the hand. From the ground to the crotch is roughly half the height, as is the distance from the pit of the throat to the tip of the outstretched middle finger. The upper and lower legs are the same length. The distances from the ground to the top of the kneecap, the kneecap to the point of the iliac (farthest forward point of the thigh bone), and from the pit of the throat to the lower line of the rectus abdominus (front abdominal muscle) are all equal.

Many authorities divide the body into three parts thus: neck to hips, hips to knee, knee to sole. They also figure that the distance from the top of the head to the pit of the throat goes into the height five and one-half times and that the distance from the sole to just below the knee is a quarter of the height. It is generally agreed that in the male figure, the elbow meets the top of the hipbone and the finger tips are normally halfway between crotch and knee.

While at birth, the center of the figure is above the navel, at two years of age the center is at the navel, and at three it has dropped to the top of the hipbone. As the child grows older, the figure center drops farther, depending on leg length. In the average grown male it is level with the pubic bone (just above the crotch); with the average female, above the pubic bone (because of her shorter leg length). The average child of three is about half adult height, at ten about three-quarters adult height. In "head" proportions, a child during its first year is about 4 heads tall. Between its first and fourth year, its fourth and ninth, and its ninth and fifteenth the child gains a head in height for each age period. This growth is indicated in Figs. 926 to 928. Also see Fig. 938, a typical child of about three (5 heads tall).

Proportions of the figure vary likewise from manhood to old age because of compression of the cartilage between the joints and the increasing tendency to stoop. Bone structure and carriage also make surprising differences. In the sketches of Figs. 918

FIGS. 931–934 · *Four carved-wood statuettes by Norman Forrest from the tourist Main Staircase, R.M.S. "Queen Mary." The simplicity of the draping and figure lines are particularly noteworthy. Courtesy Cunard White Star Lines.*

and 919, I have drawn a fairly muscular male figure; in Figs. 920 and 921, a decidedly slender and youthful female one. Male figures will vary widely from this one in appearance, depending partially upon muscular development; female figures become broader and thicker through the abdomen and hips as a result of childbearing. To show normal posture, I have sketched in Figs. 913 and 914 a series of cross sections of the male figure, identifying each on the basic sketch of Fig. 918. Note how the forward protrusion of the chest is balanced by the rearward protrusion of the buttocks. Similar balancing of the breast and buttock protrusions can be seen in the female cross sections (Figs. 916 and 917). In Fig. 916, note also how the breasts are set at an angle with the front of the torso because of the curvature of the breastbone.

Primary planes of the torso are sketched in Fig. 915, using the male figure as an example. The great plane of the chest extends from the line of the shoulders down to a line drawn across the nipples, forming a rough trapezoid almost at right angles to the sides of the body. From this plane there extends downward the triangular plane of the abdomen, with its base at the nipples, sloping inward and narrowing as it passes downward toward the crotch. This meets a plane rising from the crotch to the navel.

In back, the shoulders form the upper line of a triangular plane extending downward to the small of the waist, where it meets a wider trapezoidal plane rising from the buttocks. While the curve of the front planes is convex, that of the back ones is concave. The back planes in addition are centrally divided by the groove marking the backbone.

The female figure has somewhat similar plane structure, except that the plane of the chest slopes outward more to the nipples, and meets the planes of the side in a more gentle curve. The frontal planes are divided by the groove of the breastbone. The upper back plane likewise slopes outward more to the lower line of the shoulders, then inward to the waist, giving the greater curvature of the backbone and the greater stoop to the shoulders mentioned previously. While the male neck is short and thick, and rises firmly from the square shoulders, the female is longer, more

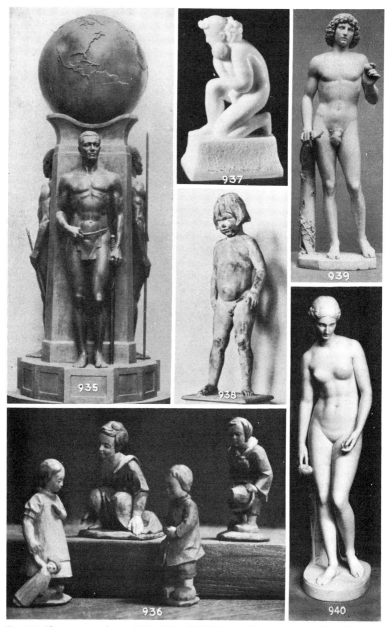

Fig. 935 · *Theme group in bronze, Hall of Man, Field Museum, Chicago, showing white, yellow, and black men. Courtesy Field Museum of Natural History.* Fig. 936 · *Four children in wood from the Lang crèche at Childrens' Library, Westbury, N.Y. See Fig. 995. Courtesy Jacqueline Overton.* Fig. 937 · *"Mother and Child," in soap. Courtesy National Soap Sculpture Committee.* Fig. 938. *"The Man Cub."* Fig. 939 · *"Adam."* Fig. 940 · *"Clytie." Figs. 938–940 courtesy Metropolitan Museum of Art.*

slender and graceful, and rises at a greater forward angle. The lines of junction of the neck with the body and the head are at an angle both with the horizontal and with the axis of the neck column. Further, and most important, the neck is tapered, as indicated in Figs. 918 and 921, so that it appears to grow like a tree from the shoulders, rather than resembling a roughly circular column simply set on top of the torso. The male neck usually tapers more decidedly because of the heavier neck muscles, and also shows a protrusion at the top, the Adam's apple.

The female figure also commonly has considerably greater slope to the plane of the lower back than does the male, caused by the thicker thighs and more rounded abdomen, which create a larger diameter at the buttocks and wider hips.

Variations in the figure due to age and improper diet are unfortunately only too common. Simply to indicate the effect of such variations, I have sketched front and side views of an older overweight male torso and of an undernourished female one. Although these shapes are obviously a long, long way from that of the "form divine," they must be understood to insure correct proportioning of a carved figure simulating an older person.

Another problem commonly faced is that of depicting a seated figure. The head proportions for such a male figure are shown in Fig. 930. The female torso, as stated previously, is in about the same proportion, but the legs and upper arms are shorter.

This lengthy discussion is a necessary prelude to any treatment of figure carving, in fact should even be supplemented by careful study of a good text on art anatomy. Careful study of art anatomy is particularly advisable if you do as many carvers do— model the figure first in clay or wax. Modeling is especially important to the woodcarver, who cannot replace a mistakenly cut section, and who must work "from the outside in," reaching the folds of the clothing before he reaches the planes of the figure itself.

The four statuettes of Figs. 931 to 934, executed in lime wood by Norman Forrest for the Tourist Main Staircase on R.M.S. "Queen Mary," are unusually good examples of simplified figure carving, with the draping so skillfully done that it does not mask

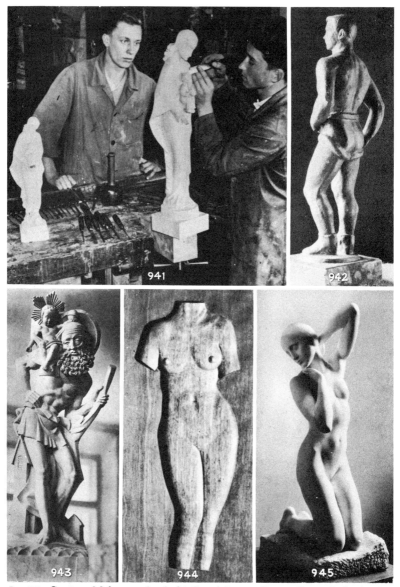

Fig. 941 · Carving a Madonna at the school in Zweisel, Bavaria. Courtesy German Railroads Information Office. Fig. 942 · A carved figure from the State Woodcarving School, Brienz, Switzerland. Fig. 943 · St. Christopher, carved at the State Carving School, Oberammergau, Germany. Courtesy German Railroads Information Office. Fig. 944 · Low-relief torso, by Gardner Wood. Fig. 945 · "Fragilina," in marble. Courtesy Metropolitan Museum of Art.

the major lines of the figures—in fact, is more nearly a veiling instead of a draping. Note the conventionalized hair of Figs. 932 to 934, and the conventionalized floral decorative motifs of Figs. 933 and 934.

One of our best-known present-day sculptors is Malvina Hoffman, who sculptured all the figures in the Field Museum's (Chicago) far-famed Hall of Man. Her theme group, symbolizing the unity of mankind, is pictured in Fig. 935. It depicts racial differences excellently. Shown are a white, a yellow, and a black man, symbolizing the three divisions of mankind.

As of possible further assistance, I have also included three famous figures, one male, one female, and one child. Figure 939 is Tullio Lombardo's "Adam," (sixteenth century); Fig. 940, William Henry Rinehart's nineteenth-century American "Clytie"; Fig. 945, Attilio Piccirilli's twentieth-century American "Fragilina"; and Fig. 938, Alexander Stirling Calder's twentieth-century "Man Cub." The "Mother and Child" of Fig. 937 is also an interesting composition, particularly because it was executed in soap. Carved by Duane B. Bryers of Virginia, Minn., it won third prize in the advanced amateur class of the Thirteenth Annual Soap Sculpture Competition. Further child figures, unusual for their expression, posing, and excellent treatment of clothing, are pictured in Fig. 936. Executed by Georg Lang of Oberammergau, Germany, for incorporation in the crèche for the Children's Library, Westbury, N. Y., they are carved in lime wood and slightly colored with flat, dull oil tones.

In contrast with American and English woodcarving schools, which commonly favor decorative panels, the German and Swiss schools favor figure carving. Figure 941 shows a scene in the German school at Zweisel, Bavaria, with one student carving a Madonna as another watches. The man of Fig. 942 was executed at the Swiss State Woodcarving School at Brienz, while the more classical St. Christopher of Fig. 943 was carved at the German State School at Oberammergau. The low-relief torso of Fig. 944 was carved in bleached mahogany by Gardner Wood, and is an excellent example of decorative treatment with simple structure.

FIG. 946 · "Singing Gondolier," by Fred Press of Boston, first-prize winner, Senior Class, 14th Annual Soap Sculpture Competition. (See also Fig. 993.) FIG. 947 · Aztec warrior, a mahogany copy by Walter F. Koch of a bust by Allan Clark. (See also Fig. 9. Fig. 947 is Mr. Koch's first carving.) FIGS. 948–956 · Winners of honorable mention awards, Advanced Amateur Class, 14th Annual Soap Sculpture Competition. Note heads in particular.

CHAPTER XIII

HEADS AND FACES · *Likenesses*

"THE human features and countenance, although composed of but some ten parts or little more, are so fashioned that among so many thousands of men there are no two in existence who cannot be distinguished one from another." So spake Pliny the Elder in his *Natural History* (Book VII, Section 8), marveling at the wonders of infinite variation in the countenance, as has many another man before him and since.

Pliny, if anything, was before his time, for only a few centuries before him the Greeks had been unable to produce any expression on the faces of their figures except the archaic (or stereotyped) smile. Smile it was, too, although it was supposed to denote grief!

In the centuries since Pliny's day, we have studied the human countenance persistently, until we have a series of rules of proportion for it, just as we have for the figure. But in the process we have found further variations—and where we couldn't find them, we've created them! To the normal differences which Pliny found, we have added such differences as are caused by race, family, carving technique (particularly important in woodcarving), and even accident or design. Even children have learned to sketch the thick lips of the Negro, the slanting eyes of the Oriental, the high-bridged nose of the Semite, and the other basic racial distinctions. In America particularly, the combination and recombination of many races have produced outstanding family distinctions—high cheekbones, round faces, or some other element of the countenance which is peculiar to a given family.

Carving technique and material together introduce many variations in the carved countenance, variations which manifest themselves particularly in the face. Soap, like clay, is suited to soft, round contours closely resembling those of the face itself. Wood, on the other hand, is more suited to flat planes, sharp, severe, geo-metric curves, and stiffer treatment in general—all designed to accentuate the grain and our basic conception of wood as a blocky material (see Fig. 947). Individual carvers have chosen to ac-centuate this blockiness in caricatures, or even, as Ossip Zadkine characteristically does, make the normally convex curves concave ones.

Variations due to accident or design include such things as the cauliflower ears of the wrestler, the broken or bent nose of the boxer, and the distended lips of the Ubangi women.

I mention all these things first in my discussion of the head and face to point out the endless variables which must be considered if you plan to produce likenesses. Basic facial proportions and methods of blocking out have already been given in Chaps. XIV and XXI, of *Whittling and Woodcarving*, and further details will be mentioned in Chap. XVII of this volume. The purpose here is simply to give the additional information necessary for you to sculpture heads and faces in the round in anything from soap to soft stone.

To review basic dimensions briefly, the head is an oval, and like the figure, has a basic unit of measurement, the width of the eye. The eyes themselves are in the middle of the head oval, viewed from the front, and are slightly less than 1 eye apart. The head itself is 5 eyes wide, the mouth 1½ eyes. The face covers the lower three-quarters of the head oval, with the nose occupying the center third (or one-fourth the total head oval). The ears are as long as the nose, and generally in line with it horizontally. The mouth is a third of the distance down from nose to chin tip.

These proportions provide a standard head, resembling no one in particular. It is the variations from these standards which produce a likeness. The longer nose, lengthened upper lip, wider mouth, and so on distinguish each man from his fellows; in fact, are the major factors in that distinction. If you copy his figure fairly generally—that is, make your carving fat if he is fat, slender if he is slender, stooped if he is stooped, and clothed as he is wont to dress, that's all that is necessary. But to obtain a likeness, the face must be an exact copy of his—even to variations between the sides (remember the Mona Lisa that has plagued analysts for centuries?)—and must even capture a fleeting characteristic expression.

Basically, the face is formed of a series of planes (Fig. 973), of which the most important are the planes of the forehead, cheeks, and chin. Once the oval (or fattened-egg shape) of the face is produced, the face can be blocked in rapidly by carving flats for the forehead, the sides of the cheeks, and the chin. Notches for the eye sockets (don't forget to leave material for carving the bulging eye) will set out the pyramid of the nose and provide the basic planes of the face. The additional planes, as sketched in Fig. 973, will work out the face elements for you. Then, if you wish, you can round up the elements. Pages 238 and 239 of *Whittling and Woodcarving* give details.

So much for the face. Now for the variations. If you are planning to carve a likeness of a living person, either make a sketch of his profile or obtain a side photograph. Either will give you his skull shape and his profile, as well as eye and ear positions, all vital in obtaining a likeness. Note that as a person grows older, the relative positions of the various elements of the countenance continue to vary. I have attempted to indicate these changes for a woman in Figs. 957 to 964, showing eight heads, the profiles at 1, 12, 20, 30, 40, 50, 70, and 85 years. Sure! Everyone you know varies from these sketches, but they serve to indicate the increase in size of the skull, the straightening of the nose, the lengthening of nose and ears, the raising of the eyes, and change of the lines of the face and the hair. Note the ear shape in particular—is it like the male ear of Figs. 974 and 975, or is it longer, set at a greater angle to the head, differently formed? Are the lips full or thin, and what is the ratio of nose-to-mouth and mouth-to-chin distances? What is the basic profile? Is it predominantly Nordic like Fig. 971, or something else? Just to indicate the possible variations, I have drawn the profiles of Figs. 965 to 972, taken from the jacket of Malvina Hoffman's 1936 book, *Heads and Tales*, which is a

[195]

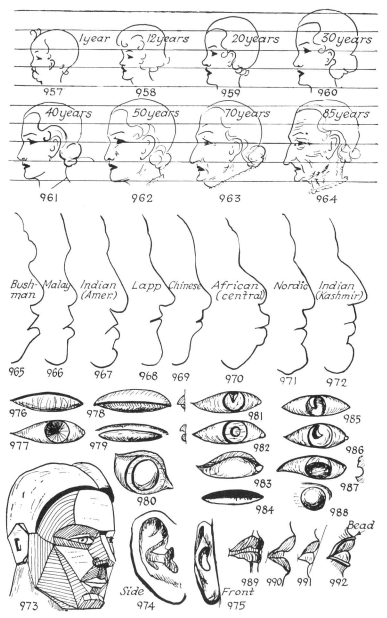

1 year 957
12 years 958
20 years 959
30 years 960
40 years 961
50 years 962
70 years 963
85 years 964

Bush-man 965
Malay 966
Indian (Amer.) 967
Lapp 968
Chinese 969
African (central) 970
Nordic 971
Indian (Kashmir) 972

976
977
978
979
980
981
982
983
984
985
986
987
988

973
Side 974
Front 975

989 990 991 992
Bead

first-class source of detailed information on racial characteristics. See also the group of Figs. 948 to 956, as well as Figs. 946 and 996.

When you have studied all these things, you can begin blocking out the head, as the carvers are doing in Figs. 994 and 998. Be sure, however, that you leave material for proper mouth and eye positions, for these two are the principal factors in determining expression. Look at the gondolier of Fig. 946, for example. See the change in lip and chin position which necessitates more material there, and the moustache which changes the whole profile from the nose downward? Unless you provide for these elements in advance, your finished face will be flat and devoid of expression.

This matter of expression is a difficult problem, particularly with children, who have few characteristic facial lines. A child's face is rounded, full of soft curves, with few or none of the lines of character which show in the face of an older person. I have included Figs. 995 and 997 as examples of children's faces, the second giving formal variations, the first showing the expressiveness obtained by Georg Lang in his crèche figures. Japanese masks, as well as the dance masks of Africa, Asia, and the South Sea islands, are particularly helpful in indicating expression. An excellent example of a Japanese mask is shown in Fig. 996; others were previously shown in Figs. 180 and 181 of *Whittling and Woodcarving*. Incidentally, such masks are often carved almost paper-thin, and have teeth, beards, and moustaches painstakingly added to accentuate the likeness.

Once all these things are understood, it is a simple enough matter to conventionalize facial details if you wish to do so. Thus the natural mouths of Figs. 989 to 992 (note particularly in Fig. 991 how the plane of the mouth slopes toward the chin, the upper lip projecting over the lower) may be modified by a narrow bead all around the lips, as the Egyptians so often finished theirs. The hair may be shown as a series of nested sine curves, as a solid, wavy mass, a series of heavy coils (as in Fig. 946), or even as a series of flat spirals clustered side by side over the surface of the head.

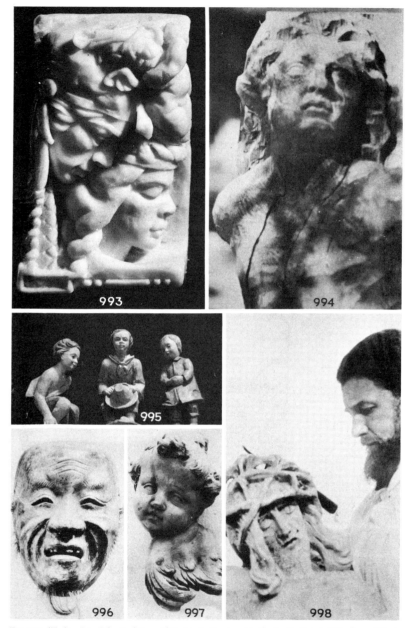

FIG. 993 · "*Indian Love,*" by Fred Press of Boston, prize-winner in the Senior Group, 13th Annual Soap Sculpture Competition. (*See also Fig. 946.*) FIG. 994 · Roughed-out figure, being carved by Josef Mayr of Oberammergau. Courtesy German Railroads Information Office. FIG. 995 · Heads of children from a Georg Lang crèche at the Childrens' Library, Westbury, N.Y. See Fig. 936. FIG. 996 · Japanese seventeenth-century mask of Kyogen, by Tenkaichi Taiko. FIG. 997 · French eighteenth-century cherub. Figs. 996, 997 courtesy Metropolitan Museum of Art. FIG. 998 · Alois Lang, Christus of the Oberammergau Passion Play in 1930 and 1934, carving a Christus. Courtesy German Railroads Information Office.

The eyes have been conventionalized more than any other feature, probably because men from time immemorial have realized their inability to capture the expression behind the oval of the eyeball. In Figs. 976 to 988, I have sketched 13 of the commoner conventionalizations of the eye, many dating all the way back to the ancient Greeks. Primitive peoples usually indicated the eye simply as a circular or hemispherical mound, quite like the modern eye of Fig. 988. The ancient Greeks, as well as the modern carvers in Figs. 946, 994, and 997, simply indicated the oval of the eyeball, as in Fig. 976, without attempting to show the pupil at all. Sometimes, this blank oval is given eye shape, as in Fig. 983, or modified by the addition of the eyelid or eyebrow, as in the modern examples of Figs. 947, 978, and 979. Or the oval may be just an incised groove, as in Fig. 984.

The iris of the eye is indicated in a similar variety of ways. A classic method is the incised cone of Fig. 977, placed on the eye-ball to give the eye the desired direction of vision, and relying upon the shadow created by the incised pyramid to represent a real eye. A modern variation in Fig. 982 shows both the pupil and the iris by setting one cylindrical depression within another. Another in Fig. 987 bulges the upper half of the iris and gouges out the lower. Still another in Fig. 981 indicates the iris with a veiner or scratch-carved circle, an incised triangle in the upper quadrant indicating the high light where the light strikes. Two variations are shown in Figs. 985 and 986, the first produced by gouging out the iris to form a bowl, except for a small curving triangle of wood projecting into the bowl and representing a high light, the second incising this triangle into the bulging surface of the iris. In some cases, the iris is depicted as a separate flat or curving plane at a level above or below that of the rest of the eye. This is done in the faun eye of Fig. 980, taken from a modern French statue, in which an oversized bowl-shaped pupil rests upon a circular plane for the iris, this being depressed below the shaped bulge of the eyeball. Note also how the whole eye has been rounded and the outer corner raised to give the figure the necessary "heathen" expression. But, as far as that is concerned, many carvers just by-pass the whole problem by lowering the lids over the eyeball, or half closing the eyes, as in Figs. 993 and 996.

For a further study of expression, see Fig. 178 and page 144 of *Whittling and Woodcarving*, where are described the variations in facial contours that create smiles, frowns, and the rest of the facial changes by which we give vent to our emotions. The subject will repay your careful study, both in the increased admiration of your friends for the finished carvings, and in the actual returns for those you choose to sell. Edwin T. Howell of West Hempstead, N. Y., for example, has built up a nice business for himself, carving heads alone—and miniature ones at that. He carves busts barely more than 2 in. high from Turkish and West Indian boxwood (pale yellow, lustrous, and almost as hard as ivory), working either from photographs or living models. He has made busts of such notables as John D. Rockefeller and J. P. Morgan—and has collected as much as $500 apiece for them. His tools are special—-miniature chisels and gouges formed from the wire of which telephone guy cables are made, and held in handles like those an engraver uses for his burins.

Whether or not you intend to make a career of carving heads or faces, you'll find it an essential and interesting part of your work. You won't be able to stay away from carving figures forever, and a figure without a head is a queer figure indeed. But don't make the mistake I had to make several times before I believed it could happen—don't carve a finished head before you shape up the body. You'll almost certainly make the head too small. It's much easier to make a head to fit a body than it is to make a body to fit a head.

Just as did the ancient Greeks, you'll find that your finished carving will show much more life if you tint it a little. The Greeks used gaudy colors, as do the modern Japanese and Chinese, but carvings are usually more effective if tinted with oil pigments brushed or rubbed on, then rubbed down until only a suggestion of color remains. Georg Lang uses this technique most effectively in such figures as those of Fig. 995.

Of course, in many cases, particularly in the harder woods, you will want to finish the head with oil and wax (Fig. 947), using no color beyond possible outlining (with pigment, ink, or pencil) of details or accenting of low-relief details, such as indicating the line of the eyebrow. Normally, however, shallow grooves will do the job better and are more in keeping with the medium.

Ivory and plastics are usually left untinted, except for polishing or allover coloring. Soap carvings can be tinted, if desired, with a solution of colored sealing wax dissolved in alcohol and brushed or swabbed on. If carefully applied, they may also be tinted with water-color pigments in a thick, creamy mixture. Daub the mix-ture on gingerly, however—don't brush it on, or you'll have colored soapsuds (see Chap. XV, *Whittling and Woodcarving*).

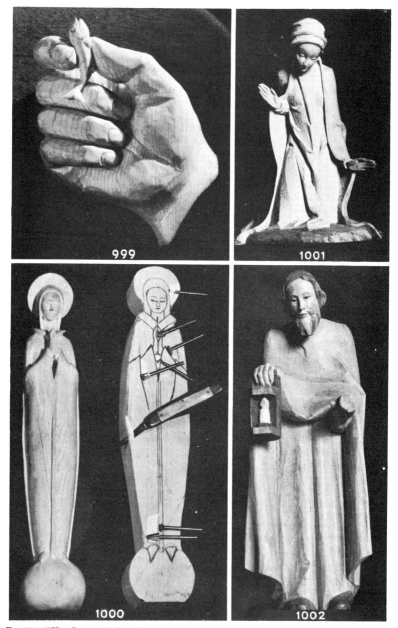

FIG. 999 · "This One DIDN'T Get Away," hand-carved from a single piece of white pine. Note how the grain accents the shape. FIG. 1000 · A carved Madonna and the blank for it, showing router tools in place. The posed hands help the composition materially. FIG. 1001 · Mary, and FIG. 1002 · Joseph, crèche figures by Georg Lang, now at the Childrens' Library, Westbury, N.Y. Courtesy Jacqueline Overton. Compare the long, slender female hands with the shorter, broader male ones.

CHAPTER XIV

THE EXTREMITIES · *Arms, Legs*

"WHO knows how sculptor on sculptor starved, with the thought in the head by the hand uncarved." Bulwer Lytton, writing thus in his *Babylonia*, pointed out again our inability to express our thoughts in carved form, to guide our hands to do what the mind's eye can see. Such common expressions as "the hand of the master," "hands of steel," and "the hand of the surgeon" are other indications of man's respect for that intricate, delicate mechanism.

Most difficult of any body element to draw or carve, the hand plays a vital part in any expression of emotion or action. The hand and arm are often more important in transmitting an idea or explaining a pose than any other element—and more likely to make that pose appear wooden if poorly done. The normal depiction of the feet is made easier by their more restricted motion, and the shoes we wear, but the leg, like the arm, can be a difficult problem. It is almost impossible to do anything approximating a perfect arm or leg without a thorough grounding in anatomy.

However, for our purposes, enough understanding of the extremities can readily be obtained. In most cases, we are carving draped arms and legs, shod feet, so that the only real problems are the hands. Although most other parts of the body can be sketched and carved readily in planes, the hand can be worked as a mass or in planes only when it is closed (see Fig. 1010).

Further, although you—and I—would say offhand that the hand is probably our most familiar feature, a little study of it from the structural point of view will reveal many things we've never noticed. For example, the body of the hand is larger on the thumb side than on the little-finger side, the palm is longer than the back of the hand, it is broader at the fingers than at the base of the thumb in most cases, and it is thicker at the wrist than at the base of the fingers. The back of the hand is flat, except near the wrist, and the whole back becomes convex when the hand is clenched. The palm is roughly a concave square, padded at the edges. The finger group tapers toward the tip or peak formed by the middle finger, and each finger also tapers and seems to lean toward the others. This latter condition is accentuated when the hand is clenched—then the finger tips point toward a common center.

There are a whole series of figure proportions based upon the numbers 3, 5, and 8, but nowhere are they more directly applicable than in the jointing of the fingers. For if the outer joint is considered as 3, the middle joint equals 5 and the inner joint equals 8 —in other words, the first joint is as long as the other two put together, *on the outside* (Fig. 1009). Inside, the greater length of the palm and its extension up halfway to the second joint of the finger makes all joints appear equal in length.

The thumb usually extends to the middle joint of the first finger, and the total length of the thumb is the same as that of the middle finger (measured outside). All fingers are generally square in cross section for the first two joints, then become triangular at the ends because of the plane created by the nail and the flesh at each side and the rounded softness of the pad. The thumb body is much heavier than that of the fingers, and doesn't taper, except beyond the last joint.

The arm and leg both taper from body to end, but leg taper is much greater. General structure of the muscular arm is quite similar to that of a large-link chain, the upper link of which is embedded in the shoulder. Muscles of the upper arm form a link at right angles to the plane of the shoulder, and the lower arm in turn forms a link at right angles to that of the upper arm. Incidentally, notice that the lower arm tapers into the wrist, which is an extended straight section that does not touch a surface upon which the arm and hand are laid flat (Fig. 1005). Unless the wrist is accurately sized and placed, the hand will look as if it were stuck upon a wristless arm.

The human foot is, of course, an arch, dividing the weight between the heel and the ball of the foot. It is broadest at the ball, and the second toe is longest, the foot tapering forward and behind the ball (Fig. 1018). The inner side of the foot rises straight in to the leg, the outer tapers in to the ankle, then rises and tapers outward into the rounded column of the leg. The anklebone projects noticeably outside, and is considerably lower outside than inside (Figs. 1013 and 1014). Also the standing leg, when viewed from the side, is bent forward above the knee, bent backward below, with the backward bend of the knee accentuating this position (Fig. 1020).

All this may assist you to understand the sketches, in which I have tried to show major outlines of the extremities in a variety of positions. Figure 1003 is simply a pattern for the hand of Fig. 999. I carved this hand of white pine for a fisherman friend, making the thumb and forefinger larger to bring out the fish as the dominant element of the carving. When completed, it was mounted on a circular blackwalnut plaque, a small silver medallion below bearing the engraved inscription, "This One DIDN'T Get Away!"

In this particular carving, grain helped materially in bringing out the lines of the hand. The piece I selected carried a small knot its full length, so I carved the hand so that this knot extended down through the middle joints of the fingers. This caused the grain lines of the piece to accent the curvature when the fingers were finally shaped. It also gave a much more realistic appearance to the palm of the hand.

Such a hand is readily blocked out as indicated in Fig. 1010, the latter as it is sketched being suitable for a door knocker or penholder. Note the spread of the knuckles, the double plane of the back of the hand, and the relative position of the thumb, which in this case is caught inside the fingers. If extended, the thumbnail would be in line with the second joint of the index finger.

This matter of grain in a highly grained piece didn't work out so well in the Madonna of Fig. 1000. When viewed from the normal eye level, the Madonna is very saintly—quite like the Georg Lang original (see Fig. 360, *Whittling and Woodcarving*). But viewed

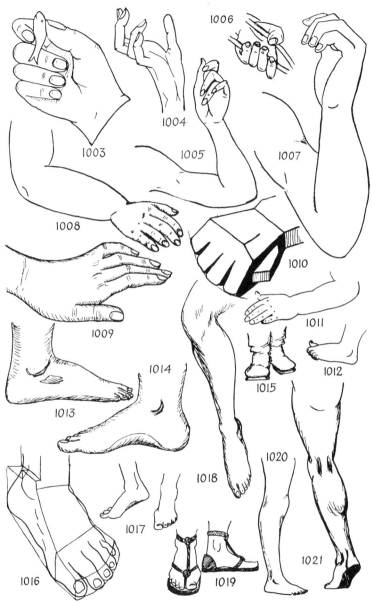

from below, as pictured here, the grain of the wood causes the corners of her mouth to appear to turn upward, so that the Madonna actually appears to smile—or even grin—as the point of view is shifted.

I have included Fig. 1000 here for two other reasons, the first that she provides an excellent example of use of the hands, arms, and legs in design, and the second because she provides an example of the use of motorized tools in carving. Note first how the sweep of her robes, the lines of her lower limbs, and the prayerful position of the hands combine to accent the saintly (properly viewed) position of the face, and her feet provide a transition element into the ball upon which she stands. At her right is a blank which will serve as a pattern, and I have also posed in their proper locations the tools that would be used with a flexible-shaft machine or a hand grinder to carve her. The little circular saw is used in outlining, as shown on her left arm, the small ball-shaped cutter for cutting out holes like that between hands and cuffs. A pointed cutter will remove the wood from between the hands. A cutter with base larger in diameter than tip will establish the line of robe joining as shown near her feet, while the actual joining line can be cut in with a burr having a diamond-shaped cross section. Carving of the halo is best done with a cylindrical burr, while the folds of the robe over the arm can be brought out conveniently with a burr having its outer diameter larger than that at the shank. Heavy shaping and rounding of the figure, as well as final carving of details of the face and hands, are best done with the knife.

As I explained in *Whittling and Woodcarving*, it is extremely important in using a power-driven tool to maintain a firm grip on it; otherwise the cutting tool will tend to "run" along the wood. Furthermore, grain will cause almost as much trouble as with hand carving, particularly if a coarse cutter is used, because the cutting edges tend to lift up the wood and split out pieces along the line of the grain. Carefully handled, however, the power-driven tool is a convenient resource for carving of this type, as well as for designs like those shown in the earlier chapters.

Now let us get back to the hand. The two crèche figures of Figs. 1001 and 1002 I included particularly because of the contrast in hand shapes. Both are by Georg Lang. Note the long, thin, tapering hand of Mary in Fig. 1001, contrasted with the shorter, broader, more powerful hand of Joseph in Fig. 1002. Although both are very simply formed, these hands certainly assist materially in showing Mary's pleasure at the infant Jesus, as well as Joseph's benevolence. The simplicity of draping on these two figures is also especially noteworthy.

To accentuate the differences between male and female hands and arms, I have sketched both in various poses. Thus Fig. 1003 shows a closed male hand, Figure, 1006 a male hand gripping a pair of tongs, and Fig. 1007 the general shape of the male hand and arm. Compare these with the more slender and graceful female hands of Figs. 1004 and 1009, as well as the female hand and arm of Fig. 1005. The female hand in general is longer, with longer, more tapering fingers, and apparently greater facility in assuming graceful poses.

Finger and hand shape, as well as differentiating the male and the female, also serve to indicate skill or profession. Thus, although often inaccurate, it is conventional to depict the hands of the surgeon or artist as extremely long and slender, and those of the workman as short, broad, and powerful.

Children's hands and arms are usually fat and chubby, the fingers being comparatively shorter than those of grownups and the lines of muscles and tendons being much less sharply defined. Thus, Fig. 1008 depicts the hand of a child of three, while Fig. 1011 shows that of a girl of six, already beginning to assume a more adult shape.

Most of the remarks relating to relative hand and arm shapes also apply to those of legs and feet. Compare the long, graceful, slender leg and foot of a woman in Fig. 1018 with the shorter, more strongly muscled male leg of Fig. 1021. Or compare the foot of Fig. 1018 with the two views of the male foot in Figs. 1013 and 1014. The foot of a child is broader, stubbier, and more shapeless, as indicated in Fig. 1012. Certain of the aborigines, particularly in the South Sea Islands, also have much greater development of the toes so that they become actually prehensile, or like shortened fingers, capable of doing almost as much. This is, of course, a result of tree climbing and similar use of the bare foot. Our confining of the feet in shoes makes them less useful to us as gripping devices, just as binding the feet of Manchu babes resulted in the "beautiful" but hobbled feet of Chinese ladies of the Old Kingdom.

To illustrate the modification of the foot when enclosed in shoes, I have sketched Figs. 1017, 1019, and 1015, the first showing the feet bare, the second showing them in sandals, and the third showing the ultimate in shapelessness—the heavy field boot of the German soldier during the World War.

Any general foot shape can be obtained by the blocking-out process illustrated in Fig. 1016, except that the central planes would be extended for a female foot. Note the wide inside plane, topped by a double plane, one crossing the instep, the other along the top surface of the toes. A side plane running along the great toe, and a curving plane along the front line of the toes, carry the blocking over to the outside, where a roughly triangular plane slopes inward to the anklebone, then runs upward to the column of the leg just above the ankle. While the outer end of the anklebone cuts through the outer plane of the foot, the inner end projects above the inner one as sketched. Figures 1013 and 1014 also bring this out, as mentioned earlier.

With this basis, you can carve the simple arms and legs required for most figures, and now have a sufficient background for considering the posing of the body in action and as draped. These will be discussed in the next chapter.

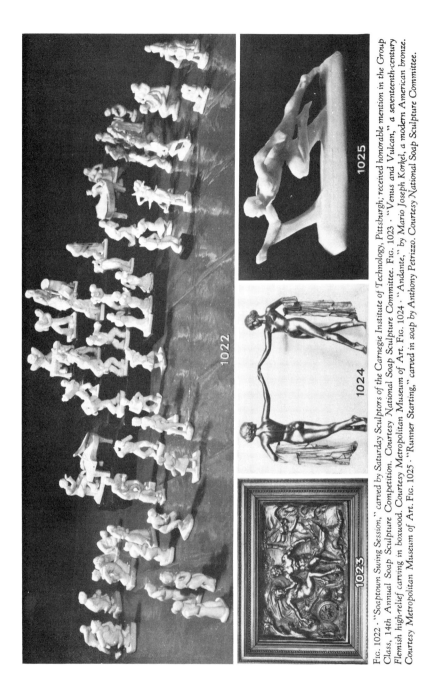

Fig. 1022 · "Soaptown Swing Session," carved by Saturday Sculptors of the Carnegie Institute of Technology, Pittsburgh; received honorable mention in the Group Class, 14th Annual Soap Sculpture Competition. Courtesy National Soap Sculpture Committee. Fig. 1023 · "Venus and Vulcan," a seventeenth-century Flemish high-relief carving in boxwood. Courtesy Metropolitan Museum of Art. Fig. 1024 · "Andante," by Mario Joseph Korbel, a modern American bronze. Courtesy Metropolitan Museum of Art. Fig. 1025 · "Runner Starting," carved in soap by Anthony Petrizzo. Courtesy National Soap Sculpture Committee.

CHAPTER XV

BODY IN ACTION · *Pose, Draping*

"**S**TIFF as a poker" and "straight as a ramrod" are laudable expressions when applied to the pose of a soldier on review, but they are just as unlaudable when applied to a carved figure. The erect body, squared shoulders, evenly balanced weight on exactly placed feet, eyes straight ahead—these are all very military, but from an artistic standpoint, most uninteresting. An artist describes such a pose as *static*—without action. Compare Major Barber's whittled soldiers in Chap. XVII, for example, with the conventional idea—see how much more interesting his are?

Spread the figure's legs, cross them, cross the arms, pose him as throwing something—do anything to avoid the rigid pose, and your carving begins to show action. As you increase the action, the figure increases correspondingly in interest. For example, look back at the postmen in Figs. 66 to 74, simple as can be, but still full of action, and consequently of interest.

"This is all easy enough to write," I can hear you say, "but posing a figure immediately introduces problems far beyond those of the simple figure proportion and detail in previous chapters. What happens to the muscles, the body elements, the clothes?"

Right! To attain real success with figure carving, you must be familiar with anatomy. If the figure is draped or clothed, you must in addition know what happens to folds of drapery when a particular pose is assumed. The posing of friends or professional models, photographs, sketches, or "sketch-models" in clay or plasticine all will help you, but close study of a good anatomy text is a sound preliminary. That is beyond the scope of this text, but let's assume you have done this if you are a student, or don't intend to if you're not, and let's get on with our carving.

FIG. 1026 · Seated girl, carved at the Swiss State Woodcarving School, Brienz, Switzerland, as was Fig. 1028. FIG. 1027 · "Mourning Madonna," an early-sixteenth-century German carving. Courtesy Metropolitan Museum of Art. FIG. 1028 · Dancing couple in modern style. FIG. 1029. Chinese warrior, a 10-in. statuette carved in wood, then gilt and trimmed in red. Over 100 years old. Courtesy Henry Groll. FIG. 1030 · Monk violinist, carved by Guido Mayr of Oberammergau. Courtesy German Railroads Information Office.

In either case, I've tried to provide enough examples, here as well as elsewhere in this book, to give a wide variety of figure poses, as well as draping in many styles. For example, there are more than 50 simple figure poses in the soap carvings of Fig. 1022. Beneath it are a woodcarving, a bronze, and a soap carving, all considerably more detailed examples. Look at the details of the drapes in Fig. 1024, for example, or the backgrounds of Fig. 1023. Or compare the seventeenth-century Flemish idea of feminine beauty in Fig. 1023 with the twentieth-century version in Fig. 1024. Or, again, compare any of these detailed figures with the roughly blocked-out soap carvings on the same page. Compare also the freedom and roundness of soap carving or bronze with the greater blockiness of the woodcarving.

The runner of Fig. 1025 is particularly interesting because the body is posed far off balance. We all think of a runner as leaning forward, and believe that the farther he is leaning forward, the faster he is moving. His very off-balance pose gives us a feeling of something impending, an actual feeling that any second that leading foot will come down, and the other one start to follow it. Like the little Negro boy in the old story, we catch ourselves watching the figure to see if it has moved. There is interest that a static figure could never win!

We all know the fundamental rules about alteration in body shape with change in position—the fact that when a boy "shows his muscle" his biceps swells to create an obvious lump on his upper arm, that various other muscles or tendons become more or less prominent in given poses. We all know also that as we "take the load off" one foot, we throw the weight of the body to one side. The hip of the leg that is carrying no weight sags and the knee bends, and the whole body shifts over the other leg until the center of gravity is over the new support—in this case the ankle of the supporting foot. A little less evident is the fact that the shoulders also move—their former straight line becomes a sloping one, with the high side actually on the *unsupported* side of the body to balance that change in center of gravity.

FIG. 1031 · "*Youth Sitting on a Cloud with the World at his Feet,*" by Robert Hodgell, *second-prize winner, Junior Class, 13th Annual Soap Sculpture Competition.* FIG. 1032 · "*Goodwill to Man,*" by E. J. Anthony, *second-prize winner, Advanced Amateur Class, 14th Annual Soap Sculpture Competition. Both courtesy National Soap Sculpture Committee.* FIG. 1033 · *Japanese statue of the Fujiwara Period (886–1186). Wood, with metal spear. Courtesy Metropolitan Museum of Art.* FIG. 1034 · *Leonhard Maderspacher roughing-out drapery on a religious figure at Oberammergau. Courtesy German Railroads Information Office.* FIGS. 1035, 1036 · *Male and female figures, two of six on the Morgan memorial plaque, Metropolitan Museum of Art, done in bronze, by Paul Manship.* FIG. 1037 · *20-in. wooden figure of Mayor LaGuardia of New York City by Warren Wheelock. Wide World Photo.*

A similar method of analysis will enable you to work out any other action pose. If you haven't a friend who will pose and you can't afford a model, pose in front of a mirror yourself and sketch what you see. Exaggerate slightly—it will help to accentuate the pose. You can study the wrinkles and folds of clothing in the same way.

You remember the old expression that "clothes make the man." In carving, they certainly help—on anything except a nude. The position of the clothes, the folds and wrinkles, even the curve of a drapery or scarf on a running figure, all may help to bring out the pose. They may go beyond that to indicate what has just happened, or what is about to happen. Again, this increases the interest of the figure. Consider, for example, the action expressed in a figure of a Spanish dancer caught just as her skirt begins or ends the swirl that is always a split second behind the motion of her body.

Often, the placing of drapery or clothing can be used to accentuate a pose, particularly if vital creases or folds are accentuated and less important elements suppressed (see Fig. 9). The usual tendency is to do too much draping, rather than too little, detailing all elements instead of limiting detail to those elements which are most important in the pose.

As an example of successful handling of two difficult problems in draping, I have included Fig. 1027, an early sixteenth-century German carving of the Swabian school. Noteworthy is the careful treatment of folds at knees and elbows—often the most difficult draping problem—and successful accentuation of the "eye" of folds reversed on themselves, as in the folds below the elbows. These "eyes" should normally project farther than the rest of the fold. Figure 1048 gives excellent examples of drapery treatment also, particularly the handling of the "eye." There is some stiffness of the drapery hanging from the arm, created largely by the unnatural folds just below the arm itself.

It is interesting to compare older treatment of drapery with that of modern figures. Compare the group of Figs. 1044 to 1049, for example, with the four R.M.S. "Queen Mary" statuettes in Chap. XII, or Figs. 1026, 1028, 1030, 1032, and 1039 in this chap-

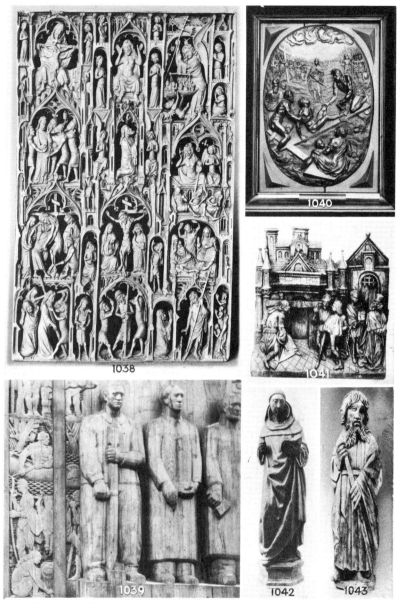

Fig. 1038 · English fifteenth-century ivory carving, "Redemption of Man." Courtesy Metropolitan Museum of Art. Fig. 1039 · A section of the woodwork at the Paris Exposition of 1938. Courtesy "Compressed Air Magazine." Fig. 1040 · "Invention of the Cross," a Flemish seventeenth-century boxwood relief. Fig. 1041 · A legendary scene in oak, Flemish late Gothic (fifteenth century). Fig. 1042 · Dutch fifteenth-century Gothic oak carving of a monk. Fig. 1043 · Oak Gothic carving of a bishop, circa 1500. Figs. 1040–1043 courtesy Metropolitan Museum of Art.

ter. The sharp break from traditional forms is particularly evident in comparing Figs. 1026 and 1027. The former, very well suited in its simplicity of outline and blockiness to the medium, has a much "lighter" appearance than the latter and much less confusing detail.

In Fig. 1028, don't fail to examine the simplified treatment of the features, as well as the angularity of the drapes carrying out the angularity of the hands. Compare this lack of detail with the extreme detail of the Chinese warrior of Fig. 1029. Not only are all the details of his armor carried out, but even the designs etched upon and worked into them. As originally made delicate carved ribbons flowed from the back of the helmet to the shoulders, the left hand apparently held a spear or sword, and the right a shield. Apparently the ancient Chinese had their left-handers too! In any case, I'm soon going to have the interesting task of attempting to replace the missing elements.

The group of Figs. 1026–1030 is also noteworthy for the treatment of the hands, particularly those of the violinist in Fig. 1030, more carefully done probably than any except those of the St. James of Fig. 1046.

Apparently, one basic attribute of the modern artist is nerve— nerve enough to forget unessential detail and to stress dominant elements of his composition. Look at Warren Wheelock's carving of Mayor LaGuardia, for example. No one but a skilled artist would have the nerve to forget buttons, pockets, and even feet to accentuate the stocky build of "The Little Flower," even though the material, lignum vitae, is sufficiently hard and close-grained for the greatest detail.

The statuette of Christ in Fig. 1032 is another example of simple modern treatment of a traditional subject. The benevolence of the figure is emphasized by the sweep of the drapery rising to the outstretched hands. Hands and face are only outlined, in comparison with the heroic figure of Christ overlooking the harbor of Rio de Janeiro, Brazil (Fig. 1056), in which they are detailed, and the treatment of drapery approximates that of the traditional figure of Fig. 1034.

FIG. 1044 · "Apostles in Prayer," Flemish early fifteenth-century oak carving. FIG. 1045 · "Worshippers," a Flemish fifteenth-century wall group. FIG. 1046 · "St. James the Great," French sixteenth-century walnut carving. FIG. 1047 · A Flemish oak carving (circa 1510) of a female saint. FIG. 1048 · "St. Magdalen," a boxwood carving of the lower Rhenish school, showing excellent drapery treatment and composition. FIG. 1049 · Flemish late-Gothic equestrian trumpeter, in oak. All courtesy Metropolitan Museum of Art.

Excellent combinations of conventional drapery and modern action are depicted in the low-relief panels of Figs. 1035 and 1036, two of a group of six by Paul Manship in his memorial plaque to J. P. Morgan in the Metropolitan Museum. An Oriental treat-ment of drapery that closely approximates the Greek is shown in the statue of Jizō, a 1,000-year-old Japanese carving (Fig. 1033).

At various times throughout this book I have mentioned other materials than wood, indicating some of the variations in treatment they introduce. To study these, examine the soap carvings of Figs. 1022, 1025, 1031, and 1032, the plaster of Fig. 1028, and the ivory of Fig. 1038, and compare them with the dozens of wood-carvings depicted.

The fifteenth, sixteenth, and seventeenth centuries are notable as the golden age of Flemish, and Flemish-inspired, figure carving. I have therefore included a number of examples, mostly religious, of Flemish work of these centuries, as well as figures from other countries influenced by the Flemish. They will repay close study, both for understanding of the carving technique and for the handling of anatomy and draping. Pierced work (Figs. 1038 and 1049) and relief carving (Figs. 1040, 1041, and 1044) as well as in-the-round designs are included. The emaciated figures of Fig. 1038, the perspective of Fig. 1041, the draping of Fig. 1044, the detail of Fig. 1046 (which walnut permits and oak makes most difficult—although Fig. 1047 almost makes a liar of me), and the treatment of the horse in Fig. 1049 are all exceptional. Don't fail to notice the conventionalized hair on the oak bishop of Fig. 1043, as well as his oversized left little finger.

For simple exercises to familiarize you with the treatment of conventional drapery forms, I have sketched a crèche group in Figs. 1050, 1051, 1053, 1055, 1057, and 1058. These figures we worked out in soap for a Christmas group, the white of the soap contrasting sharply with the usual Christmas greenery. The angels of Figs. 1053 and 1057 carry actual birthday-cake candles, which can be lighted to make the scene more effective. Because they are the center of the group, hence must be worked out in considerable detail, I have drawn two sketches of the Madonna

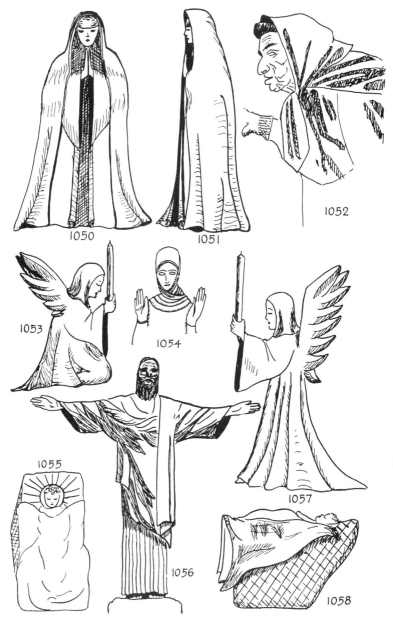

1050

1051

1052

1053

1054

1055

1056

1057

1058

(Figs. 1050 and 1051) and the Infant Jesus (Figs. 1055 and 1058). The Madonna and the standing angel of Fig. 1057 each take a full bar of soap, the kneeling angel and the Infant Jesus a half bar. Since the group includes a Madonna and child, and two of each angel pose, five bars of soap should see you through. The front view of the Madonna in Fig. 1050, and the side views of all of the figures, made twice their printed size, will serve as patterns.

To provide other examples of modern drapery treatments, I have sketched two other figures in this group. The first is the 100-ft. heroic concrete figure of Christ which stands on the 2,300-ft. crest of Corcovado overlooking the harbor of Rio de Janeiro (Fig. 1056). The second is the head of the Madonna from a carved low-relief wood panel by Ivan Meštrović, famed Yugo-Slavian sculptor. The folds of the drapery are indicated by such shallow planes that they are almost just lines. Another modern example is the workman group of Fig. 1039, composed of figures about 10 ft. high, and installed as a column decoration at the 1937 Paris Exposition. In contrast to most figures, made of a single piece of wood and hence limited by the size and shape of the available piece, these are built up of a number of wood pieces, apparently of about the same dimensions as our American 2-by-4's. As nearly as I can tell from the original picture, the figures were 5 planks thick by 7 wide—or about 9 in. thick by 26 in. wide. Here's a worth-while suggestion, rarely followed, which overcomes the normal limitations of wood—a laminated statue. The low-relief border is also noteworthy, particularly the excellent treatment of the conventionalized water under the canoe, a diamond shape incised with straight sides above and a single flat gouge curve replacing the two usual straight sides below. Here is a moderniza-tion of the diaper with a vengeance!

When you can combine action, proper draping, and true pic-turization in a wood sculpture, you really have achieved some-thing. Take, for example, the bust of the old lady in Fig. 1052 as a problem. Work out the details of her draped shawl, the lines of her face—and retain her expression, and you need have little fear of carving anything, even a statuette portrait of a friend.

〖 221 〗

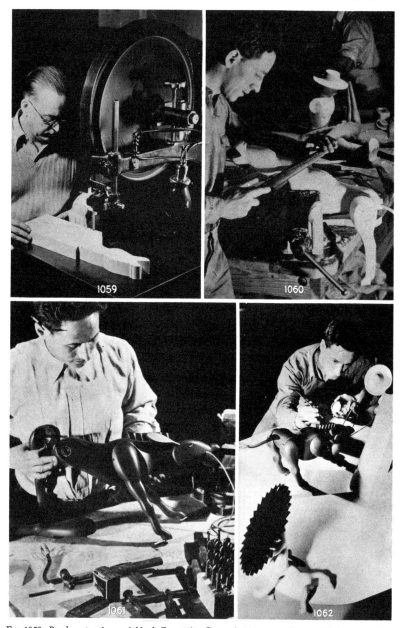

FIG. 1059 · Band sawing the rough blank. FIG. 1060 · Carver finishing partially assembled figure with a file. It has previously been carved. FIG. 1061 · Assembling the mechanized donkey. FIG. 1062 · Touching up the assembled and painted figure, which is part of the sequence depicting how silimanite is mined in the High Sierras and processed into the porcelain of spark-plug coils.

CHAPTER XVI

CARICATURES · *Grotesques*

WHAT is a caricature and what a grotesque? How do they differ? Let's go to Webster. A *grotesque* is "characterized by fantastic exaggeration or combination, especially of human and animal figures. It is fanciful, absurdly incongruous or awkward." A *caricature*, on the other hand, is "a distortion by exaggeration . . . producing a grotesque or ridiculous effect."

In simple English, a carved grotesque is fantastic, and often a combination of human and animal elements to form a figure, like the gargoyles on the Cathedral of Notre Dame (Fig. 1083). A caricature, on the other hand, simply accentuates personal characteristics or habits of an individual to point out the things people notice first about him, as, for example, W. C. Fields' nose, Chamberlain's umbrella, or Hitler's forelock and mustache.

Suffice it to say that carving either is quite a paradox. It looks simple, and isn't. The finished piece looks rough, and isn't. The effect is one of hasty "knife sketching," and isn't. Successful caricaturing takes long practice, intensive observation, and at least as careful carving as formal sculpture. You must learn what to emphasize and what to subdue, what to accept and what to reject. The principal characteristics of the subject—the things his friends (or enemies) recognize him by—are what you must bring out in your carving, the overlarge ears, the always-open mouth, the habitual slouch, the peculiar way of wearing some article of clothing. One good way to start is to write down the characteristics of the subject, making a rough list first, then rearranging it in order of importance. Then work those elements into your carving in exaggerated form, starting with No. 1, and getting in as many of the others as you can without making the finished job a pure grotesque. Often you will find, too, that some line is characteristic of the person—a loose curve of the fat man, sharp angles of the thin or penurious one, and so on. Some success-ful cartoonists (a cartoon, by the way, is a caricature on paper) insist that they can pick out some one curve or line characteristic of the subject and can produce a likeness simply by using that line or curve over and over again.

The New York World's Fair (1939) is particularly productive of caricatures, as well as of grotesques. While many critics more capable than I will call "The Tree of Life" (Fig. 1) a symbolic piece of sculpture, my vote goes for it as a grotesque because of its queer distortions and combinations of the human and tree forms. The dozens of figures in the Ford exhibit, on the other hand, I, rightly or wrongly, call caricatures. I have shown several of them here (Figs. 1063–1067), as well as the method of con-structing and carving one of the more interesting ones, the balky mule. These figures had to be simple, yet humorous and interest-ing, and in addition had to be animated to tell their story. Let's start by running through that story:

Men in every part of the world help build the motor cars which roll off Detroit assembly lines. Sources of materials, the manner in which they are obtained, and how they are processed is a dramatic story. "The Ford Cycle of Production" is the Ford Motor Company's attempt to visualize these steps. This unique exhibit comprises a huge 100-ft. turntable, weighing almost 152 tons, floating in a huge circular moat so that it can be revolved six times a minute. The exhibit shows by animated models the production and processing of 27 principal raw materials from source to finished part. There are 87 large-scale models with 142 human figures carved in wood by Willi Noell and Juan Oliver, 79 of them being mechanized later.

All forms are reduced to the simplest recognizable shapes, to unify displays and concentrate attention on essentials. Machine forms are reduced, wherever possible, to basic geometrical shapes. Models are highly stylized, with color, line, and form handled effectively in a number of different materials, including wood, glass, metal, and plastics, the basic material of course being wood.

Each unit has its own lighting scheme, with concealed lights casting bold high lights and shadows on the figures and machines.

Each display has its own base, cut to fit the steps of the turn-table, which diminish in diameter as they rise to the full height of 30 ft. Some 30,000 bd. ft. of lumber were used in building displays and platforms, each wood selected to stand up best under its particular use. Stationary and heavy parts are California sugar pine; oak, mahogany, maple, and birch are used for moving parts; and white-pine laminated panels for hollow shapes which must stand stress and yet provide space to house animating machinery. All pieces were painted inside and out to preserve them against climatic influences, which would cause shrinkage or expansion disastrous to operating mechanisms. All animating mechanism is concealed, although in some cases it was necessary to sew clothes over vital hinges or other operating elements. Animation is as simple as possible to avoid the necessity for servicing; antifriction bearings and inbuilt lubrication are incorporated in the figures so that there will be no grease staining, no failure of parts, and most important of all, no noise.

So to the carving itself. The job of producing 142 human and animal figures, as well as trees, birds, flowers, etc., uniform in style, workmanship, and finish had to be done in seven months. That made conventional methods out of the question. The work was further complicated because 79 figures had to be animated, meaning channels, joints, and sockets at heads, elbows, waists, legs, or feet, as necessary. To have a number of sculptors work on them would have resulted in as many different styles.

So the production methods for which Ford is famous were put into use. A complete ½-in. scale model of the entire turntable was made and studied. Colored drawings, half size, were made by the designer's staff, indicating more closely the intention and conception. From these the sculptors made working drawings, actual size, which were actually patterns for parts to be roughed out on the band saw, as in Fig. 1059. The technique is quite similar to that described by Major Barber in Chap. XVII.

Fig. 1063 · *Undercutter mining coal.* Fig. 1064 · *Molding headlight lenses.* Fig. 1065 · *Attendant on "triple tiger" mohair upholstery cleaner and nap raiser.* Fig. 1066 · *Chuting mined copper ore.* Fig. 1067 · *Sheep herder and flock, source of upholstery.*

Body, arms, and legs cut separately from sugar pine on the band saw, after rough shaping with a drawknife, were joined with glue and dowels to heads and necks turned on a wood lathe. After assembly, one sculptor did the actual carving, the other did finish filing (Fig. 1060) and sanding. This was followed by animation, where necessary (Fig. 1061). Plated metals and rayons were used discreetly to heighten humor and effectiveness. The figure was finished by shellacking, ground coating, hand sanding, again ground coating, again sanding, taping and airbrushing, and final application of two coats of high-grade lacquer. In some cases, noses, eyes, horns, and tails were turned, carved, or bent from plastics and added. Touching-up was done after final assembly (Fig. 1062). Some of the finished models are shown in Figs. 1063 to 1067. Here certainly is the current model of the marionette!

William Steig, cartoonist whose work is familiar to New Yorkers through his drawings of "Small Fry," has recently made his debut as a sculptor. A New Yorker from birth, educated in Public School No. 53 in the Bronx, the thirty-one-year-old cartoonist moved three years ago to Connecticut. With his brother, Henry Anton Steig, he pruned the fruit trees—and first thing you know, he was carving! The 14 resulting figures, which his family have classified as Jasons (males) and Tessies (females), are executed in mahogany, pear, apple, walnut, wild apple, orange, and tangerine.

Bearing a close resemblance to primitive African carving (Figs. 153 and 175, *Whittling and Woodcarving*), Mr. Steig's figures are good caricature, aimed at creating humor, rather than being funny, as are his cartoons. To achieve that effect, he often steps outside the bounds imposed by the purists, just as Noell and Oliver did with the Ford carvings. Steig is not above making the sequins for his "Sequinned Lady" (Fig. 1068) by driving small nails into the figure, or making her bracelets and necklace with brass nails. Other figures, the "Matriarch" of Fig. 1069, for example, actually are equipped with real bead necklaces. In addition to the knife, Steig uses the file for shaping, some of the marks still being evident.

FIG. 1068 · "Sequinned Lady," in pearwood, trimmed with nails and brass tacks. FIG. 1069 · "Matriarch," in walnut. FIG. 1070 · "Man at a Gathering," in tangerine. FIG. 1071 · "Man with the Nose," in soap, by Eve Bass. Courtesy National Soap Sculpture Committee. FIG. 1072 · "School Girl," in wild apple, with brass-tack necklace. FIG. 1073 · "Guitarist," in apple wood. FIG. 1074 · "Grotesque," by Elizabeth Philbrick. Courtesy National Soap Sculpture Committee. FIG. 1075 · "Mal de Tête," in orange wood. Photographs of Mr. Steig's carvings by Soichi Sunami.

Say what you will, he has achieved a unique and interesting result. Look at the obvious "laced-in" appearance of the "Sequinned Lady" for proof, or at the "Man at a Gathering" (Fig. 1070), obviously ill at ease, bored and uncomfortable, standing there with hands jammed into coat pockets, hoping the affair will soon be over.

Steig's own explanation of these carvings is: "In the city, one is impressed with what people *do*. In the country, where there is little activity, one becomes preoccupied with what people *are*." From which I infer that the doings of people can be readily depicted in two dimensions, but that it takes three to show what they are like inside. He hasn't decided yet whether this is a hobby or more business. His opinion is, "If it sells, it isn't a hobby." Construction times vary all the way from the business-like two days for the "Sequinned Lady" to the hobbylike two weeks for the "Guitarist" (Fig. 1073); the style varies from the straight Steig of the "Man at a Gathering" to the decidedly African-look-about-the-eyes of the "School Girl" (Fig. 1072). And look at the combination of humor and pathos of the lady with the headache in Fig. 1075!

In the same group with the Steig pieces, I have placed two interesting grotesques carved in soap, "The Man With the Nose" (Fig. 1071), by Eve Bass, Brooklyn, N. Y., the third prize winner in the Senior Class, 14th Annual Soap Sculpture Competition, and "Grotesque," by Elizabeth Anne Philbrick of Winchester, Minn., a prize winner the preceding year.

Although they are plaster models rather than the original wood-carvings, I couldn't resist including the three-dimensional playing-card royalty group of Figs. 1076 to 1079. In the Card Room of the R.M.S. "Queen Mary," they include fairly formal figures of king and knave, a formal queen, and a delightful joker. The apparent detail and obvious simplicity of the busts recommend them to any serious caricaturist. As soon as I get through writing about them, I'm going to try that joker myself!

To round out the group of caricatures and grotesques, I have included some miscellaneous figures in Figs. 1080 to 1104. They

FIG. 1076 · Knave. FIG. 1077 · King. FIG. 1078 · Queen. FIG. 1079 · Joker. All three-dimensional carica-tures in the Card Room, R.M.S. "Queen Mary." Courtesy Cunard White Star Lines.

come from such widely separated sources as the cathedrals of England and the temples of Bali, but all possess considerable merit. Figures 1080 to 1082 and 1086 are good typical examples of primitive carving, the first two coming from Nepal, India, the third from Bali, and the fourth from the prehistoric temple at Tiahuanaca, Bolivia.

The gargoyles all over the Cathedral of Notre Dame in Paris have long been famous as grotesques, as has the inscrutable Sphinx in Egypt. A typical gargoyle (this one used as a water spout) is sketched in Fig. 1083, a side view of the Sphinx in Fig. 1085. A highly conventionalized god's head done by the Mayans in Yucatan is shown in Fig. 1084.

The grotesques carved as finials, bench and desk ends, and stall elbows in various old English churches have long been famous. A few typical examples are sketched in Figs. 1091 to 1104. Figure 1091 is a king's figure from a bench end at Wiggenhall St. Mary V., Norfolk; Fig. 1092 is a heraldic north-England griffin from Manchester Cathedral; Fig. 1093, a late fifteenth-century bench-end dog from Dennington, Suffolk. The bishop of Fig. 1094 is from Berne Cathedral; the winged and feathered grotesque of Fig. 1095 is a parochial late fifteenth-century stall figure from Gresford, Denbigh. The piratelike head of Fig. 1096 is from a stall end in the fifteenth-century church at Southwold, Suffolk; the Indianlike head of Fig. 1097 is from a late fourteenth-century stall in Chester Cathedral, before America was discovered! The conventionalized ram of Fig. 1098 is a bench-end figure from Woolpit, Suffolk; the angel of Fig. 1099 is a monastic stall figure from the late fifteenth-century Beaumarais at Denbigh. Oxford Cathedral contributes the winged-cleric late fifteenth-century desk end of Fig. 1100. The angel finial of Fig. 1101 comes from Ewelme, Oxon. Occasionally, the finals of stall and bench ends incorporated grotesques like the poupee head of Fig. 1102, from Rattlesdon, Suffolk. The misericords (elaborately carved shelves under the folding stall seats to give worshippers partial support during the many standing periods in the old-English service) often incorporated grotesque figures; the heraldic dog of

Fig. 1103, from Southwold, Suffolk, is one type of end decoration for a misericord. Lastly, there is the grotesque elbow of Fig. 1104, a late fourteenth-century monastic example from Chester Cathedral.

Many romantic stories have been written about the figureheads that once graced capital ships of the great maritime nations—and even now grace the prows of the canoes of primitive South Sea Islanders. I have sketched four English and American examples of these figureheads, simply to indicate their general form. Figure 1087 is a figure of Britannia from the 110-gun "Royal Adelaide" and is now at the Devonport Naval Barracks, England. Figure 1088 is the head of Tecumseh, dear to the heart of every Annapolis midshipman. Once the figurehead for the U.S.S. "Delaware," it is now cast in bronze on the grounds at Annapolis, and is known as "The God of 2.5" because of the midshipmen's habit of pitch-ing pennies at it just before they take the examinations which must earn them a grade of 2.5 points. In sharp contrast is the figure of Columbia from the Mariners' Museum at Newport News, Va. (which has a number of these figureheads, as has Devonport), taken from a ship whose name has been lost in the mists of time. The British lion of Fig. 1090 comes from H.M.S "Hogue," a 74-gun ship of the British Royal Navy between the years of 1811 and 1865, and now at the Devonport Naval Bar-racks. This shows the most detailed carving of any figure in the group, although the thing any observer notices first is the staring, terrifying eyes. All these figures were of course elaborately painted and gilded, for it was traditional that a ship which neglected its figurehead soon met disaster.

If, after looking over these grotesques and caricatures, you are tempted to try your hand at some, check back first on Chap. XIV of *Whittling and Woodcarving*, where I have given detailed in-formation about the vagaries of the human face and figure—how a preferred expression can be obtained, for example. Similar data about animal and bird caricatures are given in Chap. XIII of the same book, so that there is little need to repeat them here.

FIG. 1105 · "*He says he'll pose for you if you'll pose for him.*" *Courtesy Richard Decker and "The New Yorker.*" FIG. 1106 · *A typical wooden Indian of fifty or sixty years ago. (See also Fig. 1118.)* FIG. 1107 · "*Have I kept you waiting?*" *Reproduced by special permission of L. Reynolds and "The Saturday Evening Post," Copyright 1938, by The Curtis Publishing Company.* FIG. 1108 · *Reclining figure by Leslie G. Bolling. Courtesy Harmon Foundation.* FIG. 1109 · *Half of a signpost in Warmbrunn, Germany, showing the old problem of girl vs. goat in a silhouette woodcarving. Courtesy German Railroads Information Office.*

CHAPTER XVII

FOLK CARVING I · *Human Figures*

"ART happens; no potentate commands it, and no hovel is safe from it." This aphorism of Whistler's is more than borne out by the facts. From Greenland to Africa, from China around the world back to China again, you'll find really artistic designs and figures carved or whittled from local materials. They may be in wood, ivory, bone, or soft stone, but most peoples produce characteristic works of art, many of them designs passed down for generations.

Perhaps this all is an outgrowth of the fact that man's original tool is the knife, and he is wont to use it idly when he has nothing more pressing to do (Fig. 1107). You can see evidences of this inherited tendency in any public park or any country store. Of course, the results vary from the classic intertwined hearts and notches in seats to really elaborate figures of people or animals. Most of the latter are traditional, coming down from father to son, and becoming identified eventually as the product of a particular family or section. And, as they say down in the Southern highlands, skill seems to "run in families." Thus we find the best examples of this informal carving coming from the Tyrolese Alps (Swiss, German, and Italian), French-Canada, Mexico, the Northeast coast of the United States, and the highland portions of North and South Carolina, West Virginia, Virginia, Tennessee, and Kentucky.

I have chosen to call this informal style "folk carving" and have included a wide variety of examples in this and the next chapter, dividing them roughly into human and animal groups. They range from the wooden Indian in Fig. 1106, America's version of the African idol of Fig. 1105, to such in-the-round figures as the Bolling reclining figure of Fig. 1108 and the German silhouette carving of Fig. 1109.

Fig. 1110 · "*Mère Marthe*" (*Swiss*) *and* "*Skipper Sam'l*" (*French-Canadian*). Fig. 1111 · *Crèche group from Oberammergau*, Fig. 1112 · *Herders at the Manger, The Children's Library, Westbury, N. Y. Figs. 1111 and 1112 Courtesy Jacqueline Overton.* Fig. 1113 · "*Dopey,*" *from* "*Snow White and the Seven Dwarfs.*" Fig. 1114 · *Typical small hand-carved figures from Italy, Switzerland, and Germany.*

During the past several years, a wide variety of whittled and carved figures have become available in this country, some stemming from our own Northeastern and Southeastern carving areas, but most of them coming from foreign sources. For example, I described in *Popular Science* in 1935 the making of the familiar pair of Fig. 1110, the first a Swiss peasant woman I called Mère Marthe, and the second a French-Canadian carving of a Yankee sea captain I called Skipper Sam'l. Both are typical of the "sketch-carved" figures turned out one after the other at almost production rates in order to meet a price market. Skipper Sam'l, for example, appeared in several stores in New York within six months of publication of the article in *Popular Science*, imported from Japan and priced at 19 cents! Here was an obvious case of copying by Japanese of an original French-Canadian figure previously produced by natives of one particular area in Canada only.

A few years ago, designs were largely regional—that is, it was readily possible to determine their source simply by looking at them. With the increase of vogue for carvings, however, many and varied designs are turned out locally, the band saw, scroll saw, and drum sander making up in production speed for the wage differential that formerly handicapped American-made carvings.

There are still entirely handmade figures turned out, however, and highly valued by their possessors. Look, for example, at the two crèche groups of Figs. 1111 and 1112, both entirely hand-carved (except for rough sawing of the blank) at Oberammergau by Georg Lang and his group. They are distinguished by strong planes which create interesting lights and shadows, as well as by excellent detailing of faces and hands. They are carved of wood of about the color of American basswood, but harder, then finished by oiling and tinting with rubbed-on and wiped-off oil colors. The figures show definitely interesting color as a result, but are not shiny or garish and the texture of the wood still shows. I used a similar finish on the Mère Marthe of Fig. 1110, in this case to allow the close grain of the fir to show through.

Fig. 1115 · *Cinderella and the Fairy*, carved by Georg Lang. *Courtesy German Railroads Information Office.* Fig. 1116 · *"Red Cap," by Leslie G. Bolling. Courtesy Harmon Foundation.* Fig. 1117 · *Whittled figures from Virginia. Courtesy M. K. Cumming.* Fig. 1118 · *Eight "cigarstore" Indians, now at the Pony Express Museum, Pasadena, Calif. Courtesy W. Parker Lyon.*

Walt Disney's animated cartoons, particularly "Snow White and the Seven Dwarfs," have been fertile fields for the sketch-carver. Disney's figures are largely compounded of circles (remember Mickey Mouse's round body, round head, and even his round ears?), but they can be readily made angular or planar, as I have done with the "Dopey" of Fig. 1113. The illustration is almost exactly half the size of the original head, which I carved from white pine and tinted as mentioned in the preceding paragraph. If you want to take a shot at it, the front and side elevations are sketched in Figs. 1145 and 1146, one with hat and one without, so you can take your choice.

This particular head of Dopey illustrates another possible use for bust carvings. It was made primarily as the head for a marionette, but with a base of sorts beneath the shoulder line so that it could be used for a desk ornament as well. Colors included flesh color for the face, with reddened nose and cheeks, red lips, blue eyes, a dull-purple cap, and a yellow sweater. This particular figure should be finished without sanding or smoothing to preserve the knife cuts. If you have a hand grinder or flexible-shaft machine, you'll find cutters useful for shaping Dopey's neck and chin, as well as hollowing out his mouth, all places difficult to reach with a penknife or standard carving tools.

In Fig. 1114 I have grouped a selection of the little knickknack figures which are now coming into this country in such profusion. The flanking peasants stand about 2 in. high, the monk about 2½ in. The latter is also commonly seen in a 5-in. figure. I have sketched him in Figs. 1140 to 1143, giving front and side profiles for this particular figure, as well as alternate head and cowl front and side views for the companion figure. The monk of Fig. 1140 is finished by staining brown, with his beard, pages of the breviary, and waist cords of his robe touched up in white. The tassels and page edges of the breviary are touched up with gilt, and his skullcap, shoes, and covers of the breviary are black. The other monk (Figs. 1142–1143) is robed in black and, of course, is beardless. The rosary is touched up with gilt, and the rest of the color scheme is the same. Either monk is made to look much more

dignified and studious by equipping him with a tiny pair of spec-
tacles bent out of a hairpin and held in place by inserting the ends
in tiny holes drilled at the sides of the nose.

The other statuettes in Fig. 1114 are principally Anri pieces
from the Italian Tyrol, except for the German musicians in the
foreground. These latter are very interesting because, although
they look carved, they are not carved at all, but are glued as-
semblies of many little turned bits of wood, cut at the proper
angles to produce the figures. The Italian peasant couple at left
and right of Fig. 1114 are fairly crude in shape, but the boy and
the redcap are quite detailed. All are finished by painting in
brilliant colors, the boy and redcap being drilled to serve as flower
holders (one hole can be seen in the top of the post against which
the boy is leaning). The whole group makes an interesting series
of figures for you to practice on—and they'll turn out to be a lot
easier to make than you expected. Make the monk first; he's the
most workmanlike figure, and besides you have patterns for him
in Figs. 1140 and 1141. I'd suggest you make him twice the size
of Fig. 1140 at first. That will give you a 5-in. monk.

There are literally dozens of figures of this type available to
suggest further figure-carving ideas. The gift department of any
store, as well as any gift shop, has them. For example, in Fig. 1117
are shown the seven members of a Negro family, as made by white
mountaineers down in Virginia and sold at a roadside souvenir
stand. While crudely done, they show a surprising amount of
character and close study of the models. Compare their simple
outlines and rounded contours with the exact precision of the
redcap in Fig. 1116, whittled by Leslie Garland Bolling, the
Negro whittler of Richmond—but more of him anon.

In *Whittling and Woodcarving*, I mentioned the ease with
which tableaus can be posed of carved figures. In previous chapters
I have shown a number of figures suitable for such groupings,
including the Soaptown Swing Session of Fig. 1022, the soap
crèche group of Figs. 1050 to 1058, etc. In Fig. 1115 is another
example, this one from Georg Lang at Oberammergau, and showing the scene where the fairy visits Cinderella for the first time.

〖 240 〗

Also, in Fig. 1106, I showed that ancestor of American folk carving, the wooden Indian. In Fig. 1118 are eight more, showing the wide variations produced by the carvers of a hundred years and more ago. Several of them are quite original conceptions of Pocahontas, the center figure is a 180-year-old figure of Piccadilly Jim advertising "Yale" cigars, and the rest are warriors. All are now in W. Parker Lyon's "Pony Express Museum," across the highway from Santa Anita racetrack, outside Pasadena, Calif. He also has nine old wooden horses, not long ago common in front of blacksmith and saddlery shops. All in-the-round figures, and usually full size, they are typical of an advertising era that believed in symbols. The wooden Indian always meant a cigar store from which could be gotten "cheroots" of Indian tobacco; the wooden horse always meant a repair shop for your horse and buggy. This era may be on the way back—look at Figs. 1165 to 1182 if you disagree! It is true that these are found only in very limited areas thus far, but you'll find inns along the highways, as well as direction signs along parkways, using the silhouette figure in wood or metal for identification again, because it's much easier to see and recognize a known silhouette than to read lettering at the speeds we travel today.

Leslie Garland Bolling, Negro shipping clerk of Richmond, Va., is one of the few whittlers who has received artistic recognition in his field. Using only the jackknife, he has produced such inter-esting figures as the reclining figure of Fig. 1108, the excellent "Redcap" of Fig. 1116, and the series of Figs. 1119 to 1126. Although he studied at Hampton Institute briefly, he has had no formal art training. Yet he has whittled many amazingly beautiful subjects covering the life and surroundings of his native rural community, and the resulting self-development of his natural talent has won the acclaim of critics. He has aimed for artistic quality rather than commercial remuneration, and has succeeded in expressing more spirit and action than is usual in whittled figures.

His technique is the same as that I have described so often before—squaring up a block of wood, drawing on two adjacent

Fig. 1119 · *Parson on Sunday.* Fig. 1120 · *Aunt Monday.* Fig. 1121 · *Sister Tuesday.* Fig. 1122 · *Mama on Wednesday.* Fig. 1123 · *On Thursday—Gossip.* Fig. 1124 · *A Workman.* Fig. 1125 · *Cousin on Friday.* Fig. 1126 · *Cooking on Saturday. All courtesy Harmon Foundation.*

faces the front and side views of the figure to be carved, sawing it out with a scroll saw, and completing the modeling with his jackknife. Here, incidentally, is proof that no elaborate tools are required, for Bolling has only a furnished room containing, in addition to the usual bed, bureau, and chairs, a desk with a vise and his scroll saw. The rest of his tools he carries in his pocket.

Through the courtesy of the Harmon Foundation, an organiza' tion founded to foster culture among the colored people, I am able to show a number of examples of Bolling's work, probably the most interesting being the series representing the days of the week, shown in Figs. 1119 to 1123, 1125 and 1126. They include "Parson on Sunday," catching the minister at the moment of vehement discourse, leaning over his pulpit to emphasize a point (Fig. 1119); "Aunt Monday" at the washtub (Fig. 1120); "Sister Tuesday" doing the ironing (Fig. 1121); "Mama on Wed' nesday" doing the mending (Fig. 1122); "Gossip on Thursday" over the back fence (Fig. 1123); "Cousin on Friday" scrubbing the floor (Fig. 1125); "Cooking on Saturday" showing the turkey being put in the oven and pots and kettles on top of the stove (Fig. 1126).

The "Redcap" of Fig. 1116 is one of Mr. Bolling's more recent figures (made in 1937), and shows his tremendous improvement. Another more ambitious figure is "The Workman" of Fig. 1124. Praise from such artists as Carl Van Vechten have aided Mr. Bolling in having a one-man show at the Richmond Academy of Art in 1935; exhibits at the National Negro Exhibition in the Smithsonian Institute, Washington, D. C., in 1933; at the College Art Association, 1933; at the Virginia Artists' Exhibition, 1934; at the Richmond Artists' Exhibition, 1934; at the New Jersey State Museum in 1935; and several exhibitions sponsored by the Harmon Foundation both in New York and in traveling shows. It is particularly noteworthy that Mr. Bolling has secured all this recognition without catering to the contemporary belief that sculpture, whether in wood, stone, or metal, must be completely rounded off and sanded until the tool marks are lost. Further, he

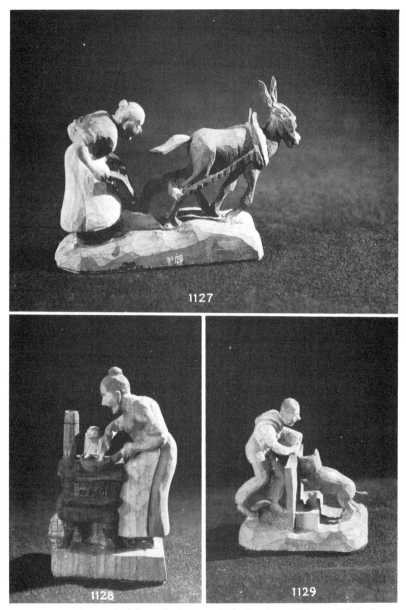

FIGS. 1127–1129 · *Figures whittled out of buckeye or poplar by Tom Brown of Pleasant Hill Academy in Tennessee. Illustration from "Handicrafts of the Southern Highlands," by Allen H. Eaton. By permission of the publisher, the Russell Sage Foundation.*

goes back to the Greek precedents in coloring his figures slightly to emphasize centers of interest.

In the Southern highlands—mountainous areas of Kentucky, Tennessee, West Virginia, North and South Carolina, and Virginia—the mountain peoples have retained many of the customs and sayings of several hundred years ago. In their isolation, they have developed a wide variety of homecrafts, which various groups and organizations are now assisting in developing and spreading. Important among these crafts are whittling and woodcarving, particularly the former. Subjects are local people and animals, often grouped to make up complete rustic scenes. As is usual under such conditions of development, local woods are used, the pieces often being finished with bits of other materials. A complete chapter dealing with the people, their types of carved pieces, and the materials they use, will be found in *Handicrafts of the Southern Highlands*, by Allen H. Eaton, who with the publishers, the Russell Sage Foundation, has permitted me to reproduce three of his illustrations here.

Figures 1127 to 1129 were whittled by Tom Brown, instructor at Pleasant Hill Academy, Tenn. Mr. Brown works at high speed, using native woods such as pine, poplar, cedar, and buckeye. Most of the pieces are left unfinished except for slight tinting. Cedar pieces are usually oiled also. Among other mountain schools and groups where whittling is taught are the John C. Campbell Folk School, Brasstown, N. C.; Jack Knife Shop, Berea College, Ky.; Whittler's Club, Gilbert Henry Community Center, Crab Orchard, Ky.; Tryon Toy Makers and Wood-Carvers, Biltmore, N. C.; and the Woodcrafters and Carvers at Gatlinburg, Tenn.

In contrast to rough, angular figures like Fig. 1127, made at Pleasant Hill, the Campbell carvers use principally fruit woods, apple being commonest, with some holly, maple, walnut, and cherry, and their finished figures are smoothed, waxed, and hand-rubbed. Tryon carvers use walnut, oak, and similar "furniture woods," producing fine furniture with such American motifs as the pine cone, galax leaf, dogwood leaf, blossom, and berry. Even the women in some areas whittle, making so-called "pop-

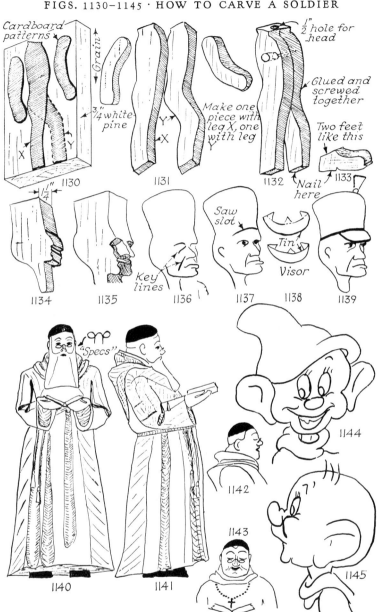

Cardboard patterns

Grain

3/4" white pine

X
Y

Y
X

1/4" 1130

Make one piece with leg X, one with leg Y

Y
X

1131

1/2" hole for head

Glued and screwed together

Two feet like this

Nail here

1132   1133

1134

1135

Key lines

1136

Saw slot

1137

Tin

Visor

1138

1139

"Specs"

1140   1141

1142

1143

1144

1145

pets," which are dolls whittled of buckeye or some similar fine and close-grained wood, then clothed and given hair made of mole, squirrel, or other fur. Further examples of the work of people in these areas can be seen in the door of Fig. 892, the animals of Figs. 1188 to 1190, and the bear of Fig. 1191, the latter a specialty of D. L. Millsaps of Damascus, Va. I have sketched one or two of the interesting patterns in Figs. 1184 to 1186, the two bears being typical of the designs of Mr. Millsaps, the peacock of Fig. 1185 being a design carved from memory by Ross Corn of South Carolina while he was a student at Berea College, and the fox another example of Pleasant Hill work.

Several years ago, *Life* published a series of photographs of some unusual whittled soldier figures. The whittler, Major Henry A. Barber, now American military attaché in Havana, Cuba, has kindly consented to permit me to illustrate several groups of his figures (Figs. 1146–1151). Here's his description of how he makes them:

"I start with a piece of 1-in. white pine like Fig. 1130 (actually about $\frac{3}{4}$ in. thick). I place on it cardboard patterns as shown, making the body of two thicknesses, one with leg X, the other with leg Y. When these are sawed out on the band saw, I get the equivalent of Fig. 1131.

"Heads I generally saw out of $1\frac{1}{4}$-in. white pine, in silhouette like Fig. 1134. The body is screwed together after gluing, as shown in Fig. 1132, the screws being countersunk and hidden with plastic wood. At the top of the 'collar,' I bore a $\frac{1}{2}$-in. hole for the neck. Feet are sawed out individually, to the shape sketched in Fig. 1133, then are secured to the ends of the legs with $1\frac{1}{2}$-in. brads.

"When all this rough work is done, the real fun starts. I can now carve, which of course is really just taking off the corners and shaping the figure 'the way it should look.'

"Faces are the most fun. I keep the cheek line in mind, and start at the nose. My first cuts give me the result shown in Fig. 1135. Another good guide is the key line from the nostril to the corner of the mouth (Fig. 1136), which controls the expression of the

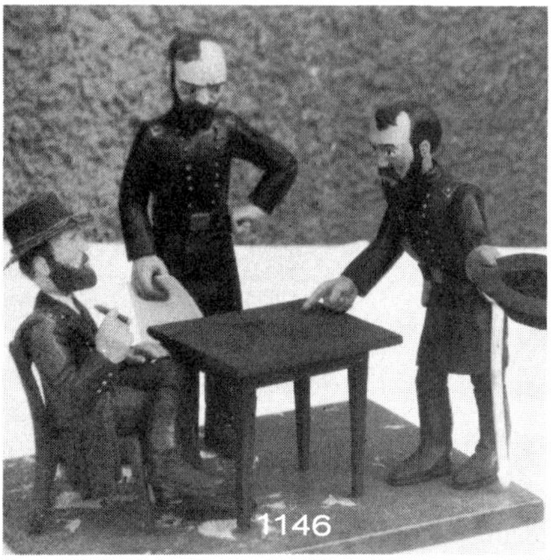

Fig. 1146 · Grant, Meade, and Sheridan at the Wilderness, 1864. Fig. 1147 · Color guard, 30th Infantry, U.S.A., 1936. Fig. 1148 · Sergeant, 1836. Fig. 1149 · Captain, 1836. Fig. 1150 · Volley fire by squad, 1836. Fig. 1151 · Machine gunners at drill, 1936.

figure—giving a grin or a severe look, depending upon how it is placed. Another key line is that under the eye. With these two placed, I can start rounding up the face, for the rest of it sort of falls into place as I carve (Fig. 1137).

"I carve accessories separately—cartridge boxes, rifles, etc. The cap visor I generally make of tin or cardboard because it is so thin, using a pattern like those in Fig. 1138 and setting it into a saw slot as sketched in Fig. 1137. The little tin tabs I bend down a little, so that the visor will slope downward when it is glued in place. Stick that in, and there you are (Fig. 1139)!"

The groups of Figs. 1146 to 1151 show where we are. And I think I can do no better than quote Major Barber's amusing captions, picture by picture. Here they are:

Figure 1146: "Grant, Meade (with papers) and Sheridan. Sheridan knows how to win the war. Grant is amused, Meade cynical. P.S. Sheridan got his request for the cavalry to be detached under him, and defeated and killed Stuart (Wilderness, 1864)."

Figure 1147: "Color Guard, 30th Infantry, U.S.A. (1936). Note: The flags are wood, too, and the whole group was carved with one blade of a jackknife" (clip shape).

Figure 1148: "Sergeant—1836. His chevron is *not* rank, but five years' service. Rank is indicated by his long epaulettes and three buttons on his sleeve instead of two."

Figure 1149: "Captain—1836. Here's the man the Sergeant is saluting, and he is returning the salute."

Figure 1150: "Volley fire by a squad in three ranks" (a drill, 1936). The Sergeant of Fig. 1148 and the Captain of Fig. 1149 go with this group.

Figure 1151: "Machine gunners at drill (1936). The man at the gun (No. 1) must mount and lay (aim) the gun and *load* it in 40 sec. He is about to flunk his test, because No. 3 (with the ammunition boxes) was asleep on the job. The Corporal is saying things. The young Lieutenant, just out of West Point, sees only the stop watch."

1152

Revolution

1153

1812

1154

Mexican War

1155

Civil War

1156

Spanish American

1157

World War

1158

Christmas Carolers

John
Barleycorn
1159

Sairey
Gamp
1160

Old
Charley
1161

Simon, the
Cellarer
1162

Dick
Turpin
1163

Parson
Brown
1164

In case all this has interested you in trying a soldier or two of your own, I have sketched Major Barber's series of figures which depict the changes in the uniform since the Revolutionary War. As far as possible, I have tried to retain the series of facial expressions he gave them also, as well as the details of uniform and equipment.

As an interesting Christmas group, I have sketched the carolers of Fig. 1158, based on those modeled in clay by H. Armstrong Roberts. Here is an excellent opportunity for modeling in wood, soap, or plastic, and developing three decidedly different expressions, as well as working out a heavy, an average, and a light figure.

As suggestions for caricatured expressions, try to locate one of the Royal Doulton character jugs. They represent such famous figures in English history as John Barleycorn (Fig. 1159), Sairey Gamp (Fig. 1160), Old Charley (Fig. 1161), Simon the Cellarer (Fig. 1162), Dick Turpin (Fig. 1163), and Parson Brown (Fig. 1164).

In the days when most citizens could not read, it was advisable for the up-and-coming innkeeper—or indeed for the purveyor of anything—to make his business known by some appropriate sign. America had the wooden Indian and the wooden horse, old English inns had their elaborately shaped signs, and so on. Now, it appears that there is to be some revival of the pictorial sign, or at least so hopes William P. Zegel, Long Island carver, who is producing the signs shown in front of his shop in Fig. 1165. The story is that Mr. Zegel began producing these trade-symbol figures to barter them for meats and groceries. Now the demand has grown to such an extent that Mr. Zegel is faced with a production problem, for he works without the aid of machines, and does a considerable amount of detail shaping of his silhouette figures in addition to the painting. Besides those shown, he has made dogs in other poses, chefs, etc. Don't fail in Fig. 1165 to notice the treed bear and the beauty-shop operator, as well as the old Gloucester fisherman, the hunter and his dog, and the two butchers with chops impending.

FIG. 1165 · *Carved sales figures by William P. Zegel. Meisel from Monkemeyer photo.* FIG. 1166 · *Heroic figures framing a bar doorway in Detroit. Photograph courtesy B. C. Brosheer.* FIG. 1167 · *Carved figure from a signboard showing the way to one of the peaks of the Swiss Alps. Courtesy State Woodcarving School, Brienz, Switzerland.* FIG. 1168 · *Roadside sign in Lenzkirch, Germany.* FIG. 1169 · "*To the Railroad Station,*" *in Warmbrunn, Germany.* FIG. 1170 · "*To Friedrichshain,*" *Island of Sylt, Germany.* FIG. 1171 · "*To the High Woods,*" *a figure of a Pathfinder, German equivalent of the American Boy Scout. Figs. 1168–1171 courtesy German Railroads Information Office.*

In Detroit a year ago, I saw the pair of heroic carved figures of Fig. 1166. Each 7 or 8 ft. high, they flank the entrance to a restaurant and bar, advertising its two leading sales items and exhibiting unusual skill in the execution of the carving detail.

These are at least two American examples of the development of carved signs which visitors remark about so often in Switzerland and Germany. In Switzerland, the carving of these silhouette or cutout signs, slightly modeled, is taught at the State Carving School at Brienz. Figure 1167 is an example of the work done there, and was originally set up to point the way to one of the peaks of the Alps.

In 1908, Privy Councillor Fuellner of Warmbrunn, Germany, suggested that road and other signposts could be made interesting and characteristic. Following his suggestion, these carefully carved signs have appeared in increasing numbers throughout the country. The sign from Lenzkirch, in the Black Forest, is a particularly good example (Fig. 1168). This one points the way to four adjacent towns. (My informant failed to tell me whether or not the two figures on the Neustadt-Bonndorf arm imply any particular reflection on the feminine population of these two towns.) The two hurrying figures of Fig. 1169 are, of course, atop a sign pointing "Zum Bahnhof"—to the station—in Warmbrunn itself.

Most of these signboards come from the Woodcarving Academy at Warmbrunn, where they are carved out of pine 2½ to 3 in. thick, to allow plenty of depth for modeling. The one shown in Fig. 1170, for example, is quite elaborately shaped. It is atop a sign pointing the way to Friedrichshain (Frederick's Grove) near Westerland on the North Sea island of Sylt. Next it, in Fig. 1171, is the figure of the Pathfinder, German equivalent of the American Boy Scout, pointing the way "Nach dem Hochwald" —to the high woods.

I have sketched a number of other similar signs in Figs. 1172 to 1182, and Fig. 1187, including both Swiss and German examples. Figures 1172, 1177, 1179, 1180, 1181, and 1187 are Swiss, Fig. 1181 being elaborately modeled and pointing the way to the

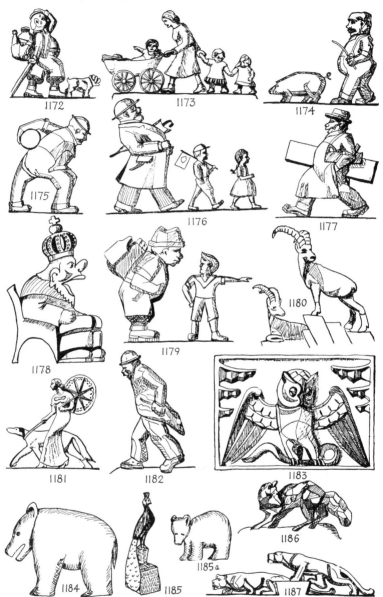

Figs. 1172, 1177, 1179–1181, 1183, and 1187 are Swiss; Figs. 1173–1176, 1178, and 1182 are German, and Figs. 1184–1186 American

public park. Figure 1187, as would be expected, shows the way to the local zoo, as does Fig. 1180.

Among the German group, Fig. 1178 is particularly interesting. This old caricature of a German king appears in a number of forms, sometimes as a silhouette modeled as shown here, some-times as an in-the-round figure. In any case, he makes a most amusing figure upon which to try your skill.

From the Swiss State Woodcarving School at Brienz* also comes the owl plaque of Fig. 1183, quite a modern conception of the owl catching a serpent in a pine forest. Figures 1184 to 1186 are examples of folk carving from the American Southern highlands, and have been previously mentioned.

* Brienz is the center of the Swiss woodcarving industry, started there by Christian Fischer in 1816. The school, established in 1884, became a department of the Industrial Museum, Canton of Berne, in 1928, when Fritz Fruschi was appointed head instructor. Most of the 450 present Brienz carvers were once students there.

Prospective students take a rigid examination for aptitude, for the Canton supports the school. Total tuition for the course is only 50 francs (about $12). First-year work is devoted to *Heimarbeit* (home articles—vases, trays, bowls, etc.). The next two years deal with ornamental sculpture, and the final period (one to two years) with animal and figure sculpture. Even advanced students make replicas of figures carved by an expert, for crea-tive work comes last of all. The town provides a small zoo for original animal subjects.

Throughout the course, students are taught drawing, modeling, portraiture, perspec-tive, and composition. But above all they learn to become imaginative and individualistic, in contrast with the thousands of peasant carvers in the surrounding *Bernese Oberland*, whose work is usually mediocre and commercial, copying endlessly designs handed down from father to son for centuries.

Other instructors there include Albert Buehlmann (for 44 years), Emil Thomann, Hans Huggler-Wyss, Karl Binder, Baumann, Ruef, Staehli, and Paul Huggler. Thomann and his three assistants, one his son, concern themselves solely with religious subjects, usually for Swiss churches (for commercial work is done here too, and best work of advanced students is also sold to aid the Museum). Paul Huggler is the leading representative of the traditional naturalistic school. Hans Huggler-Wyss, the outstanding member of wood-carving's No. 1 family, developed expressionism in 1914—carving in a simplified, expres-sive form. He carves a figure with a few long, flowing lines, in the manner so many of the Brienz carvings show, which brings out the natural beauty of wood so well.

Introduced only about two years ago, the signposts in this style, pictured here, thus far have been sold only to towns or resorts. The same expressionistic technique is being adapted to signs for shops and taverns.

The whole venture reflects Fruschi's philosophy to his 18 present students: "Perhaps you will experience no great financial success, but remain true to your work and it will remain true to you. It will make your life a rich and happy one."

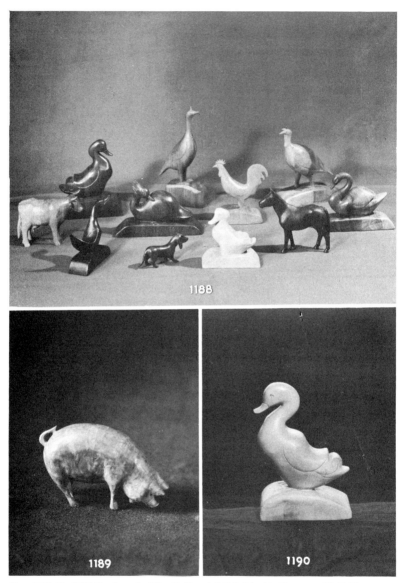

FIGS. 1188–90 · *Whittling from the John C. Campbell Folk School in Brasstown, N. C. Illustration from "Handicrafts of the Southern Highlands," by Allen H. Eaton. By permission of the publisher, The Russell Sage Foundation.*

CHAPTER XVIII

FOLK CARVING II · *Animals, Birds*

MAN'S first carvings were apparently of animals. Where
Danzig now stands, neolithic men carved pieces of amber
into the likenesses of animals four or five thousand years ago. In
the Woldenburg district of Pomerania, Germany, almost as long
ago, some prehistoric man carved a likeness of a horse. And
further south, about 2300 B.C., a Sumerian in Mesopotamia
carved a steer out of bone. Remember, too, that the cave drawings
of Spain and Southern France are of animals.

It is only to be expected that man would thus depict the
animals which he respected and feared—but which provided
food. It is only to be expected also that he would deify them and
make images to them to worship, or even to assure success in the
chase—his major occupation. It is further to be expected that
certain animals would become holy or tabooed, as are the cows of
India today or the swine in Biblical times.

With such a background of tradition, it would be indeed surprising if much of the folk carving of modern man were not of
animals. From the crude images of primitive peoples of Africa
and the South Sea Islands to the most exact and expert carvings
of the most accomplished sculptors is a wide step—but carvings
of animals bridge them.

Many of the whittlers of our Southern highlands have chosen
animal subjects, as Figs. 1127 to 1129 and 1188 to 1191 prove.
They range from the lowly and familiar hog, cow, and cock to the
horse, dachshund, wild turkey, and swan. An especially good
design is the bear of Fig. 1191. Figures 1184 to 1186 in the previous chapter show additional ones. Many are traditional designs
which have been handed down from father to son for generations,
certain designs seeming to run in certain families. W. J. Martin,

〖 257 〗

FIG. 1191 · Bear, carved out of native holly wood by D. L. Millsaps of Damascus, Va. Illustration from "Handicrafts of the Southern Highlands," by Allen H. Eaton. By permission of the publisher, the Russell Sage Foundation. FIG. 1192 · Bison, from a Swiss signpost. Courtesy State Woodcarving School, Brienz, Switzerland, as is Fig. 1194. FIG. 1193 · Skiing dog from the Italian Tyrol. FIG. 1194 · Bear, from a Swiss signpost. FIG. 1195 · Four backwoods American figures carved from white pine. FIG. 1196 · Some Typical Southern carved animals. Courtesy M. K. Cumming.

venerable whittler of the John C. Campbell Folk School in Brass-town, N. C., for example, produces wild turkeys of apple wood—birds that many younger people have never seen but that he has either seen alive or in a carved statuette. Ross Corn sat down and whittled a peacock like one he had seen somewhere 12 years before. D. L. Millsaps of Damascus, Va., specializes in bears—as Fig. 1191 bears eloquent witness. For other examples, turn to Mr. Eaton's book, from which these were taken.

The carvings of Figs. 1188 to 1190, in accordance with Campbell School methods, are sanded smooth and polished, but many carvers, both of this and other lands, prefer the rough, angular finish left by the knife or carving tools. The bison of Fig. 1192 and the bear of Fig. 1194, from the Swiss school at Brienz, are excellent examples of this technique. The suggestions of fur on these figures, produced by simple veiner lines, are particularly worth study, as well as the gouge grooves showing muscle masses on the bison and the simplicity of the posing of both animals. Both are signpost figures pointing the way to the local zoo, thus are low-relief silhouettes. A third animal from the same source, performing the same service, and made by the same technique is the mountain sheep of Fig. 1200.

Common commercial figures vary just as widely in their method of finishing, all showing again the power of tradition. Photographs of three groups from widely varying sources are shown in Figs. 1193, 1195, and 1196. The balky donkey, giraffe, hound dog, and dachshund of Fig. 1195 also show to advantage the rough, angular, knife-cut finish preferred by many whittlers, particularly skilled folk carvers, and produced without the artistic direction that developed the carefully finished pieces of Figs. 1188 to 1190 or the "studied" angular pieces from Switzerland.

The skiing wire-haired terrier of Fig. 1193 comes from the Italian Tyrol, and incidentally shows an interesting small-gouge roughening of the coat to simulate the wirehair's clipped fur. Like the backwoods American figures of Fig. 1195, the dog is finished by shellacking, providing a shine which may make dusting

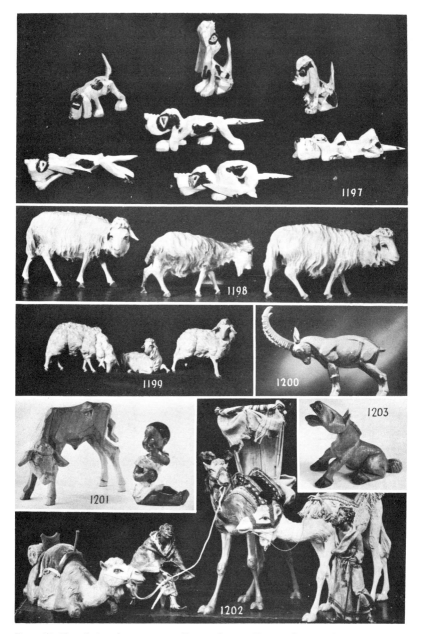

FIG. 1197 · *Hugo the hound, in seven poses.* FIGS. 1198, 1199 · *Five carved sheep and a goat, part of the crèche at The Children's Library, Westbury, N. Y. Courtesy Jacqueline Overton.* FIG. 1200 · *Bighorn sheep, from a Swiss signpost. Courtesy State Woodcarving School, Brienz, Switzerland.* FIG. 1201 · *Boy and calf. By Georg Lang of Oberammergau.* FIG. 1202 · *Camel caravan. Figs. 1201, 1202 courtesy German Railroads Information Office.* FIG. 1203 · *Conventionalized horse, in white pine.*

easier but certainly doesn't help to bring out the texture of the wood of which he is carved. Because he is a commercial figure, too, the skis and the ski poles are made separately and glued on, a process which makes the gorge of any law-abiding whittler rise.

Figure 1196 shows a wide variety of Southern animal figures, made principally from local fruit woods, many undoubtedly from some of the sources previously mentioned. They introduce several animal figures not previously shown, however, the Airedale, rabbit, pelican, fawn, goose, and squirrel, as well as several different poses of burros and hogs.

From Oberammergau come the sheep and the goat of Figs. 1198 and 1199, showing to advantage the detailed technique of these skilled carvers. Compare their naturalistic carving with the stylized bighorn sheep of Fig. 1200, or the blocky conventionalizing on the horse in Fig. 1203. The latter, incidentally, I whittled from white pine in order to show grain lines after finishing by simple oiling and waxing. The original was an Italian Tyrol carving. Round up his contours and he can be made very successfully in soap or plastic.

Also from Oberammergau come the bull calf and child of Fig. 1201 and the caravan of Fig. 1202. The latter is unusual as an Oberammergau piece in being finished with fabric bridles and saddles on the camels, as well as robes on the camel driver and supplicating slave. The pieces do, however, show the careful attention to detail and excellent treatment of surface representation that characterize the carvings of Georg Lang.

I have left until now any mention of Fig. 1197, because it is my intention to explain the making of this particular dog in detail, as illustrative of the methods used in producing any of the other pieces. Hugo is just a long, lanky "houn' dawg," but he's quite particular of his poses—in fact has each one named separately. Along the top line, from left to right, are "Snuffing," "Baying," and "Huh?" In the center is "Stuck Up," and along the lower line, "On His Way," "Hurryin'," and "Snoozing," again from left to right. Through the courtesy of *Popular Mechanics*, I have been permitted to reproduce here both the illustrations and data

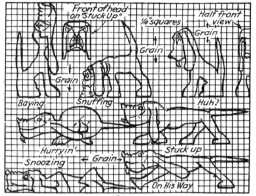

1204

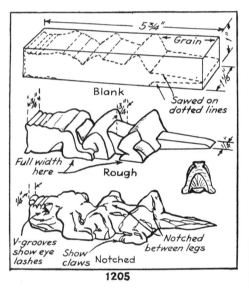

1205

1206

FIG. 1204 · Patterns for the seven poses of Hugo the hound, Fig. 1197, with details of head, grain direction, etc. Copy these on block, square by square, to any desired size. FIG. 1205 · The three major steps in making "Snoozing." Block is 1⅛ in. thick. Final notching after rough shaping should be done "crudely" to give angular effect. FIG. 1206 · Same series of steps in making "Snuffing" pose. The blank is sawed out with a fine-tooth fretsaw or bandsaw, then shaped as shown.

on Hugo. To retain the flavor of the original, I'm reproducing it here just as I originally wrote it, except for necessary changes and deletions.

Hugo is produced in all seven acts with just a pocketknife and some pieces of straight-grained white pine. He's finished with a few careful daubs of brown or black paint. In Fig. 1197 he's posing for you, and doing it very casually and creditably, as you see, but there are several details that he's fussy about. Notice, for example, his wrinkled nose, a personal characteristic that he is probably rather jealous of because it shows up in all his poses. Hugo's body is angular, very much so, and being a good model, he takes pains to emphasize it. In doing this he's really trying his best to make it easy for you to carve his profile, because rough cutting of a sawed profile block gives just the body characteristics needed. Hugo has huge feet, and what's more—he's proud of them. You won't have to look far in the details to see that. Another reason Hugo has posed specially for his pictures is to show you that his tail is just as much a part of his personality as is his wrinkled nose.

Now, as you see in Figs. 1204, 1205, and 1207, all the poses are just variations, the variables being the ear position and general body shape. Whittle any one from 1⅛-in. straight-grained white pine or basswood. Just see that Hugo's tail points in the direction of the grain. Starting with Fig. 1205, draw ¼-in. squares on one flat face of the block, and transfer the pattern for the desired Hugo pose from Fig. 1204, square by square. Saw out the blank on the dotted lines in Fig. 1204 to get the profile. Then just follow through the three steps sketched in Fig. 1205.

Any other pose can be done in the same way. "Hurryin'," "Stuck Up," and "On His Way" are not sketched in body detail because they are so similar to the others. However, Fig. 1208 shows the arrangement of the feet on "Hurryin'," the foot arrangement on "Stuck Up," and details of the face. Note that here, as on "Snoozing" in Fig. 1205, the eye is not a complete diamond, but just a straight line at the base of the flat surface on which the eye is carved.

〚 263 〛

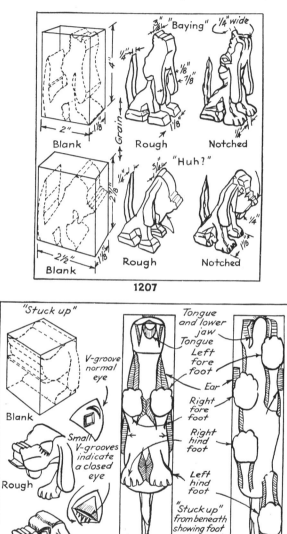

1207

1208

FIG. 1207 · *The three steps in making the "Baying" and "Huh?" poses. Notice extended tongue in both cases, details of nostrils and nose wrinkles, and rough notching of square corners on legs, back, and tail. Grain in each case runs in direction of tail.* FIG. 1208 · *Details of special elements in three Hugo poses. At left is the method of carving the "Stuck Up" head; in the center the arrangement of the feet and legs on "Hurryin'," and at right a similar view of the foot arrangement on "Stuck Up."*

As shown in the details, particularly in Fig. 1206, the full width of the block is always used for Hugo's huge feet. The body should be between ¾ and ⅞ in. thick, the head ¾ in., which allows ⅟₁₆ in. on each side for the ears to project from the head. Thin the neck down to ⅜ in. or even a little less to make Hugo's head appear larger. Cut large V notches to break up the flat surfaces and indicate the joints—don't use small notches because they'll make Hugo look like he has a shaggy coat. And don't smooth the edges; whittle them crudely (which is harder than it sounds), and leave them that way. Notches also indicate Hugo's claws and his wrinkled nose.

Paint on Hugo's spots or not, as you will—then use him for a desk, mantel, knickknack corner, coffee table, dresser, or other ornament, as a book-end element, or for any of the dozens of other uses which may occur to you. If you want Hugo bigger, choose a larger block and make your original squares larger— ½-in. squares make Hugo twice as big (and ⅛ in. squares half as big—if you dare). And if you want to polish him, use mahogany, walnut, or maple instead of pine. But in any case, don't sandpaper Hugo—you'll round off all his character.

That'll do for Hugo. With the same general set of instructions, you can make any of the animals of Fig. 1195, varying the pose similarly if you wish. And of course the instructions for copying the patterns by using enlarging grills or checkerboards apply equally well to any of the animals here shown or to anything in any other chapter of the book. And, what's more, the others will do any of the jobs suggested above for Hugo.

Each year, I'm surprised all over again when the prize winners of the Annual Soap Sculpture Competition are announced. Entries vary from the simplest pieces to the most elaborate bits of sculpture, many being worthy of reproduction in some enduring material (I understand that one is selected each year for reproduction in pottery). A number of the prize winners have been pictured in appropriate places throughout this book, and in Figs. 1209 to 1231 are 23 more, all small subjects, but each so well done that it is deserving of an individual figure number.

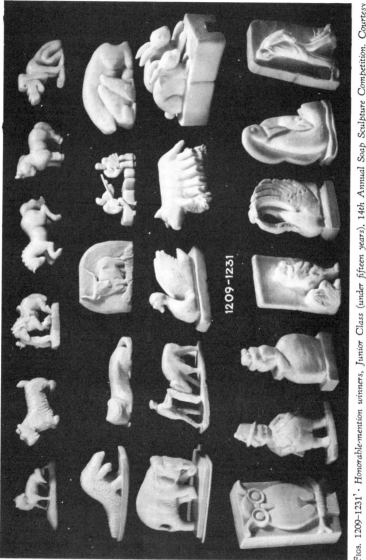

1209-1231

FIGS. 1209–1231[1]. Honorable-mention winners, Junior Class (under fifteen years), 14th Annual Soap Sculpture Competition. Courtesy National Soap Sculpture Committee.

This entire group won honorable mention in the Fourteenth Annual Competition in the Junior Class, for each was made by a child under fifteen years of age! If children of that age can produce such unusual pieces in soap, certainly we older ones can produce their equivalent, in soap, wood, plastics, or even ivory.

Here, too, is certainly a wide enough variety to meet almost any need. Subjects range from the conventionalized owl at lower left to the naturalistic boy next him, with foxes, horses, cow-punchers, dogs, cats, steers, bears, elephants, swans, bullfighters, pigs, rabbits, and a French peasant figure thrown in.

Should your journeys happen to take you to the vicinity of Warren, N.H., be certain to visit the Morse Museum there for carving ideas. Mrs. Ira Morse has an unusual collection of carved African figures in wood and ivory, as well as exceptionally fine East Indian ivory carvings. The prizes of her safaris, however, are her *mwikos*, the little tribal totems formerly made and worshiped by East African tribes. They are excellent naturalizations of African animals, carved in a wide variety of woods. Members of a family or tribe formerly forswore the meat of their own *mwiko* or totem animal. Intermarriage of families, with consequent prohibition of an increasing number of meats, finally forced the breakdown of the system, but the *mwikos* themselves remain—in Mrs. Morse's collection.

Figs. 1232–1234 (Right) · Two poses of Neanderthal man and one of Cro-Magnon man, the first artist. Fig. 1235 (Far right) · Elotheres. Figs. 1236–1237 · Primitive elephant with young. Fig. 1238 · Mastodon. Fig. 1239 (Lower left) · Trachodon, the duck-billed dinosaur. Fig. 1240 (Bottom) · Triceratops, a harmless herbivore. Fig. 1241 (Center) · Diplodocus, one of the family of largest dinosaurs, the sauropods. Fig. 1242 (Far right) · Pteranodon, one of the later forms of pterodactyl. Fig. 1243 (Lower right) · Stegosaurus, strange and fierce looking, but a herbivore. All carved to scale from ivory by Japanese craftsmen for the Harrington Collection. Photographs courtesy Department of Geology, Princeton University.

1232–1243

CHAPTER XIX

ANIMALS AND BIRDS · *Naturalistic*

STRICTLY speaking, the subjects of the first 30 figures in this chapter are neither animals nor birds, but their ancestors. However, they are such excellent examples of carving in ivory—and to scale at that—that they belong in any compilation of modern examples.

All are specimens from the George Harrington collection of 67 ivory models carved by Japanese craftsmen to a scale of 1 to 96. They are now on loan to the Geology Department of Princeton University, from which Mr. Harrington was graduated in 1939. Executed over a period of years to scale drawings which Mr. Harrington collected, they were paid for from his annual birthday and Christmas presents.

Actual size of the carvings is about two-thirds that shown. Each is tremendously detailed, including not only the general outlines and anatomical details of the subject, but also the markings and folds of the skin. All the carvings shown except the diplodocus of Fig. 1241 are single-piece; the diplodocus is in three parts, head and neck, body and legs, and tail.

On the facing page, the upper three figures are early human beings, apparently two Neanderthal men and one Cro-Magnon. The latter eventually overcame and succeeded his predecessor. Neanderthal man, living from 20,000 to 40,000 years ago, had crude weapons; Cro-Magnon man had much finer ones, some in fact being tools with which he did the first carving. He is also responsible for the first cave paintings. In general, he was quite similar to ourselves in height and build; while the Neanderthal man was shorter (largely because of short lower limbs) and stockier, averaging about 5 ft. 4 in. high.

Undoubtedly, primitive man would have been scared to death by some of the prehistoric animals shown with him here, but fortunately most of them preceded him by a good many hundreds of thousands of years. The dinosaurs, which were the really big reptiles inhabiting the earth in the Mesozoic epoch, were gone millions of years before man entered the scene. Let's just pause for a moment to sketch prehistoric times so that we can identify these specimens. Dinosaurs first appeared during the Triassic period, then grew progressively larger through the Jurassic and Cretaceous. With the close of the Mesozoic epoch, which included these three periods, the dinosaurs died out, and the ancestors of our familiar modern animals appeared, developing progressively through the Oligocene, Miocene, Pliocene, Pleistocene, and recent periods of the Cenozoic epoch. Just for example, man didn't even begin to evolve until the Pleistocene period. For a detailed picture of this development, see *Before the Dawn of History*, by Charles R. Knight (Whittlesey House, 1935).

Now to our ivory carvings and their identification. Figure 1235 is an elothere, of the Miocene period, a curious, somewhat piglike, formidable creature which has no direct descendants. Figures 1236 and 1237 are primitive elephants; Fig. 1238 is the American mastodon, whose curious tusk formation is not duplicated in any African or Indian form.

The remaining specimens pictured in the group are from the far earlier Jurassic and Cretaceous periods. The trachodont of Fig. 1239 is a duck-billed, wading dinosaur of the Cretaceous period. Like the triceratops of Fig. 1240, it was herbivorous. The triple horns and neck plates of the latter were only for protection. Just above him, in Fig. 1241, is a diplodocus, one of the larger dinosaurs, which grew as much as 60 to 70 ft. long. Behind the diplodocus is the stegosaurus in Fig. 1242, strangest of the dinosaurs and an exclusively American reptile. Apparently his alternated scales and other armaments were only for defense, too, because he was an herbivore. Above him, in Fig. 1242, is one of the later forms of pterodactyl, those bird ancestors that varied from the size of a sparrow to a 20-ft. wingspread. They had three-clawed fingers at the "wrist joint," and a wing membrane over the "fingers." It is this whole group that inspired several recent oil-company advertising campaigns, which, as I recall, included stirring pictures of battles between these harmless and stupid noncarnivorous Jurassic and Cretaceous reptiles! In the first place, they were too quiet and peace-loving to fight, and in the second, they lived hundreds of thousands of years apart.

It is rather difficult to point out individual members of the next group, although some are worth identification. At the top (Figs. 1244-1250) is a protoceratops family, this being the dinosaur most noted because it laid the dinosaur eggs which created such a stir a few years ago. An inhabitant of what is now the Gobi Desert, it grew to 6 or 8 ft. in length during the Cretaceous period—so those dinosaur eggs were some millions of years old!

The peculiar animal to the left and below protoceratops is the titanothere, of the Oligocene period, a huge animal standing almost 8 ft. at the shoulder (Fig. 1251). At his right is an ancestor of the hippopotamus, of about the same period. Below and to the left is smilodon, the saber-toothed tiger (Fig. 1253), which was a terror to early man as well as to many of the slower and larger mammals of his period. The next two represent forms with which I am not familiar, although Fig. 1254 appears to be an ancestor of the camel or llama and Fig. 1255 an ancestor of the elephant or tapir. Figure 1256 is the 5-ft. 4-in. Neanderthal man for scale, standing next to a prehistoric four-horned deer (Fig. 1257).

In the left-hand corner are Figs. 1258 (megathere, the giant ground sloth), and Fig. 1259 (glyptodont, the early armadillo). These two roamed North and South America in comparatively recent times, probably some of the most peculiar creatures seen by primitive man, and the latter, at least, so encased in horny armor that he was well protected even against the saber-toothed tiger.

At their right, in Fig. 1260, is the moropus, huge herbivore, which is a misfit judged by any standards. It had long, powerful forelimbs and feet armed with huge, curved, fairly blunt claws, the latter apparently not of the least use. Like elothere, moropus is of the Miocene period.

Figs. 1244–1260 · *Further ivory carvings from the Harrington Collection, Department of Geology, Princeton University. Reproduced with permission.*

So much for the reptiles and primitive mammals. Let us now jump, for the sake of contrast, to something quite modern, and stylized at that. I refer to the hen of Fig. 1261 and the polar bear of Fig. 1265, neither a woodcarving by any means, but both offering suggestions in ways of stylizing familiar birds and animals. The hen is in gray marble, the polar bear in white, and both were sculptured by modern French artists.

The Swiss State Woodcarving School at Brienz, examples from which have been shown in several preceding chapters, partic-ularly in Chap. XVIII, is the source of three more naturalistic poses in Figs. 1262, 1263, and 1266. The life and action of the horse group are particularly noteworthy, as is the treatment of nostrils and manes. The bighorn sheep of Fig. 1263 is a more static pose, but with plenty of apparent power and life. Compare the treatment of muscle bulges on the sheep with those of the horses of Fig. 1262 or the cows of Fig. 1266. The latter is a partic-ularly reposeful group, coming nearer to that famous American phrase about "contented cows" than anything I have previously seen. Here is a different form of surface finish also—completely covered with small flat gouge or firmer marks which make it undeniably a thing of wood, yet preserve every detail of the animals themselves.

Several quite professional animal carvings were submitted in the most recent soap-sculpture competitions. Examples are shown in Figs. 1264 and 1267 to 1270. The "Elephant Pyramid" of Fig. 1264, won third prize in the Advanced Amateur Class of the Fourteenth Annual Soap Sculpture Competition (1938). Carved by Harry F. May of Tacoma, Wash., it is a decidedly imaginative pose.

The mouse on the cheese in Fig. 1267, won a $75 prize in the Thirteenth Annual Competition the preceding year. Carved by Elizabeth Anne Philbrick of Winchester, Mass., it shows careful study of mouse habits and combination of this with an unusual, but very appropriate, pedestal and an imaginative idea.

Excellent stylizing of an old fable is the "Hare and Tortoise" of Fig. 1268, second prize winner, Senior Class, in the Fourteenth

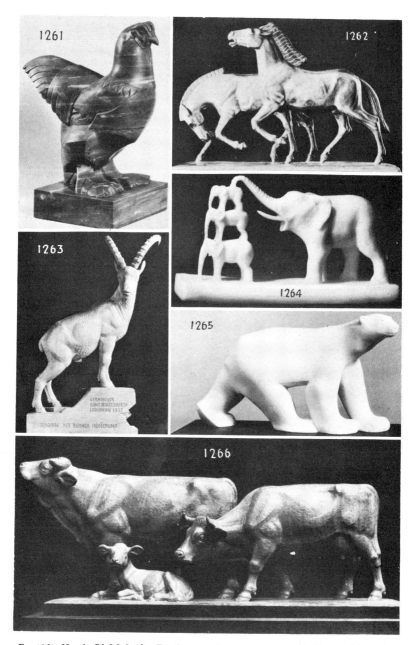

FIG. 1261 · Hen, by Ed. M. Sandoz. French, twentieth century, in gray marble. Courtesy Metropolitan Museum of Art. FIG. 1262 · Equine group. Courtesy State Woodcarving School, Brienz, Switzerland. FIG. 1263 · Bighorn sheep, also carved at Brienz. FIG. 1264 · "Elephant Pyramid," carved in soap by Harry F. May, Tacoma, Wash., and third-prize winner, Advanced Amateur Class, 14th Annual Soap Sculpture Competition. Courtesy National Soap Sculpture Committee. FIG. 1265 · Polar bear, in white marble, by Francois Pompon, modern French. Courtesy Metropolitan Museum of Art. FIG. 1266 · Bovine family, carved at Brienz.

Competition. Compare the streamlined suggestion of speed by the designing of the hare, and the slower, more plodding aspect of the rounded and more conventional tortoise.

Close observation of animal habits is again the answer in the steer carving of Fig. 1269. This figure of the animal, back to "The Blizzard," won young Betty Keeran of Goodland, Kans., first prize in the Junior Group, 1937 competition. Her highly naturalistic rendering compares with the stylized treatment of the "Grotesque Elephant" of Fig. 1270, second prize winner in the Advanced Amateur group, of the same competition.

Enough of soap and ivory carving. Figures 1271 and 1272 show two excellent figures, the first a stylized foal whittled from white pine and one of a series of recent poses emanating from Maine and French Canada, and the second a spaniel whittled from a similar wood, and chiefly noteworthy for the realistic appearance of its coat produced by continuous notching of the surface. Pose and proportions are quite naturalistic. If you wish to try either of these figures, the side views are sketched in Figs. 1274 and 1279. Because the foal's head is turned at 90 degrees to the side, I have sketched a side view of the head in Fig. 1280.

This matter of surface treatment is an important one, for by proper handling of the surface you can give both a distinctive and a natural appearance to the carving—or either alone, as desired. In the endeavor to show comparisons, I have sketched several typical treatments in Figs. 1274, 1279, 1282, 1284, and 1289. The first is the allover notching just referred to, an excellent way to show the coat of a long-haired dog or other animal, provided the axis of the notch runs in the same direction as the length of the hair.

Figure 1279 shows conventional angular finish of a whittled piece, with strong planes and sharp angles unsoftened with sandpaper. Contrast it with the rounded and smoothed figure of Fig. 1289—then make your own choice. Figure 1282 is sketched from a plaque carved at the Swiss School at Brienz. Here the texture of the sheep's wool is simulated by a series of small circles cut side by side into the "woolly" part of the coat. Figure

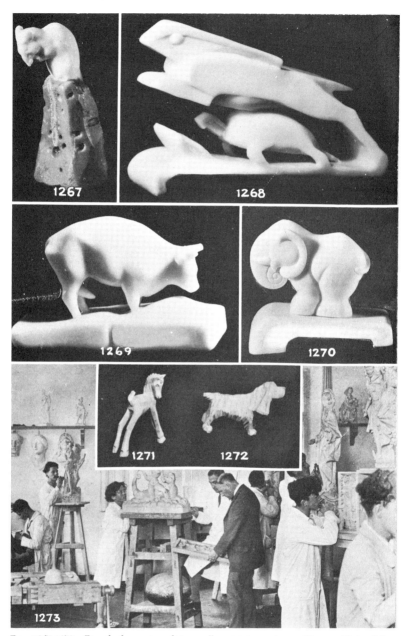

FIGS. 1267–1270 · *Four further soap sculptures, all contest-prize winners. Courtesy National Soap Sculpture Committee.* FIG. 1267 · *"The Connoisseur," by Elizabeth Anne Philbrick, Winchester, Mass.* FIG. 1268 · *"Hare and Tortoise," by Yukio Taskiro, Santa Maria, Calif.* FIG. 1269 · *"The Blizzard," by Betty Keeran, Goodland, Kans.* FIG. 1270 · *"Grotesque Elephant," by Tom Stevens, Los Angeles, Calif.* FIG. 1271 · *Foal, in white pine. (See Figs. 1279–1280.)* FIG. 1272 · *Spaniel. (See Fig. 1274.)* FIG. 1273 · *A typical wood-sculpture studio, this one in the State Woodcarving School, Oberammergau Germany. Courtesy German Railroads Information Office.*

1284, taken from a clay sculpture of a zebra by Kurt Schwerdfeger, shows a method of simulating zebra stripes which can be adapted quite readily to woodcarving. He has simply channeled out the stripes by making parallel grooves. This can be done in wood with a fairly wide, fairly flat gouge. Channels or flutes which conform to the lines and actual striping of the animal's body will give a very effective finish.

I also mentioned previously the small gouge marks which serve to give an interesting roughness to the coats of the cows in the Swiss study of Fig. 1266. A number of other treatments were shown in Chap. XVIII, probably most outstanding of which were the deeper gouge marks which D. L. Millsaps worked into the surface of the bear of Fig. 1191. The skiing terrier of Fig. 1193 shows a surface finished with gouge marks somewhat between these two examples in depth. Some indication of what can be done to suggest surfaces of the subject with just a few simple lines is shown in the bear of Fig. 1194, the bison of Fig. 1192, and the bighorn sheep of Fig. 1200, all from the Swiss School at Brienz. An American example is the drake of Fig. 1190, in which two veiner lines adequately delineate the lines of the wing and tail feathers.

As of possible assistance in your carving of animals, I have sketched several recent dog-show prize winners, Fig. 1275 being a Dalmatian, Fig. 1276 a Scotch terrier, and Fig. 1277 a Sealyham. Any of them is simple to blank out and make from these sketches, and you can adapt the surface to suit yourself.

The horse of Fig. 1278 is an alternate for that of Fig. 1279, the first being of the stocky workhorse-colt variety so popular in Czecho-Slovak (that was) pottery. The camel of Fig. 1281, in addition to its simple stylizing of head and body detail, is also of interest for another reason. It is by far the oldest carving of any shown in this chapter, being of stone, in heroic size, and placed on the road to the tomb of Emperor Yung Lo, north of Peiping. Though 500 years old, it would do credit to some of our modern stylists.

1274

1275

1276

1277

1280

1278

1279

1281

1283

1282

1284

1285

1286

1287

1288

1289

The birds and animals of Figs. 1283 and 1285 to 1289 are like-wise in stone, but I think of decided value to woodcarvers because of their simplicity and ready adaptability to wood. All come from the Levi L. Barbour memorial fountain in Detroit, and were sculptured by Marshall Fredericks, instructor in model-ing at the Cranbrook Academy of Art. Figure 1283 is a grouse, Fig. 1285 a rabbit, Figs. 1286 and 1287 a hawk, and Fig. 1288 an otter. These figures, in black granite, surround the figure of the gazelle (Fig. 1289) done in green bronze. It is interesting to note that Mr. Fredericks had a very definite plan in selecting these particular animals for his composition. Belle Isle Park, in which it is placed, is thronged by children, who can understand a subject like this as well as a grownup. The four subordinate figures include two birds and two animals, two predatory and two non-predatory, but all show the grace and beauty of animals native to the territory. The leaping gazelle is caught in its most signifi-cant movement. The whole composition teaches another valuable lesson quickly and easily—adapt your subject to those who must understand it.

A blocky stylized figure, originally in white Italian marble, is "Porky the Pig," Figs. 1290 to 1298, which I have included here as a final example to show how any figure may be copied. This figure is adaptable to a wide variety of materials, including wood, soap, plastics, ivory, or soft stone. White pine or basswood is, of course, easiest to carve, but mahogany, walnut, or similar harder woods will take a better oiled and waxed finish.

Porky is sawed from a block $1\frac{3}{4}$ by 2 by 4 in., with the grain running the long way. Outline his legs with the tip of the knife blade, and whittle the wood away around them $\frac{3}{16}$ in. deep, except for the cheek, which is only $\frac{1}{8}$ in. Now lay out the back "hump." Note that it tapers both above and under his belly from tail to nose. Then roughshape the face and ears and deepen the notches at Porky's joints, rounding all sharp lines—particularly if you use soap or plastics instead of wood. Accent the ears by a groove all around in front and at the side. Porky's eyes are half cones in a little hollow, his nostrils drilled holes (see Fig. 1296).

[279]

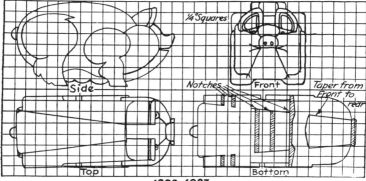

1290-1293

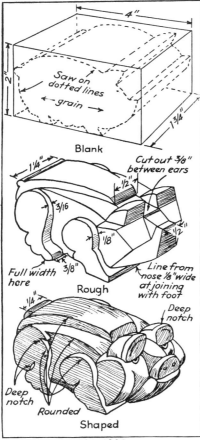

Blank

Saw on dotted lines

grain

4"

2"

1 3/4"

Rough

1 1/4"

Cutout 3/8" between ears

1/2"

3/16

1/8"

1/2"

1"

Full width here

3/8"

Line from nose 1/8" wide at joining with foot

Shaped

1/4"

Deep notch

Deep notch

Rounded

1294-1296

1297

1298

Figs. 1290–1293 · The four sides of Porky the Pig. He requires a $1\frac{3}{4} \times 2 \times 4$-in. block. Figs. 1294–1296 · Steps in carving Porky. Note dimensions of indentations on the "rough." Figs. 1297 and 1298 · Porky in soap and in fir, oiled and waxed.

HOW TO ENLARGE A DESIGN

THE simplest method of enlarging any design or pattern given in preceding chapters is by means of the "checkerboard," or copying grill. It was extensively used in *Whittling and Wood-carving*, but I have avoided it in this text because of the added confusion of the grill lines over a detailed drawing.

To begin with, almost all the drawings here reproduced were twice their present size as originally sketched, so let us assume that you wish to return the drawing to its original size. Draw a grill or checkerboard of $\frac{1}{8}$-in. squares on tracing paper (or other paper that you can see through), place it on the drawing in the text, and trace the principal lines and outlines. Then on another sheet, or on the wood itself, draw a similar grill of $\frac{1}{4}$-in. squares, and on it repeat the smaller drawing, square for square. That's all there is to it as you can see from Figs. 1290 to 1293 at left.

To enlarge in any other proportion—for example, to fit a given space or a given block—divide the area into the same num-ber of squares horizontally and vertically as you have in your base drawing, making squares of a size necessary to accomplish this. Then trace as before. To a very limited extent, a drawing may be lengthened or widened by making a grill of oblongs instead of squares.

Of course, the simplest way to enlarge or to reduce any sketch or photograph you plan to copy is to photostat it, if there is a photostating laboratory near by. A clear photostat will give you practically all the detail of the original and in the exact size you require.

Proportioning dividers are helpful in checking during the progress of carving from a model or sketch of different size.

BIBLIOGRAPHY

These books will be found sources of more detailed information in the subjects beneath which they are listed.

Ornament and Design

Speltz, Alexander. *Styles of Ornament*. Bruno Hessling G. M. b. H., Berlin, 1904. (Now available in a newer, English edition.) Dover

Meyer, Franz Sales. *Handbook of Ornament*. 1888. (Originally *Ornamentas Formenlehre*, a folio of ornamental forms.) Dover

The Acanthus Motive in Decoration. Metropolitan Museum of Art, New York, 1934.

Gothic Woodcarving

Howard, F. E. and Crossley, F. H. *English Church Woodwork*. B. T. Batsford, Ltd., London, 1917.

Oettinger, Karl. *Altdeutsche Bildschnitzer der Ostmark (Old German Woodcarvers of Austria)*. Verlag Anton Schroll & Co., Vienna. 104 full-page photographs.

During 1939, several German publishers published inexpensive, pocket-size, paper-bound pamphlets of photographs of the work of great German artists. Those on woodcarvers are:

Gerstenberg, Kurt. *Riemenschneider im Taubertal*. Infel-Verlag, Leipzig, 1939. 47 photographs.

Von Lorck, Dr. Carl. *Tilman Riemenschneider*. Kanter-Verlag, Königsberg, 1939. 60 photographs.

Von Reitzenstein, A. *Das Meisterwerk—Riemenschneider*. Gustav Weise Verlag, Berlin, 1939. 20 photographs.

———, *Das Meisterwerk—Veit Stoss*. Gustav Weise Verlag, Berlin, 1939. 20 photographs.

Mountain Carving

Eaton, Allen H. *Handicrafts of the Southern Highlands*. Russell Sage Foundation, New York, 1937.

Handicrafts of the Tyrol. In three volumes, extensively illustrated in color. Printed in German.

[282]

BIBLIOGRAPHY

Human Figure

Vanderpoel, John H. *The Human Figure*. Bridgman Publishers, Inc., Pelham, N. Y., 1935. Dover

Perard, Victor. *Anatomy and Drawing*. Victor Perard, New York.

Portraiture

Brinckmann, A. E. *Annie Höfken-Hempel—Das Werk der Bildhauerin*. Atlantis-Verlag, Berlin and Zurich, 1937. 24 full-page photographs of this contemporary's portrait heads of Germany's great.

Racial Characteristics

Hoffman, Malvina. *Heads and Tales*. Charles Scribner's Sons, New York.

Handbook to the Ethnographical Collections, 2d ed. Printed by the British Museum, 1925. 293 illustrations and 20 plates.

Various booklets and postcard sets of the Field Museum of Natural History, Chicago.

Furniture Carving Motifs

DeBles, Arthur. *Genuine Antique Furniture*. Garden City Publishing Company, Garden City, N. Y., 1929.

Cescinsky, Herbert and Hunter, George Leland. *English and American Furniture*. Garden City Publishing Company, Garden City, N. Y.

INDEX

A CATALOGUE OF SELECTED DOVER BOOKS
IN ALL FIELDS OF INTEREST

A CATALOGUE OF SELECTED DOVER BOOKS
IN ALL FIELDS OF INTEREST

AMERICA'S OLD MASTERS, James T. Flexner. Four men emerged unexpectedly from provincial 18th century America to leadership in European art: Benjamin West, J. S. Copley, C. R. Peale, Gilbert Stuart. Brilliant coverage of lives and contributions. Revised, 1967 edition. 69 plates. 365pp. of text.

21806-6 Paperbound $3.00

FIRST FLOWERS OF OUR WILDERNESS: AMERICAN PAINTING, THE COLONIAL PERIOD, James T. Flexner. Painters, and regional painting traditions from earliest Colonial times up to the emergence of Copley, West and Peale Sr., Foster, Gustavus Hesselius, Feke, John Smibert and many anonymous painters in the primitive manner. Engaging presentation, with 162 illustrations. xxii + 368pp.

22180-6 Paperbound $3.50

THE LIGHT OF DISTANT SKIES: AMERICAN PAINTING, 1760-1835, James T. Flexner. The great generation of early American painters goes to Europe to learn and to teach: West, Copley, Gilbert Stuart and others. Allston, Trumbull, Morse; also contemporary American painters—primitives, derivatives, academics—who remained in America. 102 illustrations. xiii + 306pp. 22179-2 Paperbound $3.00

A HISTORY OF THE RISE AND PROGRESS OF THE ARTS OF DESIGN IN THE UNITED STATES, William Dunlap. Much the richest mine of information on early American painters, sculptors, architects, engravers, miniaturists, etc. The only source of information for scores of artists, the major primary source for many others. Unabridged reprint of rare original 1834 edition, with new introduction by James T. Flexner, and 394 new illustrations. Edited by Rita Weiss. 6⅝ x 9⅝.

21695-0, 21696-9, 21697-7 Three volumes, Paperbound $13.50

EPOCHS OF CHINESE AND JAPANESE ART, Ernest F. Fenollosa. From primitive Chinese art to the 20th century, thorough history, explanation of every important art period and form, including Japanese woodcuts; main stress on China and Japan, but Tibet, Korea also included. Still unexcelled for its detailed, rich coverage of cultural background, aesthetic elements, diffusion studies, particularly of the historical period. 2nd, 1913 edition. 242 illustrations. lii + 439pp. of text.

20364-6, 20365-4 Two volumes, Paperbound $6.00

THE GENTLE ART OF MAKING ENEMIES, James A. M. Whistler. Greatest wit of his day deflates Oscar Wilde, Ruskin, Swinburne; strikes back at inane critics, exhibitions, art journalism; aesthetics of impressionist revolution in most striking form. Highly readable classic by great painter. Reproduction of edition designed by Whistler. Introduction by Alfred Werner. xxxvi + 334pp.

21875-9 Paperbound $2.50

THE ARCHITECTURE OF COUNTRY HOUSES, Andrew J. Downing. Together with Vaux's *Villas and Cottages* this is the basic book for Hudson River Gothic architecture of the middle Victorian period. Full, sound discussions of general aspects of housing, architecture, style, decoration, furnishing, together with scores of detailed house plans, illustrations of specific buildings, accompanied by full text. Perhaps the most influential single American architectural book. 1850 edition. Introduction by J. Stewart Johnson. 321 figures, 34 architectural designs. xvi + 560pp.

22003-6 Paperbound $4.00

LOST EXAMPLES OF COLONIAL ARCHITECTURE, John Mead Howells. Full-page photographs of buildings that have disappeared or been so altered as to be denatured, including many designed by major early American architects. 245 plates. xvii + 248pp. 7⅞ x 10¾. 21143-6 Paperbound $3.50

DOMESTIC ARCHITECTURE OF THE AMERICAN COLONIES AND OF THE EARLY REPUBLIC, Fiske Kimball. Foremost architect and restorer of Williamsburg and Monticello covers nearly 200 homes between 1620-1825. Architectural details, construction, style features, special fixtures, floor plans, etc. Generally considered finest work in its area. 219 illustrations of houses, doorways, windows, capital mantels. xx + 314pp. 7⅞ x 10¾. 21743-4 Paperbound $4.00

EARLY AMERICAN ROOMS: 1650-1858, edited by Russell Hawes Kettell. Tour of 12 rooms, each representative of a different era in American history and each furnished, decorated, designed and occupied in the style of the era. 72 plans and elevations, 8-page color section, etc., show fabrics, wall papers, arrangements, etc. Full descriptive text. xvii + 200pp. of text. 8⅜ x 11¼.

21633-0 Paperbound $5.00

THE FITZWILLIAM VIRGINAL BOOK, edited by J. Fuller Maitland and W. B. Squire. Full modern printing of famous early 17th-century ms. volume of 300 works by Morley, Byrd, Bull, Gibbons, etc. For piano or other modern keyboard instrument; easy to read format. xxxvi + 938pp. 8⅜ x 11.

21068-5, 21069-3 Two volumes, Paperbound $10.00

KEYBOARD MUSIC, Johann Sebastian Bach. Bach Gesellschaft edition. A rich selection of Bach's masterpieces for the harpsichord: the six English Suites, six French Suites, the six Partitas (Clavierübung part I), the Goldberg Variations (Clavierübung part IV), the fifteen Two-Part Inventions and the fifteen Three-Part Sinfonias. Clearly reproduced on large sheets with ample margins; eminently playable. vi + 312pp. 8⅛ x 11. 22360-4 Paperbound $5.00

THE MUSIC OF BACH: AN INTRODUCTION, Charles Sanford Terry. A fine, non-technical introduction to Bach's music, both instrumental and vocal. Covers organ music, chamber music, passion music, other types. Analyzes themes, developments, innovations. x + 114pp. 21075-8 Paperbound $1.25

BEETHOVEN AND HIS NINE SYMPHONIES, Sir George Grove. Noted British musicologist provides best history, analysis, commentary on symphonies. Very thorough, rigorously accurate; necessary to both advanced student and amateur music lover. 436 musical passages. vii + 407 pp. 20334-4 Paperbound $2.75

TWO LITTLE SAVAGES; BEING THE ADVENTURES OF TWO BOYS WHO LIVED AS INDIANS AND WHAT THEY LEARNED, Ernest Thompson Seton. Great classic of nature and boyhood provides a vast range of woodlore in most palatable form, a genuinely entertaining story. Two farm boys build a teepee in woods and live in it for a month, working out Indian solutions to living problems, star lore, birds and animals, plants, etc. 293 illustrations. vii + 286pp.

20985-7 Paperbound $2.50

PETER PIPER'S PRACTICAL PRINCIPLES OF PLAIN & PERFECT PRONUNCIATION. Alliterative jingles and tongue-twisters of surprising charm, that made their first appearance in America about 1830. Republished in full with the spirited woodcut illustrations from this earliest American edition. 32pp. $4\frac{1}{2}$ x $6\frac{3}{8}$.

22560-7 Paperbound $1.00

SCIENCE EXPERIMENTS AND AMUSEMENTS FOR CHILDREN, Charles Vivian. 73 easy experiments, requiring only materials found at home or easily available, such as candles, coins, steel wool, etc.; illustrate basic phenomena like vacuum, simple chemical reaction, etc. All safe. Modern, well-planned. Formerly *Science Games for Children.* 102 photos, numerous drawings. 96pp. $6\frac{1}{8}$ x $9\frac{1}{4}$.

21856-2 Paperbound $1.25

AN INTRODUCTION TO CHESS MOVES AND TACTICS SIMPLY EXPLAINED, Leonard Barden. Informal intermediate introduction, quite strong in explaining reasons for moves. Covers basic material, tactics, important openings, traps, positional play in middle game, end game. Attempts to isolate patterns and recurrent configurations. Formerly *Chess.* 58 figures. 102pp. (USO) 21210-6 Paperbound $1.25

LASKER'S MANUAL OF CHESS, Dr. Emanuel Lasker. Lasker was not only one of the five great World Champions, he was also one of the ablest expositors, theorists, and analysts. In many ways, his Manual, permeated with his philosophy of battle, filled with keen insights, is one of the greatest works ever written on chess. Filled with analyzed games by the great players. A single-volume library that will profit almost any chess player, beginner or master. 308 diagrams. xli x 349pp.

20640-8 Paperbound $2.75

THE MASTER BOOK OF MATHEMATICAL RECREATIONS, Fred Schuh. In opinion of many the finest work ever prepared on mathematical puzzles, stunts, recreations; exhaustively thorough explanations of mathematics involved, analysis of effects, citation of puzzles and games. Mathematics involved is elementary. Translated by F. Göbel. 194 figures. xxiv + 430pp. 22134-2 Paperbound $3.00

MATHEMATICS, MAGIC AND MYSTERY, Martin Gardner. Puzzle editor for Scientific American explains mathematics behind various mystifying tricks: card tricks, stage "mind reading," coin and match tricks, counting out games, geometric dissections, etc. Probability sets, theory of numbers clearly explained. Also provides more than 400 tricks, guaranteed to work, that you can do. 135 illustrations. xii + 176pp.

20338-2 Paperbound $1.50

AMERICAN FOOD AND GAME FISHES, David S. Jordan and Barton W. Evermann. Definitive source of information, detailed and accurate enough to enable the sportsman and nature lover to identify conclusively some 1,000 species and sub-species of North American fish, sought for food or sport. Coverage of range, physiology, habits, life history, food value. Best methods of capture, interest to the angler, advice on bait, fly-fishing, etc. 338 drawings and photographs. 1 + 574pp. 6⅝ x 9⅜.

22383-1 Paperbound $4.50

THE FROG BOOK, Mary C. Dickerson. Complete with extensive finding keys, over 300 photographs, and an introduction to the general biology of frogs and toads, this is the classic non-technical study of Northeastern and Central species. 58 species; 290 photographs and 16 color plates. xvii + 253pp.

21973-9 Paperbound $4.00

THE MOTH BOOK: A GUIDE TO THE MOTHS OF NORTH AMERICA, William J. Holland. Classical study, eagerly sought after and used for the past 60 years. Clear identification manual to more than 2,000 different moths, largest manual in existence. General information about moths, capturing, mounting, classifying, etc., followed by species by species descriptions. 263 illustrations plus 48 color plates show almost every species, full size. 1968 edition, preface, nomenclature changes by A. E. Brower. xxiv + 479pp. of text. 6½ x 9¼.

21948-8 Paperbound $5.00

THE SEA-BEACH AT EBB-TIDE, Augusta Foote Arnold. Interested amateur can identify hundreds of marine plants and animals on coasts of North America; marine algae; seaweeds; squids; hermit crabs; horse shoe crabs; shrimps; corals; sea anemones; etc. Species descriptions cover: structure; food; reproductive cycle; size; shape; color; habitat; etc. Over 600 drawings. 85 plates. xii + 490pp.

21949-6 Paperbound $3.50

COMMON BIRD SONGS, Donald J. Borror. 33⅓ 12-inch record presents songs of 60 important birds of the eastern United States. A thorough, serious record which provides several examples for each bird, showing different types of song, individual variations, etc. Inestimable identification aid for birdwatcher. 32-page booklet gives text about birds and songs, with illustration for each bird.

21829-5 Record, book, album. Monaural. $2.75

FADS AND FALLACIES IN THE NAME OF SCIENCE, Martin Gardner. Fair, witty appraisal of cranks and quacks of science: Atlantis, Lemuria, hollow earth, flat earth, Velikovsky, orgone energy, Dianetics, flying saucers, Bridey Murphy, food fads, medical fads, perpetual motion, etc. Formerly "In the Name of Science." x + 363pp.

20394-8 Paperbound $2.00

HOAXES, Curtis D. MacDougall. Exhaustive, unbelievably rich account of great hoaxes: Locke's moon hoax, Shakespearean forgeries, sea serpents, Loch Ness monster, Cardiff giant, John Wilkes Booth's mummy, Disumbrationist school of art, dozens more; also journalism, psychology of hoaxing. 54 illustrations. xi + 338pp.

20465-0 Paperbound $2.75

How to Know the Wild Flowers, Mrs. William Starr Dana. This is the classical book of American wildflowers (of the Eastern and Central United States), used by hundreds of thousands. Covers over 500 species, arranged in extremely easy to use color and season groups. Full descriptions, much plant lore. This Dover edition is the fullest ever compiled, with tables of nomenclature changes. 174 full-page plates by M. Satterlee. xii + 418pp. 20332-8 Paperbound $2.75

Our Plant Friends and Foes, William Atherton DuPuy. History, economic importance, essential botanical information and peculiarities of 25 common forms of plant life are provided in this book in an entertaining and charming style. Covers food plants (potatoes, apples, beans, wheat, almonds, bananas, etc.), flowers (lily, tulip, etc.), trees (pine, oak, elm, etc.), weeds, poisonous mushrooms and vines, gourds, citrus fruits, cotton, the cactus family, and much more. 108 illustrations. xiv + 290pp. 22272-1 Paperbound $2.50

How to Know the Ferns, Frances T. Parsons. Classic survey of Eastern and Central ferns, arranged according to clear, simple identification key. Excellent introduction to greatly neglected nature area. 57 illustrations and 42 plates. xvi + 215pp. 20740-4 Paperbound $2.00

Manual of the Trees of North America, Charles S. Sargent. America's foremost dendrologist provides the definitive coverage of North American trees and tree-like shrubs. 717 species fully described and illustrated: exact distribution, down to township; full botanical description; economic importance; description of subspecies and races; habitat, growth data; similar material. Necessary to every serious student of tree-life. Nomenclature revised to present. Over 100 locating keys. 783 illustrations. lii + 934pp. 20277-1, 20278-X Two volumes, Paperbound $6.00

Our Northern Shrubs, Harriet L. Keeler. Fine non-technical reference work identifying more than 225 important shrubs of Eastern and Central United States and Canada. Full text covering botanical description, habitat, plant lore, is paralleled with 205 full-page photographs of flowering or fruiting plants. Nomenclature revised by Edward G. Voss. One of few works concerned with shrubs. 205 plates, 35 drawings. xxviii + 521pp. 21989-5 Paperbound $3.75

The Mushroom Handbook, Louis C. C. Krieger. Still the best popular handbook: full descriptions of 259 species, cross references to another 200. Extremely thorough text enables you to identify, know all about any mushroom you are likely to meet in eastern and central U. S. A.: habitat, luminescence, poisonous qualities, use, folklore, etc. 32 color plates show over 50 mushrooms, also 126 other illustrations. Finding keys. vii + 560pp. 21861-9 Paperbound $3.95

Handbook of Birds of Eastern North America, Frank M. Chapman. Still much the best single-volume guide to the birds of Eastern and Central United States. Very full coverage of 675 species, with descriptions, life habits, distribution, similar data. All descriptions keyed to two-page color chart. With this single volume the average birdwatcher needs no other books. 1931 revised edition. 195 illustrations. xxxvi + 581pp. 21489-3 Paperbound $5.00

POEMS OF ANNE BRADSTREET, edited with an introduction by Robert Hutchinson. A new selection of poems by America's first poet and perhaps the first significant woman poet in the English language. 48 poems display her development in works of considerable variety—love poems, domestic poems, religious meditations, formal elegies, "quaternions," etc. Notes, bibliography. viii + 222pp.

22160-1 Paperbound $2.00

THREE GOTHIC NOVELS: THE CASTLE OF OTRANTO BY HORACE WALPOLE; VATHEK BY WILLIAM BECKFORD; THE VAMPYRE BY JOHN POLIDORI, WITH FRAGMENT OF A NOVEL BY LORD BYRON, edited by E. F. Bleiler. The first Gothic novel, by Walpole; the finest Oriental tale in English, by Beckford; powerful Romantic supernatural story in versions by Polidori and Byron. All extremely important in history of literature; all still exciting, packed with supernatural thrills, ghosts, haunted castles, magic, etc. xl + 291pp.

21232-7 Paperbound $2.50

THE BEST TALES OF HOFFMANN, E. T. A. Hoffmann. 10 of Hoffmann's most important stories, in modern re-editings of standard translations: Nutcracker and the King of Mice, Signor Formica, Automata, The Sandman, Rath Krespel, The Golden Flowerpot, Master Martin the Cooper, The Mines of Falun, The King's Betrothed, A New Year's Eve Adventure. 7 illustrations by Hoffmann. Edited by E. F. Bleiler. xxxix + 419pp.   21793-0 Paperbound $3.00

GHOST AND HORROR STORIES OF AMBROSE BIERCE, Ambrose Bierce. 23 strikingly modern stories of the horrors latent in the human mind: The Eyes of the Panther, The Damned Thing, An Occurrence at Owl Creek Bridge, An Inhabitant of Carcosa, etc., plus the dream-essay, Visions of the Night. Edited by E. F. Bleiler. xxii + 199pp.   20767-6 Paperbound $1.50

BEST GHOST STORIES OF J. S. LEFANU, J. Sheridan LeFanu. Finest stories by Victorian master often considered greatest supernatural writer of all. Carmilla, Green Tea, The Haunted Baronet, The Familiar, and 12 others. Most never before available in the U. S. A. Edited by E. F. Bleiler. 8 illustrations from Victorian publications. xvii + 467pp.   20415-4 Paperbound $3.00

MATHEMATICAL FOUNDATIONS OF INFORMATION THEORY, A. I. Khinchin. Comprehensive introduction to work of Shannon, McMillan, Feinstein and Khinchin, placing these investigations on a rigorous mathematical basis. Covers entropy concept in probability theory, uniqueness theorem, Shannon's inequality, ergodic sources, the E property, martingale concept, noise, Feinstein's fundamental lemma, Shanon's first and second theorems. Translated by R. A. Silverman and M. D. Friedman. iii + 120pp.   60434-9 Paperbound $1.75

SEVEN SCIENCE FICTION NOVELS, H. G. Wells. The standard collection of the great novels. Complete, unabridged. *First Men in the Moon, Island of Dr. Moreau, War of the Worlds, Food of the Gods, Invisible Man, Time Machine, In the Days of the Comet.* Not only science fiction fans, but every educated person owes it to himself to read these novels. 1015pp   20264-X Clothbound $5.00

A HISTORY OF COSTUME, Carl Köhler. Definitive history, based on surviving pieces of clothing primarily, and paintings, statues, etc. secondarily. Highly readable text, supplemented by 594 illustrations of costumes of the ancient Mediterranean peoples, Greece and Rome, the Teutonic prehistoric period; costumes of the Middle Ages, Renaissance, Baroque, 18th and 19th centuries. Clear, measured patterns are provided for many clothing articles. Approach is practical throughout. Enlarged by Emma von Sichart. 464pp. 21030-8 Paperbound $3.50

ORIENTAL RUGS, ANTIQUE AND MODERN, Walter A. Hawley. A complete and authoritative treatise on the Oriental rug—where they are made, by whom and how, designs and symbols, characteristics in detail of the six major groups, how to distinguish them and how to buy them. Detailed technical data is provided on periods, weaves, warps, wefts, textures, sides, ends and knots, although no technical background is required for an understanding. 11 color plates, 80 halftones, 4 maps. vi + 320pp. 6⅛ x 9⅛. 22366-3 Paperbound $5.00

TEN BOOKS ON ARCHITECTURE, Vitruvius. By any standards the most important book on architecture ever written. Early Roman discussion of aesthetics of building, construction methods, orders, sites, and every other aspect of architecture has inspired, instructed architecture for about 2,000 years. Stands behind Palladio, Michelangelo, Bramante, Wren, countless others. Definitive Morris H. Morgan translation. 68 illustrations. xii + 331pp. 20645-9 Paperbound $3.50

THE FOUR BOOKS OF ARCHITECTURE, Andrea Palladio. Translated into every major Western European language in the two centuries following its publication in 1570, this has been one of the most influential books in the history of architecture. Complete reprint of the 1738 Isaac Ware edition. New introduction by Adolf Placzek, Columbia Univ. 216 plates. xxii + 110pp. of text. 9½ x 12¾. 21308-0 Clothbound $10.00

STICKS AND STONES: A STUDY OF AMERICAN ARCHITECTURE AND CIVILIZATION, Lewis Mumford.One of the great classics of American cultural history. American architecture from the medieval-inspired earliest forms to the early 20th century; evolution of structure and style, and reciprocal influences on environment. 21 photographic illustrations. 238pp. 20202-X Paperbound $2.00

THE AMERICAN BUILDER'S COMPANION, Asher Benjamin. The most widely used early 19th century architectural style and source book, for colonial up into Greek Revival periods. Extensive development of geometry of carpentering, construction of sashes, frames, doors, stairs; plans and elevations of domestic and other buildings. Hundreds of thousands of houses were built according to this book, now invaluable to historians, architects, restorers, etc. 1827 edition. 59 plates. 114pp. 7⅞ x 10¾. 22236-5 Paperbound $3.50

DUTCH HOUSES IN THE HUDSON VALLEY BEFORE 1776, Helen Wilkinson Reynolds. The standard survey of the Dutch colonial house and outbuildings, with constructional features, decoration, and local history associated with individual homesteads. Introduction by Franklin D. Roosevelt. Map. 150 illustrations. 469pp. 6⅝ x 9¼. 21469-9 Paperbound $4.00

AGAINST THE GRAIN (A REBOURS), Joris K. Huysmans. Filled with weird images, evidences of a bizarre imagination, exotic experiments with hallucinatory drugs, rich tastes and smells and the diversions of its sybarite hero Duc Jean des Esseintes, this classic novel pushed 19th-century literary decadence to its limits. Full unabridged edition. Do not confuse this with abridged editions generally sold. Introduction by Havelock Ellis. xlix + 206pp.   22190-3 Paperbound $2.00

VARIORUM SHAKESPEARE: HAMLET. Edited by Horace H. Furness; a landmark of American scholarship. Exhaustive footnotes and appendices treat all doubtful words and phrases, as well as suggested critical emendations throughout the play's history. First volume contains editor's own text, collated with all Quartos and Folios. Second volume contains full first Quarto, translations of Shakespeare's sources (Belleforest, and Saxo Grammaticus), Der Bestrafte Brudermord, and many essays on critical and historical points of interest by major authorities of past and present. Includes details of staging and costuming over the years. By far the best edition available for serious students of Shakespeare. Total of xx + 905pp.
21004-9, 21005-7, 2 volumes, Paperbound $7.00

A LIFE OF WILLIAM SHAKESPEARE, Sir Sidney Lee. This is the standard life of Shakespeare, summarizing everything known about Shakespeare and his plays. Incredibly rich in material, broad in coverage, clear and judicious, it has served thousands as the best introduction to Shakespeare. 1931 edition. 9 plates. xxix + 792pp.   (USO) 21967-4 Paperbound $3.75

MASTERS OF THE DRAMA, John Gassner. Most comprehensive history of the drama in print, covering every tradition from Greeks to modern Europe and America, including India, Far East, etc. Covers more than 800 dramatists, 2000 plays, with biographical material, plot summaries, theatre history, criticism, etc. "Best of its kind in English," *New Republic.* 77 illustrations. xxii + 890pp.
20100-7 Clothbound $8.50

THE EVOLUTION OF THE ENGLISH LANGUAGE, George McKnight. The growth of English, from the 14th century to the present. Unusual, non-technical account presents basic information in very interesting form: sound shifts, change in grammar and syntax, vocabulary growth, similar topics. Abundantly illustrated with quotations. Formerly *Modern English in the Making.* xii + 590pp.
21932-1 Paperbound $3.50

AN ETYMOLOGICAL DICTIONARY OF MODERN ENGLISH, Ernest Weekley. Fullest, richest work of its sort, by foremost British lexicographer. Detailed word histories, including many colloquial and archaic words; extensive quotations. Do not confuse this with the Concise Etymological Dictionary, which is much abridged. Total of xxvii + 830pp. 6½ x 9¼.
21873-2, 21874-0 Two volumes, Paperbound $6.00

FLATLAND: A ROMANCE OF MANY DIMENSIONS, E. A. Abbott. Classic of science-fiction explores ramifications of life in a two-dimensional world, and what happens when a three-dimensional being intrudes. Amusing reading, but also useful as introduction to thought about hyperspace. Introduction by Banesh Hoffmann. 16 illustrations. xx + 103pp.   20001-9 Paperbound $1.00

ALPHABETS AND ORNAMENTS, Ernst Lehner. Well-known pictorial source for decorative alphabets, script examples, cartouches, frames, decorative title pages, calligraphic initials, borders, similar material. 14th to 19th century, mostly European. Useful in almost any graphic arts designing, varied styles. 750 illustrations. 256pp. 7 x 10. 21905-4 Paperbound $4.00

PAINTING: A CREATIVE APPROACH, Norman Colquhoun. For the beginner simple guide provides an instructive approach to painting: major stumbling blocks for beginner; overcoming them, technical points; paints and pigments; oil painting; watercolor and other media and color. New section on "plastic" paints. Glossary. Formerly *Paint Your Own Pictures.* 221pp. 22000-1 Paperbound $1.75

THE ENJOYMENT AND USE OF COLOR, Walter Sargent. Explanation of the relations between colors themselves and between colors in nature and art, including hundreds of little-known facts about color values, intensities, effects of high and low illumination, complementary colors. Many practical hints for painters, references to great masters. 7 color plates, 29 illustrations. x + 274pp.
20944-X Paperbound $2.75

THE NOTEBOOKS OF LEONARDO DA VINCI, compiled and edited by Jean Paul Richter. 1566 extracts from original manuscripts reveal the full range of Leonardo's versatile genius: all his writings on painting, sculpture, architecture, anatomy, astronomy, geography, topography, physiology, mining, music, etc., in both Italian and English, with 186 plates of manuscript pages and more than 500 additional drawings. Includes studies for the Last Supper, the lost Sforza monument, and other works. Total of xlvii + 866pp. 7⅞ x 10¾.
22572-0, 22573-9 Two volumes, Paperbound $10.00

MONTGOMERY WARD CATALOGUE OF 1895. Tea gowns, yards of flannel and pillow-case lace, stereoscopes, books of gospel hymns, the New Improved Singer Sewing Machine, side saddles, milk skimmers, straight-edged razors, high-button shoes, spittoons, and on and on . . . listing some 25,000 items, practically all illustrated. Essential to the shoppers of the 1890's, it is our truest record of the spirit of the period. Unaltered reprint of Issue No. 57, Spring and Summer 1895. Introduction by Boris Emmet. Innumerable illustrations. xiii + 624pp. 8½ x 11⅝.
22377-9 Paperbound $6.95

THE CRYSTAL PALACE EXHIBITION ILLUSTRATED CATALOGUE (LONDON, 1851). One of the wonders of the modern world—the Crystal Palace Exhibition in which all the nations of the civilized world exhibited their achievements in the arts and sciences—presented in an equally important illustrated catalogue. More than 1700 items pictured with accompanying text—ceramics, textiles, cast-iron work, carpets, pianos, sleds, razors, wall-papers, billiard tables, beehives, silverware and hundreds of other artifacts—represent the focal point of Victorian culture in the Western World. Probably the largest collection of Victorian decorative art ever assembled—indispensable for antiquarians and designers. Unabridged republication of the Art-Journal Catalogue of the Great Exhibition of 1851, with all terminal essays. New introduction by John Gloag, F.S.A. xxxiv + 426pp. 9 x 12.
22503-8 Paperbound $4.50

VISUAL ILLUSIONS: THEIR CAUSES, CHARACTERISTICS, AND APPLICATIONS, Matthew Luckiesh. Thorough description and discussion of optical illusion, geometric and perspective, particularly; size and shape distortions, illusions of color, of motion; natural illusions; use of illusion in art and magic, industry, etc. Most useful today with op art, also for classical art. Scores of effects illustrated. Introduction by William H. Ittleson. 100 illustrations. xxi + 252pp.

21530-X Paperbound $2.00

A HANDBOOK OF ANATOMY FOR ART STUDENTS, Arthur Thomson. Thorough, virtually exhaustive coverage of skeletal structure, musculature, etc. Full text, supplemented by anatomical diagrams and drawings and by photographs of undraped figures. Unique in its comparison of male and female forms, pointing out differences of contour, texture, form. 211 figures, 40 drawings, 86 photographs. xx + 459pp. 5⅜ x 8⅜.

21163-0 Paperbound $3.50

150 MASTERPIECES OF DRAWING, Selected by Anthony Toney. Full page reproductions of drawings from the early 16th to the end of the 18th century, all beautifully reproduced: Rembrandt, Michelangelo, Dürer, Fragonard, Urs, Graf, Wouwerman, many others. First-rate browsing book, model book for artists. xviii + 150pp. 8⅜ x 11¼.

21032-4 Paperbound $2.50

THE LATER WORK OF AUBREY BEARDSLEY, Aubrey Beardsley. Exotic, erotic, ironic masterpieces in full maturity: Comedy Ballet, Venus and Tannhauser, Pierrot, Lysistrata, Rape of the Lock, Savoy material, Ali Baba, Volpone, etc. This material revolutionized the art world, and is still powerful, fresh, brilliant. With *The Early Work,* all Beardsley's finest work. 174 plates, 2 in color. xiv + 176pp. 8⅛ x 11.

21817-1 Paperbound $3.00

DRAWINGS OF REMBRANDT, Rembrandt van Rijn. Complete reproduction of fabulously rare edition by Lippmann and Hofstede de Groot, completely reedited, updated, improved by Prof. Seymour Slive, Fogg Museum. Portraits, Biblical sketches, landscapes, Oriental types, nudes, episodes from classical mythology—All Rembrandt's fertile genius. Also selection of drawings by his pupils and followers. "Stunning volumes," *Saturday Review.* 550 illustrations. lxxviii + 552pp. 9⅛ x 12¼.

21485-0, 21486-9 Two volumes, Paperbound $10.00

THE DISASTERS OF WAR, Francisco Goya. One of the masterpieces of Western civilization—83 etchings that record Goya's shattering, bitter reaction to the Napoleonic war that swept through Spain after the insurrection of 1808 and to war in general. Reprint of the first edition, with three additional plates from Boston's Museum of Fine Arts. All plates facsimile size. Introduction by Philip Hofer, Fogg Museum. v + 97pp. 9⅜ x 8¼.

21872-4 Paperbound $2.00

GRAPHIC WORKS OF ODILON REDON. Largest collection of Redon's graphic works ever assembled: 172 lithographs, 28 etchings and engravings, 9 drawings. These include some of his most famous works. All the plates from *Odilon Redon: oeuvre graphique complet,* plus additional plates. New introduction and caption translations by Alfred Werner. 209 illustrations. xxvii + 209pp. 9⅛ x 12¼.

21966-8 Paperbound $4.00

EAST O' THE SUN AND WEST O' THE MOON, George W. Dasent. Considered the best of all translations of these Norwegian folk tales, this collection has been enjoyed by generations of children (and folklorists too). Includes True and Untrue, Why the Sea is Salt, East O' the Sun and West O' the Moon, Why the Bear is Stumpy-Tailed, Boots and the Troll, The Cock and the Hen, Rich Peter the Pedlar, and 52 more. The only edition with all 59 tales. 77 illustrations by Erik Werenskiold and Theodor Kittelsen. xv + 418pp. 22521-6 Paperbound $3.50

GOOPS AND HOW TO BE THEM, Gelett Burgess. Classic of tongue-in-cheek humor, masquerading as etiquette book. 87 verses, twice as many cartoons, show mischievous Goops as they demonstrate to children virtues of table manners, neatness, courtesy, etc. Favorite for generations. viii + 88pp. 6½ x 9¼. 22233-0 Paperbound $1.25

ALICE'S ADVENTURES UNDER GROUND, Lewis Carroll. The first version, quite different from the final *Alice in Wonderland,* printed out by Carroll himself with his own illustrations. Complete facsimile of the "million dollar" manuscript Carroll gave to Alice Liddell in 1864. Introduction by Martin Gardner. viii + 96pp. Title and dedication pages in color. 21482-6 Paperbound $1.25

THE BROWNIES, THEIR BOOK, Palmer Cox. Small as mice, cunning as foxes, exuberant and full of mischief, the Brownies go to the zoo, toy shop, seashore, circus, etc., in 24 verse adventures and 266 illustrations. Long a favorite, since their first appearance in St. Nicholas Magazine. xi + 144pp. 6⅝ x 9¼. 21265-3 Paperbound $1.75

SONGS OF CHILDHOOD, Walter De La Mare. Published (under the pseudonym Walter Ramal) when De La Mare was only 29, this charming collection has long been a favorite children's book. A facsimile of the first edition in paper, the 47 poems capture the simplicity of the nursery rhyme and the ballad, including such lyrics as I Met Eve, Tartary, The Silver Penny. vii + 106pp. 21972-0 Paperbound $1.25

THE COMPLETE NONSENSE OF EDWARD LEAR, Edward Lear. The finest 19th-century humorist-cartoonist in full: all nonsense limericks, zany alphabets, Owl and Pussycat, songs, nonsense botany, and more than 500 illustrations by Lear himself. Edited by Holbrook Jackson. xxix + 287pp. (USO) 20167-8 Paperbound $2.00

BILLY WHISKERS: THE AUTOBIOGRAPHY OF A GOAT, Frances Trego Montgomery. A favorite of children since the early 20th century, here are the escapades of that rambunctious, irresistible and mischievous goat—Billy Whiskers. Much in the spirit of *Peck's Bad Boy,* this is a book that children never tire of reading or hearing. All the original familiar illustrations by W. H. Fry are included: 6 color plates, 18 black and white drawings. 159pp. 22345-0 Paperbound $2.00

MOTHER GOOSE MELODIES. Faithful republication of the fabulously rare Munroe and Francis "copyright 1833" Boston edition—the most important Mother Goose collection, usually referred to as the "original." Familiar rhymes plus many rare ones, with wonderful old woodcut illustrations. Edited by E. F. Bleiler. 128pp. 4½ x 6⅜. 22577-1 Paperbound $1.25

DESIGN BY ACCIDENT; A BOOK OF "ACCIDENTAL EFFECTS" FOR ARTISTS AND DESIGNERS, James F. O'Brien. Create your own unique, striking, imaginative effects by "controlled accident" interaction of materials: paints and lacquers, oil and water based paints, splatter, crackling materials, shatter, similar items. Everything you do will be different; first book on this limitless art, so useful to both fine artist and commercial artist. Full instructions. 192 plates showing "accidents," 8 in color. viii + 215pp. 8⅜ x 11¼. 21942-9 Paperbound $3.50

THE BOOK OF SIGNS, Rudolf Koch. Famed German type designer draws 493 beautiful symbols: religious, mystical, alchemical, imperial, property marks, runes, etc. Remarkable fusion of traditional and modern. Good for suggestions of timelessness, smartness, modernity. Text. vi + 104pp. 6⅛ x 9¼. 20162-7 Paperbound $1.25

HISTORY OF INDIAN AND INDONESIAN ART, Ananda K. Coomaraswamy. An unabridged republication of one of the finest books by a great scholar in Eastern art. Rich in descriptive material, history, social backgrounds; Sunga reliefs, Rajput paintings, Gupta temples, Burmese frescoes, textiles, jewelry, sculpture, etc. 400 photos. viii + 423pp. 6⅜ x 9¾. 21436-2 Paperbound $4.00

PRIMITIVE ART, Franz Boas. America's foremost anthropologist surveys textiles, ceramics, woodcarving, basketry, metalwork, etc.; patterns, technology, creation of symbols, style origins. All areas of world, but very full on Northwest Coast Indians. More than 350 illustrations of baskets, boxes, totem poles, weapons, etc. 378 pp. 20025-6 Paperbound $3.00

THE GENTLEMAN AND CABINET MAKER'S DIRECTOR, Thomas Chippendale. Full reprint (third edition, 1762) of most influential furniture book of all time, by master cabinetmaker. 200 plates, illustrating chairs, sofas, mirrors, tables, cabinets, plus 24 photographs of surviving pieces. Biographical introduction by N. Bienenstock. vi + 249pp. 9⅞ x 12¾. 21601-2 Paperbound $4.00

AMERICAN ANTIQUE FURNITURE, Edgar G. Miller, Jr. The basic coverage of all American furniture before 1840. Individual chapters cover type of furniture—clocks, tables, sideboards, etc.—chronologically, with inexhaustible wealth of data. More than 2100 photographs, all identified, commented on. Essential to all early American collectors. Introduction by H. E. Keyes. vi + 1106pp. 7⅞ x 10¾. 21599-7, 21600-4 Two volumes, Paperbound $11.00

PENNSYLVANIA DUTCH AMERICAN FOLK ART, Henry J. Kauffman. 279 photos, 28 drawings of tulipware, Fraktur script, painted tinware, toys, flowered furniture, quilts, samplers, hex signs, house interiors, etc. Full descriptive text. Excellent for tourist, rewarding for designer, collector. Map. 146pp. 7⅞ x 10¾. 21205-X Paperbound $2.50

EARLY NEW ENGLAND GRAVESTONE RUBBINGS, Edmund V. Gillon, Jr. 43 photographs, 226 carefully reproduced rubbings show heavily symbolic, sometimes macabre early gravestones, up to early 19th century. Remarkable early American primitive art, occasionally strikingly beautiful; always powerful. Text. xxvi + 207pp. 8⅜ x 11¼. 21380-3 Paperbound $3.50

LAST AND FIRST MEN AND STAR MAKER, TWO SCIENCE FICTION NOVELS, Olaf Stapledon. Greatest future histories in science fiction. In the first, human intelligence is the "hero," through strange paths of evolution, interplanetary invasions, incredible technologies, near extinctions and reemergences. Star Maker describes the quest of a band of star rovers for intelligence itself, through time and space: weird inhuman civilizations, crustacean minds, symbiotic worlds, etc. Complete, unabridged. v + 438pp. 21962-3 Paperbound $2.50

THREE PROPHETIC NOVELS, H. G. WELLS. Stages of a consistently planned future for mankind. *When the Sleeper Wakes,* and *A Story of the Days to Come,* anticipate *Brave New World* and *1984,* in the 21st Century; *The Time Machine,* only complete version in print, shows farther future and the end of mankind. All . .ow Wells's greatest gifts as storyteller and novelist. Edited by E. F. Bleiler. x + 335pp. (USO) 20605-X Paperbound $2.50

THE DEVIL'S DICTIONARY, Ambrose Bierce. America's own Oscar Wilde— Ambrose Bierce—offers his barbed iconoclastic wisdom in over 1,000 definitions hailed by H. L. Mencken as "some of the most gorgeous witticisms in the English language." 145pp. 20487-1 Paperbound $1.25

MAX AND MORITZ, Wilhelm Busch. Great children's classic, father of comic strip, of two bad boys, Max and Moritz. Also Ker and Plunk (Plisch und Plumm), Cat and Mouse, Deceitful Henry, Ice-Peter, The Boy and the Pipe, and five other pieces. Original German, with English translation. Edited by H. Arthur Klein; translations by various hands and H. Arthur Klein. vi + 216pp.
20181-3 Paperbound $2.00

PIGS IS PIGS AND OTHER FAVORITES, Ellis Parker Butler. The title story is one of the best humor short stories, as Mike Flannery obfuscates biology and English. Also included, That Pup of Murchison's, The Great American Pie Company, and Perkins of Portland. 14 illustrations. v + 109pp. 21532-6 Paperbound $1.25

THE PETERKIN PAPERS, Lucretia P. Hale. It takes genius to be as stupidly mad as the Peterkins, as they decide to become wise, celebrate the "Fourth," keep a cow, and otherwise strain the resources of the Lady from Philadelphia. Basic book of American humor. 153 illustrations. 219pp. 20794-3 Paperbound $1.50

PERRAULT'S FAIRY TALES, translated by A. E. Johnson and S. R. Littlewood, with 34 full-page illustrations by Gustave Doré. All the original Perrault stories— Cinderella, Sleeping Beauty, Bluebeard, Little Red Riding Hood, Puss in Boots, Tom Thumb, etc.—with their witty verse morals and the magnificent illustrations of Doré. One of the five or six great books of European fairy tales. viii + 117pp. 8⅛ x 11. 22311-6 Paperbound $2.00

OLD HUNGARIAN FAIRY TALES, Baroness Orczy. Favorites translated and adapted by author of the *Scarlet Pimpernel.* Eight fairy tales include "The Suitors of Princess Fire-Fly," "The Twin Hunchbacks," "Mr. Cuttlefish's Love Story," and "The Enchanted Cat." This little volume of magic and adventure will captivate children as it has for generations. 90 drawings by Montagu Barstow. 96pp.
(USO) 22293-4 Paperbound $1.95

THE RED FAIRY BOOK, Andrew Lang. Lang's color fairy books have long been children's favorites. This volume includes Rapunzel, Jack and the Bean-stalk and 35 other stories, familiar and unfamiliar. 4 plates, 93 illustrations x + 367pp.
21673-X Paperbound $2.50

THE BLUE FAIRY BOOK, Andrew Lang. Lang's tales come from all countries and all times. Here are 37 tales from Grimm, the Arabian Nights, Greek Mythology, and other fascinating sources. 8 plates, 130 illustrations. xi + 390pp.
21437-0 Paperbound $2.50

HOUSEHOLD STORIES BY THE BROTHERS GRIMM. Classic English-language edition of the well-known tales — Rumpelstiltskin, Snow White, Hansel and Gretel, The Twelve Brothers, Faithful John, Rapunzel, Tom Thumb (52 stories in all). Translated into simple, straightforward English by Lucy Crane. Ornamented with headpieces, vignettes, elaborate decorative initials and a dozen full-page illustrations by Walter Crane. x + 269pp.
21080-4 Paperbound $2.50

THE MERRY ADVENTURES OF ROBIN HOOD, Howard Pyle. The finest modern versions of the traditional ballads and tales about the great English outlaw. Howard Pyle's complete prose version, with every word, every illustration of the first edition. Do not confuse this facsimile of the original (1883) with modern editions that change text or illustrations. 23 plates plus many page decorations. xxii + 296pp.
22043-5 Paperbound $2.50

THE STORY OF KING ARTHUR AND HIS KNIGHTS, Howard Pyle. The finest children's version of the life of King Arthur; brilliantly retold by Pyle, with 48 of his most imaginative illustrations. xviii + 313pp. 6⅛ x 9¼.
21445-1 Paperbound $2.50

THE WONDERFUL WIZARD OF OZ, L. Frank Baum. America's finest children's book in facsimile of first edition with all Denslow illustrations in full color. The edition a child should have. Introduction by Martin Gardner. 23 color plates, scores of drawings. iv + 267pp.
20691-2 Paperbound $2.50

THE MARVELOUS LAND OF OZ, L. Frank Baum. The second Oz book, every bit as imaginative as the Wizard. The hero is a boy named Tip, but the Scarecrow and the Tin Woodman are back, as is the Oz magic. 16 color plates, 120 drawings by John R. Neill. 287pp.
20692-0 Paperbound $2.50

THE MAGICAL MONARCH OF MO, L. Frank Baum. Remarkable adventures in a land even stranger than Oz. The best of Baum's books not in the Oz series. 15 color plates and dozens of drawings by Frank Verbeck. xviii + 237pp.
21892-9 Paperbound $2.25

THE BAD CHILD'S BOOK OF BEASTS, MORE BEASTS FOR WORSE CHILDREN, A MORAL ALPHABET, Hilaire Belloc. Three complete humor classics in one volume. Be kind to the frog, and do not call him names . . . and 28 other whimsical animals. Familiar favorites and some not so well known. Illustrated by Basil Blackwell. 156pp.
(USO) 20749-8 Paperbound $1.50

JOHANN SEBASTIAN BACH, Philipp Spitta. One of the great classics of musicology, this definitive analysis of Bach's music (and life) has never been surpassed. Lucid, nontechnical analyses of hundreds of pieces (30 pages devoted to St. Matthew Passion, 26 to B Minor Mass). Also includes major analysis of 18th-century music. 450 musical examples. 40-page musical supplement. Total of xx + 1799pp.
(EUK) 22278-0, 22279-9 Two volumes, Clothbound $15.00

MOZART AND HIS PIANO CONCERTOS, Cuthbert Girdlestone. The only full-length study of an important area of Mozart's creativity. Provides detailed analyses of all 23 concertos, traces inspirational sources. 417 musical examples. Second edition. 509pp. (USO) 21271-8 Paperbound $3.50

THE PERFECT WAGNERITE: A COMMENTARY ON THE NIBLUNG'S RING, George Bernard Shaw. Brilliant and still relevant criticism in remarkable essays on Wagner's Ring cycle, Shaw's ideas on political and social ideology behind the plots, role of Leitmotifs, vocal requisites, etc. Prefaces. xxi + 136pp.
21707-8 Paperbound $1.50

DON GIOVANNI, W. A. Mozart. Complete libretto, modern English translation; biographies of composer and librettist; accounts of early performances and critical reaction. Lavishly illustrated. All the material you need to understand and appreciate this great work. Dover Opera Guide and Libretto Series; translated and introduced by Ellen Bleiler. 92 illustrations. 209pp.
21134-7 Paperbound $1.50

HIGH FIDELITY SYSTEMS: A LAYMAN'S GUIDE, Roy F. Allison. All the basic information you need for setting up your own audio system: high fidelity and stereo record players, tape records, F.M. Connections, adjusting tone arm, cartridge, checking needle alignment, positioning speakers, phasing speakers, adjusting hums, trouble-shooting, maintenance, and similar topics. Enlarged 1965 edition. More than 50 charts, diagrams, photos. iv + 91pp. 21514-8 Paperbound $1.25

REPRODUCTION OF SOUND, Edgar Villchur. Thorough coverage for laymen of high fidelity systems, reproducing systems in general, needles, amplifiers, preamps, loudspeakers, feedback, explaining physical background. "A rare talent for making technicalities vividly comprehensible," R. Darrell, *High Fidelity*. 69 figures. iv + 92pp. 21515-6 Paperbound $1.00

HEAR ME TALKIN' TO YA: THE STORY OF JAZZ AS TOLD BY THE MEN WHO MADE IT, Nat Shapiro and Nat Hentoff. Louis Armstrong, Fats Waller, Jo Jones, Clarence Williams, Billy Holiday, Duke Ellington, Jelly Roll Morton and dozens of other jazz greats tell how it was in Chicago's South Side, New Orleans, depression Harlem and the modern West Coast as jazz was born and grew. xvi + 429pp.
21726-4 Paperbound $2.50

FABLES OF AESOP, translated by Sir Roger L'Estrange. A reproduction of the very rare 1931 Paris edition; a selection of the most interesting fables, together with 50 imaginative drawings by Alexander Calder. v + 128pp. 6½x9¼.
21780-9 Paperbound $1.25

MATHEMATICAL PUZZLES FOR BEGINNERS AND ENTHUSIASTS, Geoffrey Mott-Smith. 189 puzzles from easy to difficult—involving arithmetic, logic, algebra, properties of digits, probability, etc.—for enjoyment and mental stimulus. Explanation of mathematical principles behind the puzzles. 135 illustrations. viii + 248pp.
20198-8 Paperbound $1.75

PAPER FOLDING FOR BEGINNERS, William D. Murray and Francis J. Rigney. Easiest book on the market, clearest instructions on making interesting, beautiful origami. Sail boats, cups, roosters, frogs that move legs, bonbon boxes, standing birds, etc. 40 projects; more than 275 diagrams and photographs. 94pp.
20713-7 Paperbound $1.00

TRICKS AND GAMES ON THE POOL TABLE, Fred Herrmann. 79 tricks and games— some solitaires, some for two or more players, some competitive games—to entertain you between formal games. Mystifying shots and throws, unusual caroms, tricks involving such props as cork, coins, a hat, etc. Formerly *Fun on the Pool Table*. 77 figures. 95pp.
21814-7 Paperbound $1.00

HAND SHADOWS TO BE THROWN UPON THE WALL: A SERIES OF NOVEL AND AMUSING FIGURES FORMED BY THE HAND, Henry Bursill. Delightful picturebook from great-grandfather's day shows how to make 18 different hand shadows: a bird that flies, duck that quacks, dog that wags his tail, camel, goose, deer, boy, turtle, etc. Only book of its sort. vi + 33pp. 6½ x 9¼.   21779-5 Paperbound $1.00

WHITTLING AND WOODCARVING, E. J. Tangerman. 18th printing of best book on market. "If you can cut a potato you can carve" toys and puzzles, chains, chessmen, caricatures, masks, frames, woodcut blocks, surface patterns, much more. Information on tools, woods, techniques. Also goes into serious wood sculpture from Middle Ages to present, East and West. 464 photos, figures. x + 293pp.
20965-2 Paperbound $2.00

HISTORY OF PHILOSOPHY, Julián Marías. Possibly the clearest, most easily followed, best planned, most useful one-volume history of philosophy on the market; neither skimpy nor overfull. Full details on system of every major philosopher and dozens of less important thinkers from pre-Socratics up to Existentialism and later. Strong on many European figures usually omitted. Has gone through dozens of editions in Europe. 1966 edition, translated by Stanley Appelbaum and Clarence Strowbridge. xviii + 505pp.   21739-6 Paperbound $3.00

YOGA: A SCIENTIFIC EVALUATION, Kovoor T. Behanan. Scientific but non-technical study of physiological results of yoga exercises; done under auspices of Yale U. Relations to Indian thought, to psychoanalysis, etc. 16 photos. xxiii + 270pp.
20505-3 Paperbound $2.50